Neopluralism

STUDIES IN GOVERNMENT
AND PUBLIC POLICY

Neopluralism
The Evolution of Political Process Theory

Andrew S. McFarland

University Press of Kansas

Publication made possible, in part, by gifts from the Institute for the Humanities, Mary Beth Rose, Director, and the Institute of Government and Public Affairs, Jack Knott, Director, both located at the University of Illinois, Chicago.

© 2004 by the University Press of Kansas
All rights reserved

Published by the University Press of Kansas (Lawrence, Kansas 66045), which was organized by the Kansas Board of Regents and is operated and funded by Emporia State University, Fort Hays State University, Kansas State University, Pittsburg State University, the University of Kansas, and Wichita State University

Library of Congress Cataloging-in-Publication Data
McFarland, Andrew S., 1940–
   Neopluralism : the evolution of politcal process theory / Andrew S. McFarland.
     p. cm.—(Studies in government and public policy)
   Includes bibliographical references and index.
     ISBN 978-0-7006-1309-0 (cloth : alk. paper)—ISBN 978-0-7006-1310-6 (pbk.: alk. paper)
     1. Political planning—United States. 2. Pluralism (Social sciences)—United States.
3. Power (Social sciences)—United States. 4. Pressure groups—United States.
I. Title. II. Series.
   JK468.P64M33 2004
   320.973'01—dc22   2003020209

British Library Cataloguing-in-Publication Data is available.

Printed in the United States of America

10 9 8 7 6 5 4 3 2 1

The paper used in this publication meets the minimum requirements of the American National Standard for Permanence of Paper for Printed Library Materials Z39.48-1984.

In memory of a leading political science researcher, Jack L. Walker Jr., and of a leading social science publisher, Edward Artinian

Contents

Preface   ix

1. Pluralism Reconsidered   1
2. Basic Ideas of Pluralism   15
3. The Multiple-Elite Theory   32
4. Neopluralism   40
5. Social Movements   62
6. Policymaking and Political Time   78
7. The Political Process and Planning   104
8. Issues and Power   124
9. The Boundaries of Pluralism   147
10. Conclusion   158

References   179

Index   193

Preface

This book summarizes and advances the earlier research of my career. My first book, *Power and Leadership in Pluralist Systems* (1969), was an analysis and friendly critique of the pluralist theory of the 1960s, written from within the theory itself. One obvious weakness of the pluralist theory was its lack of treatment of the logic of collective action—the tendency for a few of those with high stakes in a policy to organize and lobby, while a diffused public was not so organized. To investigate this lobbying problem, I went to Washington, D.C., to study public interest groups, most of them newly formed, and published *Public Interest Lobbies: Decision Making on Energy* (1976) and, eventually, *Common Cause: Lobbying in the Public Interest* (1984). Since some public interest groups, particularly environmentalist groups, had developed significant power, I became interested in how this power could be coordinated with the need for economic development, publishing *Cooperative Pluralism: The National Coal Policy Experiment* (1993).

In doing the research and writing for those three books about lobbying and policymaking in Washington, I saw myself as building on a research tradition initiated by such pluralists as Robert A. Dahl, Charles E. Lindblom, and Herbert Simon. I believed that many other researchers were also participating in this endeavor. However, many scholars do not admit the existence of such a research tradition or, if they do, dismiss it as irrelevant. Thus, I am writing a book to set this record straight and to argue that the pluralist research tradition has been developing into a more general theory of political process. As this becomes more clearly understood, future research and theorizing in the field will become even more productive.

I wish to express my thanks to Frank Baumgartner and Randall Strahan for their extraordinary help in improving an earlier draft of this manuscript, although neither should be held responsible for the final draft. John Kingdon and Tony Orum also read the draft and made many suggestions that I adopted. Members of the Political Science Department at Penn State made several helpful criticisms when I gave a presentation at their departmental seminar. Similarly, members of my own Department of Political Science at the University of Illinois at Chicago helped clarify my assumptions at a departmental seminar. Alba Alexander and Dennis Judd commented on parts of this work, a Ph.D. dissertation by Carla Knorowski helped develop it (see the bibliography), and James Nell straightened out my WordPerfect.

I was able to write a rough-draft manuscript while supported by a sabbatical leave from the College of Liberal Arts and Sciences of the University of Illinois at Chicago.

Chapter 6 is a revised version of my 1991 article "Interest Groups and Political Time: Cycles in America," *British Journal of Political Science* 21:257–84, used with the permission of Cambridge University Press.

1
Pluralism Reconsidered

The aim of this book is to further the consideration and development of a theory of the political process. By a "theory of the political process" I mean a general approach to answering these questions: How is public policy made in this area of action? Which persons, groups, or organizational units have power in this area of public policy? What do interest groups do in this area of public policy? The answers refer to patterns of conflict, cooperation, and strategy, things we regard as "political," thereby implying a "political process."

I do not believe that there will ever be a single theory of political science, or even a single theory of domestic politics. I do think that political science is developing several general theories about or approaches to the study of politics. Among such approaches I include rational choice theory (Riker, 1982); institutional theory, whether rational choice or that which is predominantly not rational choice (e.g., Lijphart, 1999); attitudinal theory, based on the study of individuals and social psychology (Sniderman, Brody, and Tetlock, 1991); and neo-Weberian theory, emphasizing the state, bureaucracy, comparative history, and the interaction of rational goal-seeking and cultural factors in political motivation (Skocpol, 1979; Linz and Stepan, 1996).* All these are coherent theoretical efforts, with a history that spans generations, and each is directed to answering a set of questions about politics. Neither the discipline nor I have a set list of such general approaches to the study of politics; one hopes that such a list could be restricted to relatively few theories, perhaps six or eight. But the point is clear: I think that a political process theory will join such a short list of important general approaches to study. First, however, we must clear up some confusion about the development of this theory.

My argument is that political process theory has been developing over the last fifty years, but this development is not widely recognized. The major reason for this lack of recognition is that the basics of theory building were stated by "pluralists," flourishing in American political science in the 1960s. The most valuable and long-lasting element of pluralist thought was the framework of a theory of political process, but this important contribution

---

* These general *theories about* or *approaches to* the study of politics should be distinguished from *theories of,* such as theories of democracy or theories of political parties, which pertain to a definite subject matter.

was misconstrued and confused in the sharp controversy about the application of pluralist theory to power in America. It is now time to clarify this confusion. Pluralist theory needs to be reconsidered from the perspective of political process theory.

Readers may be interested in political science theory, in specific research projects in political science, or in both. Others may appreciate a framework to organize what a lot of political science has been about. I will address these issues.

For those focusing on theory, I believe that the theory of political process has been slowly developing since the publication of David Truman's *The Governmental Process* in 1951. This book is smaller than Truman's landmark work, and there are other books similar to it, but my hope is that it will have an audience among those who like my way of organizing a large body of research into a body of thought. I am part of a collective of researchers about American interest groups and public policy that likely numbers over 500 since 1980. My own distinctive contribution is perhaps an understanding of the position of the pluralist theories of the 1960s with regard to interest group and policy research conducted in the last generation.

I want to communicate an optimistic note to some readers who may be disappointed at the state of research in the area of political process. Although I am somewhat frustrated at the slow pace of accumulation, I am heartened by advances in the study of power especially. I think we have reached the stage of accepted textbook knowledge in discussions of models of power such as elitism, pluralism, neopluralism, corporatism, and statism. Political process researchers have achieved this major accomplishment, in addition to making advances in the study of interest groups, some of which overlap with advances in the study of power.

I am not hesitant to use the term *advances*. I am opposed, however, to a careless use of Thomas Kuhn's *The Structure of Scientific Revolution* (1962) in describing research in political science. Kuhn sees science as progressing through a series of paradigmatic shifts, in which a qualitatively new theory replaces the old within a generation. The criticism of pluralist theory of the 1960s should not lead scholars to think that its basic assumptions (discussed later) should be, or actually have been, rejected by political scientists. Instead, I believe there has been a research sequence from David Truman (1951) to Robert Dahl (1961b) to Theodore Lowi (1969, 1979) to neopluralists (e.g., Walker, 1991) that has led to an accumulation of knowledge in the understanding of political process. The neopluralist theory is internally coherent and effectively incorporates earlier work in the field. Good new research is produced that can be referenced to this framework (see chapter 4). Thus, there has been a research sequence, not a paradigm shift, leading me to be optimistic about the accumulation of knowledge in this field.

As noted, pluralist theory needs to be reconsidered because the controversy about democracy and pluralism in America (circa 1970) obscured the links between the pluralists and later developments in political process theory. This separation is as if one cut off the head of an icon; what is left is not as impressive as it should be. Accordingly, I am violating the "name no federal building after a living person" norm. It seems to me that, as a group, Bentley, Truman, Dahl, Lindblom, and several of their leading adherents are comparable to one of the major figures in social theory—Durkheim, let us say. I see Durkheim's contribution to be less than that of Weber, Marx, or Adam Smith, but greater than that of Michels and the Italian elitists, for instance. This is my view of these four pluralists, taken as a group. As the adjective *Durkheimian* has been meaningful for a century of research, so the term *pluralist* will also be meaningful for a century or more.

In addition to an interest in social science theory, some readers will look to this book to provide guidance on priorities for research projects. Using the framework of neopluralism that I develop, I attempt to do this. As I discuss in more detail later, general research on power (defined as intended influence) seems largely finished, and the next priority within the framework is research on the relationship between power and issue construction. Many researchers already agree with this, so to be more specific, I endorse the project of using frame analysis from sociology as a way to study issues (see chapter 8). Again, I am not unique in this conclusion; the Penn State interest group project does work along these lines (Baumgartner, Berry, Hojnacki, Kimball, and Leech, 2000).

Another research area that developed in the 1990s should be finished within the neopluralist framework. This is the theory of the policy niche, developed from empirical observation that there may be hundreds of policy areas, quite specific in nature, in which very few interest groups are active (e.g., regulation of cesium production). (See Browne, 1990; Gray and Lowery, 1996; Baumgartner and Leech, 2001.)

In the latter part of chapter 5, I look to social movement theory to provide research ideas for understanding the periods of sudden change in public policy, now known as "punctuation." For those not enamored of social science methods, I point out in chapter 6 that political process theory can be tied to historical studies, as power in policy areas varies through time.

A further type of research, not now popular among students of domestic policy, is the study of cooperation among actors who also have conflicting goals (Quirk, 1989), or what I term "cooperative pluralism." This area of political action overlaps with the theory of planning and the political process, an academic study that could be brought into the political process framework. The study of cooperation within mixed-motive "games" is old hat in the field of international relations and might be applied to domestic politics (Jervis, 2002). I have done some research in this area, so I am not solely an advice giver (McFarland, 1993).

Specific research can and will be done in applying models of power to various policymaking situations. Such research is not likely to bring major changes in the theory of power, but it can prove illuminating to those whose lifelong commitment is to some profession or particular policy area. One example is applying theories of power to an understanding of the politics of regulating physician and nurse anesthesiologists, a question obscure to political scientists but vital to many thousands of professionals, to millions of patients, and to all those concerned with health expenditures (Larson, forthcoming). It is not especially prestigious for political scientists to carry out such "applied political science," but such research may be quite valuable to practitioners of specialized professions. Political process theory has a rich variety of potential applications, equal to the applications of political attitudinal research to electoral campaigns.

Social science theory and research as theater calls for an audience with rarefied tastes. But for such aficionados, the development of political process theory presents an interesting and involving narrative.

For the rest of this chapter and in the next chapter, I present an overview of political process theory. In addition, I present a compressed treatment of the pluralist theory of the 1960s. I want to avoid "déjà vu all over again," and it would be easy to say too much about pluralism. Those who would enjoy spending more time with pluralism can sample the earlier works of Robert A. Dahl (1956, 1957, 1958, 1961a, 1961b). To avoid more déjà vu, I do not have a separate section dealing with the criticisms of pluralism; these criticisms are discussed throughout the book, where relevant. Readers are reminded, however, that the core criticisms are Olson's (1965) theory of collective action (probably known to most readers), Lowi's article in *World Politics* (1964a) and his book *The End of Liberalism* (1969, 1979), "The Two Faces of Power" article (Bachrach and Baratz, 1962), and perhaps Pateman's (1970) book on participation.

FOUR BASIC ASSUMPTIONS

Political process theory, and the pluralist theory of power of the 1960s, may be said to have four basic assumptions. They are briefly outlined here and developed further in the course of the book.

The first assumption is that the political process model is normally relevant to questions concerning power, policymaking, and interest groups in some field of action. The political process model is demonstrated in American political science by two books considered to be landmark theoretical statements of previous generations: Arthur F. Bentley's *The Process of Government* (1908/1967) and David Truman's *The Governmental Process* (1951). The Bentley-Truman idea viewed the political process as characterized by a combination of the following elements: (1) empirical observation indicates a large number of agents having causal impact; (2) these agents are seen as groups and individuals representing group interests; (3) the numerous agents interact and affect one another's behavior; (4) the numerous agents act to pursue their interests, defined according to the agents' own definitions of interest, although sometimes this needs to be inferred from behavior; (5) interests are not taken as given, but frequently change in the process of interaction among the agents over time; and (6) implicit by the foregoing, empirical observation should be made over a period sufficient to understand fluctuations in power, interest groups, and policymaking activities. As a result, a political process model is complex; it has many units, many interrelationships that shift over time, and interests (goals) that are frequently redefined by the interacting agents.

The question remains as to the scope of the coverage of the political process model. Bentley, the pioneering theorist of process, argued that it covered everything in politics: interest groups, elections, institutions, political culture, and, presumably, "judicial process." Forty-four years later, disciplinary leader Truman basically argued the same thing, although he may have been hesitant to apply the process model to the entire scope of judicial institutions. However, ten years later, embodying the views of the pluralist theory of power, Dahl in *Who Governs?* (1961b) restricted the process model, at least implicitly, to bargaining among elites, interest groups, and policymaking, with the rules of electoral institutions, along with the outcomes of political process, components in the analysis of power. Another leading political pluralist, Charles E. Lindblom, apparently agreed with such restrictions on the applicability of the process model but preferred to study the area of elite bargaining, interest groups, and policymaking, regarded as covered by political process models such as Lindblom's partisan mutual adjustment and incremental decision-making (Lindblom, 1959, 1965; Braybrooke and Lindblom, 1963). In general, since 1961, researchers in the pluralist or neopluralist tradition of study accept a process model as basic but restrict its scope, as we see in the work of Dahl.

A second assumption of political process theory, as stated by the pluralists of the 1960s, is the definition of political power in terms of causation. That is, A has power over B to the extent that A causes changes in B's behavior in the direction of A's intentions. For instance, Dahl would study the urban renewal decision-making process and find that the New Haven mayor tended to realize his intentions by getting other actors to do what he wanted. Dahl (1961b) defines this as political power. Power here is seen as causing changes in the behavior of others. Clearly there is a sticky issue of the role of intentions. An actor might cause changes in the behavior of others simply by acting, but those changes might not be ones favored by the original actor. In such cases, most would speak of the actor exercising "influence" by causing changes in behavior, even if such changes were opposed by the actor. But it seems, following Max Weber, that it is best to use the word *power* to refer to changes intended by the actor, and to reserve *influence* to refer to any behavioral change (e.g., "he influenced the situation for the worse in terms of his goal"). Herbert Simon, James March, and Robert Dahl introduced the causal definition of power to the process model, though not at first making a distinction between power and influence. Dahl and others later came to see the distinction as necessary (Simon, 1953; March, 1955; Dahl, 1957, 1961b, 1968; McFarland, 1969, chap. 1; 2001; M. Weber, 1946).

The use of power as causation is certainly not a universal. Structural theorists tend to prefer to use *power* to refer to the control of resources, such as money and property (Polsby, 1980), or, in the realm of international relations, as military and economic capability (Morgenthau, 1964). As herein, process theorists would refer to these items as "resources" to be used in the pursuit of power; for example, military capability might be a resource used by one nation-state to threaten an opposing nation-state and make it comply with the policy of the first.

This definition of political power is readily linked to a political process model. One observes the political process and asks which of the interacting units seems to be gaining its way by persuading other units to comply. Such units are said to have power.

The third basic assumption of political process theory, as stated by pluralists of the 1960s, is that power and policy must be studied in specific domains. The political system is seen as divided into numerous separate policy areas (there may not be so many at the local level). The process theorist assumes that the structure of power and the nature of the process may vary in different policy areas. One has to observe various areas to find out. Of course, previous research may lead one to expect a particular pattern of power and process, but someone at sometime had to do an empirical study to establish such a conclusion. This third assumption represents a commitment to one view of empiricism, emphasizing the need to observe (or at least study) actual political processes and a reluctance to accept quick generalizations about power and policymaking. It is linked to the first two assumptions by postulating that power and policymaking could well vary with different policy issues (Dahl, 1958, 1961a, 1961b).

The fourth assumption of the pluralist theory of power of the 1960s, accepted by the later line of neopluralist researchers, involves the definition of the "interests" of the subjects being studied. The assumption is that researchers should accept definitions of interest as given by the subjects themselves, or perhaps as inferred and defined from observations of patterns of behavior. Clearly this assumption rules out the notion of class in the Marxist sense (Balbus, 1971). But a subjective definition of interest also rules out conceptions of quiescence—the idea that some subjects should make an issue out of something but are not observed doing so. A writer such as John Gaventa might argue that poor coal miners should be protesting working and housing conditions, even if they are not doing so, and that such quiescence is a key issue in the study of power. The pluralists of the 1960s called this the problem of "nonissues" and maintained that specifying a list of nonissues embodies value assumptions that could lead to biased research (Bachrach and Baratz, 1962; Lukes, 1974; Gaventa, 1980; Polsby, 1980).

The assumption of a subjective definition of interests seemed to be a major weakness in the pluralist theory, because many scholars believe that a discussion of political power involves an analysis of who controls the agenda of politics. Around 1970, the pluralist scholars of power were unable to deal with this argument in a satisfactory manner, a major reason why many scholars rejected their theory. But many researchers studying power, policymaking, and interest groups continued to assume a subjective definition of interests, but with a small restriction. In situations termed "market failure" by economists, units of production may impose some of the costs of production on the public as a whole; such costs are referred to as "external costs" or "externalities." The archetypal case is the polluting chimney. Neopluralist researchers then tended to restrict the subjective definition of interest assumption to include quiescence in the face of externalities as part of the analysis of power (Coase, 1960).

In other ways as well, more than thirty years of research by neopluralist researchers has limited the significance of the nonissues critique of pluralism, which thus does not constitute a major obstacle to the development of the theory of political process (see chapter 8).

The assumption of a subjective definition of interests fits with the process model, in that the observer assumes that sometimes subjects will redefine their interpretations of interest in a process of interaction with and learning from others in a political process. This might involve causality and intentionality, hence power.

TWO DIRECTIONS OF THEORY AND RESEARCH

The pluralist theory of power can be described as an answer to the question: who has power over whom and over what? As noted, the pluralist answer came in the form of a political process model, specifying patterns of power-as-causation in specific issue areas, and defining issues and interests in the manner specified by the actors. While developing toward a more general theory of the political process, research from the pluralist model branched in two directions. The first direction emphasizes observations of patterns of power and policymaking, and this theory has developed since 1970 from pluralism to neopluralism. Since 1970, such research studies have numbered at least thirty per year, totaling a thousand or more. This research is summarized in chapters 2 to 4 of this book.

The second direction of study focuses on "the power over what" aspect of the basic question. Such research emphasizes the question of power and the formation of the political agenda, and it also attempts to study how interaction among the political actors changes their definition of interests and political goals. There has been only about 10 percent as much research directed toward such questions compared with research about power and policymaking. Yet research about the formation of political issues and how political interactions affect the definition of interests is now the leading effort in studies of the political process.

The four assumptions of pluralist theory of the 1960s—the political process, power as causation, power in domains, and subjective definition of interests—constituted a foundational logic for a type of theory and research. When combined with notions of empirical scholarly practice, this pluralist foundational logic almost necessarily led to an unfolding of research practice as described below.

This foundational logic, combined with an initial research practice, immediately constituted the major approach to the study of American politics in the 1960s and was referred to as *pluralism*. However, the next stages in the unfolding of the logic and practice were viewed as a refutation of the initial theory, rather than as a further development from the initial foundation. This led to the widespread view that pluralism was dead, or at least uninteresting.

Yet from the perspective of a generation hence, the long-lasting significance of pluralism is now emerging. Pluralism constituted a foundational logic for an emerging theory of the political process. It is generally viewed as a theory of political power, perhaps one of several such theories, and often not the best one. This is a misunderstanding of the main import of pluralism. Thus, pluralist theory needs to be reconsidered.

PLURALISM AND THE UNFOLDING THEORY OF POLITICAL POWER

In this section I summarize the unfolding of the theory of power from the statement of 1960s pluralism. The second branch emanating from the pluralist assumptions, the theory of issue formation, is still being developed and is covered in chapter 8.

Focusing on the question of who has power over whom in some area of policymaking, there has been a sequence of accumulating research since the 1960s. The resulting synthesis can be called *neopluralism* and provides a basis for the statement of a theory of political process. This research sequence can be presented as the accumulation of concepts and research in a series of eleven steps.

The first five of these steps represent the pluralist theory of power of the 1960s, as elaborated in chapter 2. Earlier, I outlined four assumptions, or steps, that went into the political pluralist theory: the process model, the idea of power as causation, the idea that power and policymaking should be studied by separate issue areas, and the subjective definition of interests. Lindblom's incremental theory of political process, as stated in his conception of "partisan mutual adjustment," consists of a fifth step in this accumulating development of theory (Lindblom, 1965). His was a theory of political process, incorporating the process model as stated above, but apparently limiting the scope of the process model in the same way that Dahl limited it in *Who Governs?* (1961b). Lindblom's perspective, developed from other pluralist work at that time, incorporated a complexity of interacting political decision-makers, adjusting their goals in light of one another's goals in a process of coalition building, producing policy change in a series of increments. This proved to be an illuminating and provocative theory for the understanding of budgeting and other policy-making functions (Wildavsky, 1964b). As noted, however, the pluralists of the 1960s dropped the universalistic application of the process model by Bentley and Truman; they failed to apply the model wholeheartedly to electoral, legislative, and judicial institutions but retained its use to understand power, elite bargaining, administrative policymaking, and interest groups.

The sixth step in the process was set forth in the 1970s by scholars I call "multiple elitists," as noted in chapter 3. These writers, such as Theodore Lowi Jr., accepted the initial five steps but added a new emphasis and interpretation, that of multiple elites (Lowi, 1969, 1979). While agreeing that the pluralist power of Dahl and Lindblom might be found in a number of policy domains, the newer school of writers emphasized instances in which policy arenas came under the control of particularistic coalitions, sometimes referred to as "subgovernments." Such subgovernments consisted of mutually enhancing coalitions of executive branch agencies, congressional subcommittees and committees, and interest groups that promoted policies advancing particular economic interests at the expense of a wider public. Rather than an optimistic picture of widely fragmented power, the multiple-elite theorists viewed the American political process as fragmented into the hands of a multitude of separate elites controlling their own policy turf.

The seventh step in the sequence was Mancur Olson Jr.'s *The Logic of Collective Action* (1965), a theory that demonstrated why widely dispersed interests would not organize effectively to oppose organized groups representing the interests of a few businesses or professional groups. Why should an individual contribute to a group to get some public good that, if enacted by government, he or she would benefit from anyway? Olson's logic of collective action implied that organized groups with particularistic interests would tend to control policymaking, thereby providing a rationale for multiple-elite theory's observation that particularistic coalitions often control specific policy areas to the detriment of more widely shared interests. The discursive observations of Lowi and others could be backed up by Olson's relatively tight theory taken from economics.

But by 1980, the new multiple-elite theory was being overturned. Later researchers studying questions of power, policymaking, and interest groups usually found well-organized representation of interest groups on two or more sides of an issue, a finding repeated more than a dozen times (see chapter 4). The frequency of such findings contradicted multiple-elite theory. The research finding of a number of well-organized groups wielding power in public policy areas might be termed *neopluralism;* it is different from the original pluralist theory, in that it recognizes that subgovernments sometimes exist and that Olson's logic of collective actions has a major impact.

The eighth step in the series was research explaining why interest groups exist when we would not expect them to exist, according to Olson's theory.

Olson himself postulated that groups would form if they could give their members "selective benefits" not obtainable outside the group—material benefits such as discounted insurance or professional information, and even the benefits of socializing with a group of restricted membership (Olson, 1965). Researchers extended Olson's theory by pointing to the existence of other "interest group sustainers." These included patrons, such as government, foundations, or wealthy persons who give resources to a group (Walker, 1991). Another interest group sustainer is a policy network, a communications network of persons concerned with policymaking in some area who have high personal stakes in a policy for occupational or other reasons and therefore participate in policymaking (Heclo, 1978). A third interest group sustainer is social movements, which motivate persons to form groups in a way not explainable by Olson (see chapter 5). Political scientists came to have a better understanding of why interest groups exist even when, strictly speaking, individuals need not contribute but just act as "free riders."

The ninth step in the development of the theory of power and policymaking was the observation of the effects of social movements and, later, bringing social movement theory to bear in the neopluralist analysis. Scholars of policymaking and interest groups in the 1970s and later frequently observed that the lobbying products of social movements exercised significant power—these were the civil rights, women's, and environmentalist movements, the governmental reform groups, and so forth. Such lobbies frequently challenged the control of subgovernments, and though they were not always equal to the elite coalitions, they at least rendered the power equation more complex. Social movements lead to group mobilization in a manner not easily explained by Olson. By the 1990s, political scientists were using social movement theory to explain these phenomena (Costain and McFarland, 1998).

A tenth step in the pluralist research sequence emerged as a product of the two preceding steps. Pluralist theory had been somewhat unclear about the role of the state or, since pluralists preferred to analyze specific policy areas, the role of administrative agencies. Although early group process models tended to dissolve the state into a flow of groups in the political process, this was rejected by pluralists in the 1960s; Dahl, for instance, clearly describes autonomous action by the government of New Haven in a way not controlled by interest groups. However, this governmental autonomy was described in terms of autonomous action by individual political entrepreneurs, not by administrative structures (Dahl, 1961b; Krasner, 1984). With the emerging neopluralist picture of a welter of groups having some power, James Q. Wilson and others observed that interest group power might be found on two or more sides of an issue and that countervailing power groups might prevent the control of a policy area by a particularistic coalition. This situation enhances the ability of an administrative agency to develop policy on its own, since it is not being dominated by powerful producer groups. Hence, professional belief systems and actions of executive branch officials can have power as an independent effect on policy (J. Q. Wilson, 1980). A standoff among groups provides for some degree of state autonomy. After 1985, there would no longer be an absolute contrast between pluralist theories (now neopluralist) and state autonomy theories (Almond, 1988).

From this sequence, an eleventh idea emerged. Neopluralist writers on power and policymaking clearly recognized that the existence of many interest groups, representing several sides of an issue, does not imply an equal balance of power among interests. No one argues that a pluralist (or neopluralist) system of groups necessarily implies fair or just policymaking. Power on one side of an issue, probably representing corporate or professional elites, is often much stronger than power on other sides of the issue. After Olson's *The Logic of Collective Action,* no one can assume that some observed pattern of widespread group mobilization is an adequate expression of democracy.

WHY CONSOLIDATE?

My reconsideration of pluralist theory is a consolidation of the pluralist theory of the 1960s with two lines of research—political power and issue formation—that emanated from that theory. Why should scholars care about such theoretical consolidation?

First, such consolidation will further research. The synthesis of neopluralism presents a more attractive picture of theoretical accomplishment than the alternative: the achievements of Dahl and the pluralists denied or ignored, and the presentation of other political process research as a scattered series of arguments. For instance, many scholars see elitism, pluralism, multiple elitism, corporatism, and statism (as process theory) as contending theories rather than as different research findings in different situations, findings that can be reconciled and organized according to the four basic assumptions of pluralism stated earlier. The neopluralist synthesis, in contrast, can be considered as a basis for a new political process paradigm.

In particular, the theoretical consolidation can help develop research concerning the definition of issues. The neopluralist synthesis demonstrates the importance of such research and directs scholarly study to this question. In the study of power, the significance of issue definition was recognized as extremely important in the criticism of Dahl's pluralist paradigm, and it is useful to remember this context in designing further research in this area. It would be unfortunate if a number of young scholars were to repeat earlier research work, being forced to "reinvent the wheel" because of a disintegrated presentation of theory in the field. And the demonstration of the neopluralist synthesis could prevent a proliferation of largely unrelated commentary and research resulting in a jumble, necessitating a decade or more to sort it out.

Still another reason for theory consolidation is based on my own observation of the sociology of the research process. A consolidated theory provides a framework of meaning. It provides a place to "plug in" an individual research project or related series of projects. Simply put, a consolidated theory calls attention to various research and helps scholars remember such research. As noted later, thousands of works of research are published within the span of political process theory. If a theoretical structure is consolidated, secondary but accurate and useful pieces of research can be linked to a point on the structure. Again, such consolidation may prevent a repetition of the same research in different contexts, with the researchers and the profession unaware that such work has already been done.

This book is similar in subject matter and scope to *Basic Interests: The Importance of Groups in Politics and in Political Science* by Frank R. Baumgartner and Beth L. Leech (1998). These authors review the history of the study of American interest groups and argue that recently there has been disproportionate study of why individuals join groups in light of the logic of collective action, but not enough study of what such groups actually do in politics. Baumgartner and Leech also see the study of issue formation as at the cutting edge of the study of interest groups, and they have organized a major research effort to collect data on interest group lobbying on a number of national issues.

Baumgartner and Leech share my view about the need for a consolidation of theory, which they term a "paradigm"—Thomas Kuhn's concept, which I criticize later. The two authors state:

> Our review of the literature shows a great number of contradictions and difficulties. It should be clear that the explanation for this has very little to do with the quality of individual studies and very much to do with the lack of a shared general paradigm, a tendency to try to isolate interest-group behavior rather than integrate it into the rest of politics, and the extremely narrow empirical base on which so many studies are based. The lack of a central paradigm is not unusual in the social sciences. (Baumgartner and Leech, 1998, 179–80)

Baumgartner and Leech and I agree on another fundamental point about political process research. They point out the extraordinary misdirection in emphasis among interest group scholars, who since 1970 have given first priority to studying why persons join interest groups rather than what interest groups actually *do* after they somehow get organized. In other words, Baumgartner and Leech argue that more research should have been done about the role of interest groups in the policy process. My book demonstrates the usefulness of their argument. In this book, I focus as much on studies of the political process, and power within that process, as on the study of interest groups. With my political process focus, I am more sanguine about the progress of research, because I see a progression from pluralism through multiple elitism to neopluralism (see chapters 2 to 4). In other words, when we look at public policy, we see progress in research. Baumgartner and Leech are correct in arguing that if interest group research had been more aligned with policy research, more would have been achieved in the field of interest groups. They have organized a major national study to do this, and the argument of this book implies that their study will be successful (Baumgartner and Leech, 1998, 2000).

THE ACCUMULATION OF RESEARCH

In the case of the study of political process, my view is that research has proceeded sequentially along the lines of the eleven concepts stated above. Later research "speaks to" earlier research in a research sequence or research narrative. Most of the earlier findings have been kept, except that they are redefined as being applicable to a more limited scope of phenomena; for instance, Lowi would regard Dahl's pluralism as applying to some policy areas.

The idea of a research sequence or unbroken research narrative contrasts with the common view of research following from organizing paradigms and then experiencing "paradigm shift," in which a new paradigm completely replaces the old. In the case of political process research, we certainly find major changes in outlook if we go back and compare twenty-year periods. If I am correct in saying that the new cutting-edge research about political process involves the relationship between issue formation and power, this is a major change from early 1980s research delineating the influence of many organized groups and autonomous state agencies. But my perspective of the accumulating research sequence differs from the paradigm shift model, in that the new theories of issue formation will extend the previous neopluralist research, not replace it.

One reason for specifying the development of a research sequence is to bring order to the results of a multitude of publications, likely in the low thousands in the case of political process theory. A clear theoretical structure illuminates the contribution of thousands of research results, most of them limited in scope. If the discipline insists on a perspective of paradigm shifts, this leads to the dumping into oblivion of most previous research, even though much of it has validity, albeit limited to a narrow range of phenomena.

The perspective of the accumulating research sequence can build the confidence of political scientists in their own discipline. In the case of the political process research sequence, for instance, the next few chapters argue that political scientists actually know quite a lot about power, policymaking, and interest groups. The results of our research can be applied to hundreds, perhaps thousands, of policy areas to understand these separate political processes. If one wants to understand the regulation of accounting, for instance, we have plenty of ideas. As in this example, there can be "applied" political science. Such applied research might not be pathbreaking in terms of the discipline as a whole, but it can be very illuminating for thousands of persons amidst the policy networks in some issue area.

The consolidation of theory and research, tied to the view of research as cumulative, can enhance the morale of those who want to do research about issue formation but may be using methodological tools that are not considered sophisticated. The development of new issues in the process of political interaction might involve the application of frame analysis or symbolic interaction theory, implying direct observation of actors and counting the number of statements, or perhaps counting the number of statements from congressional hearings and other records. Upon the initial publication of Rogan Kersh's direct observation of lobbyists' activities in 2002, some political scientists were startled to realize that there had been very little such observation by scholars. No one had ever followed lobbyists through their daily activities and simply charted who they talked to and what they talked about. Such research does not involve surveys, statistics, or rational choice models, and it has been avoided by younger political scientists because it is not prestigious. However, a consolidated theory of the political process can bolster the prestige of such straightforward research, because such work is more meaningful within the context of a theory that summarizes much excellent research and writing.

CONCLUSION

Finally, let me state an assumption implied earlier. Political process theory is defined as the answers to these questions: Who has power here? How is policy made in this area? What are the activities of interest groups in this area? This obviously implies that there are other major political science theories to answer other major questions. For example, some will ask: how do authoritarian states change to democracies? This implies some type of structural theory focusing on the nature of civil society, judicial institutions, military organization, and so forth. Or one might ask: how are individuals related to political systems? Theoretical answers to this question are likely to be based on attitudinal research, theories of personality, understanding of the structuring of perception, and so forth. Rational choice theory is an attempt to use one mode of theory throughout the discipline to answer as many questions as possible. But it is the only such broad-gauged effort in our generation of research. For most, political science constitutes several different types of theory, all existing and developing simultaneously. Political process theory is one such theory, developing simultaneously with the others.

2
Basic Ideas of Pluralism

The works of Bentley, Truman, Dahl, Polsby, and Wildavsky and the earlier work of Lindblom have been styled "pluralist theory," in that such research normally found that power in the policymaking process was fragmented, or "plural," thereby disproving the results of research claiming that power was concentrated in a power elite. Although the term *pluralism* has other uses in political philosophy and comparative politics, its use in reference to these scholars is still the more common application. However, such pluralist scholarship is now widely in disrepute, and its defenders normally expect great resistance to positive observations about pluralism. These pluralists are regarded as arguing that all individuals know their own interests and that, in the American political system, all interests are capable of organizing in politics and influencing the political process in one forum or another. Pluralists are also regarded as believing that the policymaking process is a sum or aggregate of the influence pressures of the various interest groups and that such public policy is adequately representative and effective. It has been common practice to begin research publications with negative references to the pluralist model and then to demonstrate the superiority of a newer model of policymaking (Schmitter, 1974; Krasner, 1978, 26–30; Skocpol, 1985, 4).

Herein it is argued that the centrality of this interest aggregation model in pluralist theory is generally overemphasized and that more attention should be paid to other aspects of the pluralist theory. It is probably true to say that Bentley, Truman, and the associated "group theory" scholars left this notion of interest aggregation as a reasonable inference from their work. Bentley stresses group formation around economic interests as the central, driving force in the process of politics. He also stresses that political outcomes result from the interactions of numerous groups affecting one another's actions. Truman never directly states the interest aggregation model, which is supposedly central to pluralism, but it is a reasonable inference from his stress on the prevalence of the countervailing organization of groups: corporate organization will be followed by the counterorganizing of labor unions, McCarthyite organizations to attack civil liberties will be followed by counterorganizations to protect civil liberties, and so forth (Truman, 1951, chaps. 2, 4, 16).

But later pluralism rejected group theory. The most influential pluralist book, Dahl's *Who Governs?* (1961b), explicitly rejects the idea that groups are central in the political process. Thus, in the first chapter, Dahl poses the question: who governs in New Haven? He states that political scientists have nominated four types of answers: political parties, interest groups, a single ruling elite, or unattached masses, as in the mass society idea. He observes, "A superficial familiarity with New Haven (or for that matter with almost any American city) would permit one to argue persuasively that each one of these [four] theories really explains the inner workings of the city's political life" (7). But then Dahl implies that all four theories are simplistic, because each addresses few of the sixteen questions he sees as posed by the general question, who governs? In the subsequent analysis, interest groups play only a minor role, chiefly in the discussion of an ad hoc neighborhood group organized to prevent the construction of cheap housing in its area (192–97). As such, the volume *Who Governs?* clearly implies that interest groups are only a secondary element in the urban polity.

After the publication of *Who Governs?* in 1961, pluralist writers paid little attention to interest groups; pluralists instead concentrated on researching the validity of the Schumpeterian model of competing political parties restraining elected political elites. Pluralists now studied parties and elections, not interest groups. It was not surprising that the 1964 Woodrow Wilson Prize for best book in political science went to Bauer, Pool, and Dexter's *American Business and Public Policy* (1963), whose central conclusion was that interest groups have little influence on Congress. After Dahl's rejection of the general claims of group theory in 1961, no pluralist argued for the policymaking model of all interests being organized and struggling to influence public policy, shaped by the pushes and pulls of interest group forces.

Even the present-day critics of pluralism seem to agree that the uses of the power elite model to describe policymaking in the United States as a whole, or in cities and local communities, are very limited. Instead, social scientists study networks of interaction among elites (Laumann and Knoke, 1987; Heinz, Laumann, Nelson, and Salisbury, 1993). Others apply various theories of hegemony to the study of power (Miliband, 1969; Offe, 1984).

But more central to our purpose, the pluralists contributed four interrelated ideas to the study of policymaking: the process of politics, a definition of power, the concern with separate policy areas, and self-knowledge of interests. These four are closely related to the ideas of partisan mutual adjustment and incremental policy change, which, however, are not basic assumptions. My argument is that pluralist theory provided a group of assumptions and related observations that facilitated research procedures for studying the nature of policymaking. This can be understood in the context of a brief discussion of the pluralist definition of *political power*.

POWER AS SOCIAL CAUSATION

Relying on work by Herbert Simon (1953), Dahl (1957) set forth the definition of *power* for pluralist researchers. Dahl's definition relied on observations that an individual caused changes in a process of social action. Such an individual is said to have power. Of course, social action processes are typically complex; consequently, observations of power tend to be observations of complex causation for those using Dahl's definition.

From 1953 to 1975, several political scientists developed the view of power as social causation, converging with an earlier viewpoint of Max Weber (M. Weber, 1946; McFarland, 1969, 14; 2001; Orum, 2001, chap. 3). After rejecting alternative definitions, Simon (1953) cited a definition of *power* by Lasswell and Kaplan (1950): "The exercise of influence (influence process) consists in affecting policies of others than the self." In the formulation best known to political scientists, Dahl (1957, 203) stated: "My intuitive idea of power, then, is something like this: A has power over B to the extent that he can get B to do something that B otherwise would not do." James G. March (1955, 437) stated: "The set of all influence relations is here defined to be that subset of all causal relations such that the behavior of an individual appears as the terminal point in the causal linkage. Alternatively, we can say that two individuals are in an influence relation if their behaviors are linked causally."

This leads to distinctions among different types of causal relations as they relate to power. For instance, *political power* refers to causal relations among humans, not to inanimate forces that change human behavior, such as a hurricane. A second distinction, producing much confusion, is the need to distinguish situations in which the changed behavior reflects the intentions of the powerful actor. One might change the behavior of another in a way that was not intended, as when an incompetent lobbyist changes a legislator's vote to one different from that favored by the lobbyist. As noted in chapter 1, pluralist political scientists became more comfortable using the term *power* to denote the causing of change in the direction intended by the powerful actor and referring to the more general category of causing any change as *influence*.

Other examples of causal relations include power-as-suggestion: when A proposes a behavior change, B adopts the change without resistance. Another category of causal relations occurs when B resists, and A uses rewards, sanctions, or perhaps even force to get B to change his or her behavior. This is power-as-coercion (McFarland, 1969; M. Weber, 1947, 152).

Ordinary language usage blurs the clear-cut distinction between power as intended causation and influence as causation in general. English speakers sometimes distinguish between power that involves the use of force or other harsh measures and power that involves lighter measures such as persuasion or petitioning, calling the latter influence. English speakers would say that "the constituent influenced the legislator's vote by means of a technical presentation," rather than "the constituent wielded power over the legislature by a technical presentation." Since neither the political science definition of *power* nor ordinary language can be eliminated, we must be clear about such overlapping usages.

With regard to power as coercive causation, John Harsanyi (1962) emphasized the costs of exercising power and also the costs of compliance with the exercise of power. For instance, a lobbyist might change a legislator's vote with little cost if all it takes is arranging a meeting with one of the legislator's staff. Conversely, the cost is high if the lobbyist must mobilize hundreds of persons to petition the recalcitrant legislator. From the standpoint of the legislator, a vote may be "cheap," offending almost no one, or it may endanger his or her victory in the next election.

Still another causal situation occurs when A's preferences cause changes in B's preferences, causing B to act differently. This is widely known as "anticipated reactions," in which B, perhaps to please A and to avoid A's exercise of sanctions, changes his or her behavior in anticipation of what A wants, even though A did not explicitly state such preferences (Nagel, 1975).

An important, implicit aspect of defining power as causation is its link to empiricism. A statement of power then implies observations of A changing B's behavior. It rules out defining power in terms of resources (e.g., wealth or force) used to get B to comply. One first has to observe the causal relationship; then one analyzes how power was wielded.

Such resources were called by Dahl (1957) a "power base," and both he and Simon (1953) warned that the power base should not be confused with power itself. In addition, Dahl stated that power-as-causation, to be an empirically useful concept, has to be used with four concomitant dimensions of power: base, amount, domain, and scope. *Base* refers to the resources or means that A uses to cause changes in others' behavior. *Amount* denotes the idea that some instances of power produce greater changes in behavior than others. A lobbyist exercises more power when he or she changes the legislator's vote from no to yes, for instance, than if the change is only from abstain to yes. The *domain* of an actor's power consists of those persons subject to the actor's power. The *scope* of power consists of the matters subject to the actor's power.

Dahl's major contribution to the study of political power is his insistence that the domain and scope always be clearly stated in discussions of power. Or, to put it another way, an actor's power in one situation should not be generalized to postulate an equivalent power over other persons in other situations. A pharmaceutical lobbyist may have power over just one legislator or over a score of legislators regarding the regulation of generic drugs. The same lobbyist might not have equivalent power over votes about Medicare payments for prescriptions, and he or she might have no power at all over any legislators with regard to civil rights or gun control.

Scope and domain of power were key issues in the still widely remembered community power debate of the 1960s. Following the example set by Dahl in

Who Governs? (1961b), political scientists studied political power in localities by conducting case studies of public policymaking and charting which persons changed the course of events. Such studies normally found that the domain and scope of power were fragmented; different persons had power in different areas of policy. Other social scientists—mostly sociologists—followed a different conception of power, conceiving power to be the possession of wealth or high social status. Such observers usually described inequalities of wealth and status and stated this as a finding of power in a community.

In contrast, political scientists, for the most part, did not consider wealth and status to be power itself, but instead to be resources that could be used to win political power, if such wealthy or high-status persons intended to do so. But such intentions are an empirical question, in this view, and must be observed in case studies.

This famous (or notorious) controversy extended for at least a decade and was expressed in scores of books and hundreds of journal articles before the frustrated debate participants, unable to persuade one another, went on to study questions other than community power (Polsby, 1980).

A RADICAL BROOM

Using the definition of power as social causation, as well as their other basic assumptions, the pluralists attacked other forms of theorizing and perspectives on political reform. If accepted, the arguments of the pluralists would sweep aside most of the work of political scientists before their time. Although such criticism sometimes produced an impression of arrogance, one could also be impressed by the almost revolutionary inclination to "clean house" of worn-out theory.

Of course, elite theory goes out the window if the same small group of individuals does not cause behavior to change in intended directions on important political issues. It seems virtually impossible to show such a change pattern in a local community, let alone a larger political unit. Elite theory is partially saved by multiple elitism, arguing that a discrete coalition (probably a governmental agency, an interest group, and a legislative committee) controls a specific policy area, such as distributing the right to graze livestock on federal land. However, because of their turn toward the study of parties and elections, the pluralists did not go far in the study of interest groups and thus did not address the problem of subgovernments.

Pluralists insisted that the concentration of wealth or social status did not translate to political power, unless such winners in social stratification actually entered the political arena and caused changes in others' behavior. Thus, documenting a skewed pattern of control of wealth in a local community showed only that the wealthy had the potential for power, not that they actually had it, barring observations of political power as social causation (Dahl, 1961b; cf.

Lynd and Lynd, 1929, 1937; Warner and Lunt, 1941). And it seems that the wealthy are less politically active in the local community, according to many pluralist community power studies, than one might expect. Stratification theorists mostly insisted that skewed patterns of wealth and prestige constituted power, in spite of the pluralist criticism (Polsby, 1980). The more sophisticated of the stratification theorists argued that the wealthy did not need to act to cause changes in the system; they were already winners, and their position was not challenged because of the "anticipated reactions" of potential challengers, foreseeing a losing battle and a loss of resources. But the pluralist critique put stratification theory on the defensive.

Pluralists did not take Marxism very seriously as either a theory or a research procedure. Pluralists did not witness cases of owners of property and of the means of production acting together to change the course of the political process, especially in areas studied by pluralists, such as education, urban renewal, and control of party nominations. Using the subjective definition of *interest*, pluralists did not observe evidence of a widespread working-class opposition to an ownership class. Intellectual debate with the Marxists did not go very far; unfortunately, Marxists of the 1960s were still predominantly of the "original" variety, arguing that the state is epiphenomenal to the interests of the ownership class. By 1970, however, Ralph Miliband and others had put forth the neo-Marxist perspective, in which the state might sometimes act independently and the basic source of class control is in social hegemony, or the control of issues that reach the political agenda. This is the sophisticated challenge to pluralism (Miliband, 1969).

Following Bentley and Truman, the pluralists regarded constitutional rules and laws as part of the political process, thus showing a concern for political factors related to judicial appointments, for instance, but not emphasizing the study of laws as factors having a long-term stabilizing, causal impact on the political process (Dahl, 1972). Instead, the process of politics for the pluralists was the interaction of individuals, political parties, groups, and governmental agencies (including courts), in which units or individuals were seen to have more or less political power. Before the use of power as causation, Bentley and Truman regarded the group as the basic actor; after the definition, which is couched in terms of individual A affecting individual B, Dahl and others usually saw the basic actor as an individual rather than an organization (Krasner, 1978).

Thus, the pluralists regarded laws and constitutional rules as legal resources for individual actors to exhibit power in the political process. There was little point, then, in studying laws and constitutions outside the context of political process. Since such study had constituted a large part of political science before 1960, the pluralists discounted much of the previous work in the field. However, the pluralists affirmed the autonomy of institutions such as elections, legislatures, chief executives, and executive branch agencies, as discussed later in this chapter.

The pluralist broom swept out reform-oriented writing. In reply to those who wished to change the system of political parties, the system of electing presidents, participation by the poor, and participation in general in local politics or to introduce systems of administrative rationality and government planning, the pluralists cautioned that we did not yet properly understand the actual workings of American politics and policymaking. Many of the existing practices, though appearing irrational, might make sense in terms of a larger system of action. Wedded to the idea of before-and-after observation of the political process, as it is conventionally defined, the pluralists were quick to point to the lack of such observations in the writings of political reformers. And, from the basic assumptions of the pluralists, it was a double error not to study causes and effects in the political process and then to interpolate one's own values into the system, arguing that political actors would be better off if various reforms were made, even if the political actors were not advocating such reforms (Polsby, 1980).

One common type of political reform is administrative reform—advocacy of systems of planning, programming, budgeting, evaluation, administrative reorganization, systems analysis, and management by objective to make administration more rational. The Lindblom-Wildavsky criticism of such reform schemes was quite devastating (Braybrooke and Lindblom, 1963; Wildavsky, 1964b, 1979). Administration is a political process, such authors noted, with various individuals and administrative units bringing their own interests to the process. It is impossible for outside observers to state a rational outcome for the process, because the actors themselves define the values, and there is no way for the reformer to devise a system to aggregate the values of the participants in a just fashion. Instead, the pluralists argued a form of pragmatism. Let the process unfold, they argued, noting that government policy normally proceeds in step-by-step increments in sequence. The numerous participants are thus able to figure out their interests in light of the incremental development of policy. As part of this theory, policy proceeds in the direction preferred by a strong majority of the actors, and this is likely to be reasonably representative and effective policy. This is where pluralists come closest to favoring policy determined by the aggregate of interest group influences, but Lindblom and Wildavsky actually do not give much attention to interest groups and define the political process more in terms of individual politicians and leaders of administrative agencies.

Particularly at the hands of Aaron Wildavsky, this pluralist broom swept aside a multitude of proposals to reform the administrative process that were not related to the real world of administrative politics. In fact, Wildavsky and Lindblom generally believed that installing an administrative reform system would make administration less effective, since attempts to repress politics are doomed and are likely to produce unforeseen consequences.

From the pluralist point of view, elite theorists, stratification theorists, class theorists, legal scholars, government reformers, and especially administrative reformers could not relate their theories and models to observations of power in the political process. In their view, such writers were not scientific and should be either opposed or ignored. The pluralist broom was radical in its sweep.

PLURALISM AS COMPLEX CAUSATION

What was left for pluralist analysis? Given the basic assumptions of pluralism, one can anticipate the usual conclusions of pluralist studies. If power is social causation, and since we normally expect social causation to be complex, then power (social causation) will be complex. It will be "plural" (McFarland, 1969).

This is foreshadowed in the four basic assumptions of pluralism. First, the process of politics is seen as a fluid, shifting interaction of politicians, groups, governmental agencies, and political parties, all affecting one another over time. Causation or power is complex, as opposed to a model in which an elite or state agency has a great deal of influence on events. Second, as noted, power is defined as social causation when one individual changes the behavior of another individual. The aggregate of such causes and effects is likely to be complex. Third, policymaking is reduced to a multitude of separate issue areas, with several hundred at the national level and perhaps ten or twelve important areas at the local level. Power as causation seems likely to vary among the separate issue areas. Fourth, the subjective definition of *interests* enhances the complexity of the model, because it rules out theoretical procedures by which the observer classifies interests as the same, relative to some objective criteria posited by the observer. Given a subjective definition of interests, the observer cannot posit interests beforehand but must observe the subjects' own definitions. Although in some situations there may be general tendencies of interest definition, normally we observe many individuals with unusual self-definitions: the poor who identify with the rich, the rich who identify with the poor, and so forth.

A fifth major pluralist idea—not one of the four basic assumptions—is *partisan mutual adjustment* as a characteristic of a political process having numerous actors interacting in a complex fashion. Dahl's theoretical collaborator, Charles E. Lindblom, maintained that the goals of the actors within a pluralistic process are dependent on one another and are continually modified by the decision-making participants within political processes. Phrased differently, political actors do not seek to maximize their value in politics but follow "the politics of muddling through" as they modify goals, after taking into consideration the goals of others and the political feasibility of attaining their goals in politics. This is partisan mutual adjustment, with political partisans mutually adjusting their goals in light of the goals of others. In a famous derivative of Lindblom's model, the policy process exhibits incremental change—policy outputs normally change only slowly over time, because the goals and the political resources of those participating in partisan mutual adjustment are unlikely to change suddenly. Lindblom's theory of partisan mutual adjustment provided dynamics commonly described by pluralists in their studies. Later researchers in the political process tradition often found that policy systems do not exhibit incremental dynamics. Instead, they found that the policy process becomes "stuck" in multiple-elitist models (see chapter 3) or that there are decided policy "jumps" or quick changes, and that Lindblom overemphasized the frequency of incremental change (Lindblom, 1965; Hochschild, 1984; Baumgartner and Jones, 1993; see chapters 4 and 8 of this book).

Partisan mutual adjustment and incrementalism were common pluralist findings, but not basic assumptions of the pluralist model. The basic pluralist book *Who Governs?* analyzes a major, nonincremental policy change—the introduction of a massive urban renewal program by the chief executive of New Haven, Connecticut (Dahl, 1961b). Dahl stated in his American politics textbook: "Incremental change, then, can be a powerful means for transforming a society—and has been so in the United States. However, comprehensive changes also occur at times; in fact comprehensive changes are . . . associated with some of the most dramatic events in American political history" (Dahl, 1972, 297–98). Lindblom apparently expected a continuous process of incremental goal changes among actors in the policy process, and such a relatively slow modification of goals by political actors is also consistent with the pluralist model (Lindblom, 1965; Kingdon, 1984; Baumgartner, Berry, Hojnacki, Kimball, and Leech, 2000).

A pluralist political system is a complex political system having complex causation. It has a great number and variety of components, such as individuals, groups, or roles. As pluralist theorist Nelson Polsby noted: "Pluralists, who see American society as fractured into a congeries of hundreds of small special interest groups, with incompletely overlapping memberships, widely differing power bases, and a multitude of techniques for exercising influence on decisions salient to them, are not surprised at the low priority Americans give to their class memberships as a basis for social action" (Polsby, 1980, 118).

A large number of component units in the pluralist political system exercise power, defined as causing changes in the behavior of other component units. In other words, many component variables are affecting many other component variables much of the time. This is another aspect of pluralism as complex causation.

Pluralist findings generally state the variability of systemic components and their relationships through time. Again, Polsby put this very well: "Another presumption of the pluralist approach runs directly counter to stratification theory's presumption that power distributions are a more or less permanent part of the social structure. Pluralists hold that power may be tied to issues, and issues can be fleeting or persistent, provoking coalitions among interested groups and citizens ranging in their duration from momentary to semi-permanent" (Polsby, 1980, 115). Thus, within the pluralist political system, power and coalitional relationships among systemic components vary considerably over time relative to specific situations. Again we see that a pluralist political system is a complex political system.

In contrast, an elitist system has concentrated power and causation. An elitist power structure is a simple power structure: few components have causal impact on the system; power relationships are not interdependent, but spring from the action of one or few components that act as independent variables; and relationships among actors remain relatively constant over time. An elitist system is asymmetrical, being dominated by one-way action. Such systems are centralized structures, in power analysis terms.

Pluralists usually generalize that power in the American system is dispersed, widely shared, and fragmented into kaleidoscopic bits and pieces. C. Wright Mills and others (often political radicals of the Left and the Right) see power as concentrated, shared by few, and consolidated into large lumps. For instance, there is Mills's (1956) "power elite" and the detached, unrepresentative governmental elite of Senator Barry Goldwater's *The Conscience of a Conservative* (1961).

In studying American government, pluralists in the 1960s generally contrasted their observations of complex causation with some simpler model relying on an elite or with some image of concentrated causation of policy. Pluralists thus criticized the thesis that the Senate is directed by an "inner club." They pointed out that the president is at the center of a complex system of interaction within the executive branch and cannot fully control some federal agencies. Applying Lindblom's incremental theory, Wildavsky (1964b) argued that the federal budgetary process is characterized by decentralized complex power (causation), a finding agreed to by all, but he added that the budgetary process should not be centralized, because decentralized incrementalism is a valid measure of the participants' interests. Thus, finding complex causation, pluralists often argued that its replacement with centralized, simpler causation (power) might do more harm than good in achieving representativeness and effectiveness (McFarland, 1969, chaps. 1, 2).

A RESEARCH PROCEDURE

While the pluralist theory embodied the idea of complex causation within the political process, it also offered a reasonably clear research procedure that could be used by political scientists studying a variety of policies and institutions. This helps explain why pluralist theory spread so rapidly in the 1960s. Thus, for the study of American politics, there was a good basis for calling pluralism "the paradigm" or "the orthodoxy." Straightforward research procedures and results acquired the academic imprint of cutting-edge research techniques because that research was linked to impressive theorizing by leaders in the field, such as Herbert Simon, Robert Dahl, and Charles E. Lindblom.

The pluralist research procedure was based on the four basic assumptions of pluralism. These ideas implied the importance of empirical case studies of the political process. As noted, politics was defined according to the definitions of those being studied. Power was defined as an individual (possibly a unit, such as a governmental agency) causing changes in the behavior of another individual or unit. This implied the necessity of observing a flow of events. Power was seen as divisible by issue area and so could not be generalized from one issue area without empirical confirmation.

The techniques for case studies of politics were straightforward. Essentially, the scholar assembled a history of a sequence of political events. To do a history, one interviewed participants, collected documents issued by political participants, read newspapers and official records, and, if possible, directly observed political meetings and other events that were part of the history. The concern for causation did not rule out the communication of the ambience of political events; good writing and readability were valued skills.

Pluralists sometimes conducted relatively simple surveys about political participation and elections in local communities. Following Dahl, pluralists tended to pay special attention to individual politicians, their motivations, and their political strategies. Presidents, mayors, members of the U.S. Congress, state legislators, and bureaucrats were studied as political entrepreneurs assembling political resources to gain power, often to please constituents and thus to keep their jobs. City and town political organizations were another favorite topic of study; these were regarded as organizational entrepreneurs assembling resources to gain support and to win elections, sometimes thereby representing the working classes and assimilating immigrants into the American political system (Polsby, 1963, 1971; Wildavsky, 1964a, 1964b).

Such methods and concepts could be applied to most sectors of political life in America. Thus we have referred to pluralist studies of cities, local communities, and different issue areas both nationally and locally. We have seen that the president and mayors can be viewed as powerful, yet within a pluralistic system of bureaucratic politics. Political party organization can be studied in pluralistic terms. Congress and other legislatures can be studied in terms of centralization or decentralization of power. In studying federalism, one may assume a political process, divided into issue areas, and conduct empirical study of the relative power (causation) of the central government versus state and local governments (Grodzins, 1960). One can study attempts to centralize power in administrative management systems: planning, budgeting, management by objective, government reorganization, and so forth.

This pluralist political theory did achieve some success. For the next thirty years, political scientists eschewed elitist or power elite explanations of political processes. Power elite theories of community power have been supplanted. Those interested in social elites started in the 1970s to analyze elites in terms of network theory, based on aggregating the frequency of communication among individuals or units, and then depicting such communications networks as a mathematical theory of social structure (Laumann and Knoke, 1987).

The supplanting of elitist theories should not be dismissed as not significant. It seems natural for the human mind to suppose, at least initially, that complex events have simple causation, perhaps in the shape of a small group of persons. And if it has explanatory power, a simple theory is better than a complex theory—the idea of Occam's razor. Analytical discourse naturally starts with something like an elitist theory, a theory of simple causation. Demonstrating the limits of simple causal models is a contribution of lasting value to political theory.

LIMITATIONS OF PLURALIST THEORY

A first limitation of pluralist theory, one not much commented on, is that the theory has rather limited explanatory value. Even as the Simon-Dahl definition of political power was being set forth, friendly observers James G. March (1955, 1966) and William H. Riker (1964) introduced the question of "the power of power." Social causation is ordinarily very complex, and case studies are not easy to do; power as causation is thus ordinarily complex, requiring a great deal of effort to study. In contrast to an elitist model, we can be satisfied with a study demonstrating complex causation. But as elitist models lose significance, most observers want more information than that events are caused by numerous actors with reciprocal, interactive relationships that change with the issue and with time. We need new models for understanding the policy-making process.

To be fair to Dahl and to Lindblom, two important models were put forth. Following a line of thought associated with Joseph Schumpeter (1950) and Anthony Downs (1957), Dahl (1961b) asserted the importance of competition among elites to hold political power, with voters choosing among the elites. In practice, this meant an assertion of the importance of competing political parties for the maintenance of representative government; otherwise, political leaders were likely to go unchecked.

Lindblom put forth the concept of incremental political change, which he developed into a multifaceted model. This model proved very useful in understanding American budgetary processes. As mentioned earlier, incrementalism assumed that actors in the decentralized, pluralistic political process considered policy change in step-by-step increments, a process that facilitated the calculation of individual or group interests, because incremental change is relatively easy to understand. Resulting policy changes often embodied the support of a large majority of individuals and acting units and could be viewed as part of a process of representative and effective policymaking.

Pluralists could not deal with the criticism of hegemony theorists, who inquired about power as the capacity to control the political agenda or, much the same thing, the capacity to define what is political. This is discussed in chapter 8, but we can note here that pluralists, assuming the centrality of observing causal relationships, were unable to relate to hegemony theorists' assertions about "nonissues," because such assertions sprang from another theoretical paradigm that was antithetical to pluralism.

Because pluralists assumed the subjective definition of interests, and because they could not deal with the criticism of hegemony theorists, pluralism became regarded in some quarters as a status quo supporting theory. Because of the nature of their assumptions, pluralists could not criticize the current social definition of politics or suggest that other issues might be equally important as those under observable political contention. It should not be necessary to select certain leaders of pluralist thought and enumerate their own support for political reform. Suffice it to say, many viewed pluralist publications as accepting the political status quo, and in the late 1960s, this meant rejection of pluralist theory by many political scientists (see chapter 9).

The next point is surprising. Pluralists stopped studying interest groups. One of the aims of Dahl's *Who Governs?* was to show that David Truman and other group theorists exaggerated the role of interest groups in American politics. One might have thought that interest groups would be added to the extensive list of political institutions and actors studied by pluralists, using the method of finding an elitist theory and then criticizing it by constructing a case study of power and political action. But this was not done.

Relying on my own observations during the 1960s, after *Who Governs?* the pluralist view of interest groups was something like the following: (1) no interest in Bentley, rejection of the idea of group theory as central to politics, but a regard for Truman's *The Governmental Process* (1951) for its good descriptions of the political process, if the group theory aspect were ignored; (2) agreement that ordinary citizens could form ad hoc protest coalitions that could have power at the local level; (3) reliance on *American Business and Public Policy* to state that the power of interest groups over national policy was greatly exaggerated and that, in many policymaking situations, interest groups had no real power (Bauer, Pool, and Dexter, 1963); (4) an assumption in incrementalist theory that some of the interacting forces might be interest groups, somewhat in contradiction of the third point.

The pluralist theory of policymaking turned out not to be a theory of interest groups, as the viewpoint of Dahl and Lindblom supplanted the viewpoint of Truman. Certainly pluralist theory was not based on the idea that public policy is basically a struggle among interest groups, with the eventual policy being the result or vector of the pushes and pulls of interest groups.

THE PLURALISTS' VIEW OF INSTITUTIONS

With the evolution of pluralist studies in the work of Dahl, Lindblom, Wildavsky, Polsby, and others, the idea that interest groups dominated the political process was rejected. Such scholars apparently assumed that Truman and his students had conducted sufficient basic research on interest groups, so they were no longer studied by pluralists. Interest groups were, however, considered to be a routine part of the political process, although this was questioned by Bauer, Pool, and Dexter (1963).

Consequently, the pluralists considered that political institutions are one variable that influences the political process, contrary to straw-man arguments used to differentiate statist theory from pluralism. However, in discussing institutions, Dahl and his associates used a language that became obsolescent. In relation to their perspective on the behavioral revolution in the study of politics, Dahl and the pluralists discussed executive branch institutions in terms of the head of the institution, or possibly other leaders of the institution. Behaviorism focused on the study of individuals; power elite theory defined individuals as the unit, so its countertheory also defined individuals as a unit. The pluralists, of course, were reacting against a political science that seemed to describe laws and rules in textbook fashion, without investigating how laws and rules worked in practice. Therefore, as "behaviorists," the pluralists saw their task as observing how institutional roles were actually carried out, or observing individual behavior within the context of institutions (Dahl, 1961a).

In rejecting the idea that groups dominate, the pluralists considered this to be a sufficient statement about political institutions; they are important but should be studied in the context of how actors behave in relation to institutions, not in the context of how laws and rules develop over time, as is the penchant of statist theory (Skowronek, 1982). The central pluralist statement *Who Governs?* focuses on the study of power in three issue areas. The first of these is the initiation and implementation of an urban renewal program by New Haven mayor Richard Lee, believing this to be a popular program for gaining reelection. In relation to the local polity, Lee expanded the executive bureaucracy by founding a powerful urban renewal agency, and Lee himself succeeded in co-opting most civic leaders to support his "statist" urban renewal effort. In current terms, Dahl's leading case study is an example of statism, the initiation and implementation of policy change by a powerful state institution headed by a strong leader. Dahl's associate, Nelson W. Polsby, uses the language of institutionalism to describe such findings:

> The invention of the office of Development Administrator ... was the device Mayor Lee used to focus his entire city administration upon redevelopment. The job was created for Edward Logue, an energetic, aggressive, and able lawyer-administrator.... In New Haven ... the Development Ad-

ministrator enjoyed unique powers because of the Mayor's commitment to urban redevelopment.... The major substantive decisions on urban redevelopment were made by Logue, Lee, and H. Ralph Turner, executive director of the Redevelopment Agency. Most of these decisions were made in secret.... One of the most striking things about Mayor Lee's urban redevelopment program was his ability to induce economic and status leaders of top rank in the community to "front" for the activities of the professional development staff.... In this case, the people behind the scenes were professionals in City Hall, who formulated their extensive programs largely in secret. (Polsby, 1980, 73, 89)

In the language of a later generation, we would say that this is action by "the local state," which in turn is constrained by laws and rules of the national state: "First, rather strict rules and regulations were prescribed by the Housing and Home Finance Agency which granted the federal share of the costs of redevelopment programs. These regulations covered items such as [the five aspects of renewal policy listed]" (Polsby, 1980, 74).

The second area for the study of power is education policymaking. Again, political institutions are found to be important, although they are acting within the context of interest groups and political officials:

Most decisions in public education, then, were made by educational administrators, more or less hierarchically. A set of particularly significant decisions was made in a process of negotiation in which the Mayor was a central figure. Other sets of significant decisions were made by means of negotiations within the Board of Education, among a cohesive group on the Board, and the superintendent and miscellaneous interest groups, and between the Board and the superintendent, and still other decisions were made by negotiation between party leaders and educational administrators. (Polsby, 1980, 79)

This passage typifies pluralist thought: political institutions are important, although there are other causal factors in policymaking.

The third of the three areas studied in *Who Governs?* is political nominations. I would say that elections are a political institution. This idea is certainly central to the treatment of institutions in rational choice theory, but it seems to be avoided in the historical statism sort of institutionalism (Riker, 1982).

Dahl's other major pluralist work, *Preface to Democratic Theory* (1956), also treats institutions as a major variable, and not just a dependent variable. In particular, the existence of the U.S. Senate, with its allocation of voting by state, is seen as a central factor in influencing policy outcomes. Throughout this work Dahl is concerned with the questions of how laws and rules regulating elections affect political outcomes.

Another important branch of pluralism is the incrementalist theory of the policy process, developed by Lindblom and applied by Wildavsky in his pathbreaking study of budgeting and appropriations. In such studies, institutions are seen as important, although they are usually concretized in terms of interacting individual decision-makers, often representing governmental agencies and their policies. Again, these were studies of role behavior (incremental decision-making) in the context of institutions. Implicitly dismissing group theory, Lindblom, Wildavsky, and such writers felt no need to state that institutions, with their rules and laws, are an important variable in the political process. Wildavsky's budgeting study assumes that the framework of the organization of Congress and the rules of the appropriations process are important. When Wildavsky became disappointed with changes in the budgeting process that led to deficit spending, he proposed fixing the situation with an institutional change—a constitutional amendment to balance the budget (Braybrooke and Lindblom, 1963; Lindblom, 1965; Wildavsky, 1964b, 1980). Of course, Wildavsky thought that the rules of institutions are an important factor in policy outcomes.

Nelson W. Polsby is normally regarded as a leading spokesman for the pluralist point of view, a role that he accepted (Polsby, 1980). This pluralist actually devoted most of his career to the study of institutions, particularly the U.S. Congress. Polsby is quite adamant that institutions are important and basic to the understanding of politics. In 1971 he wrote:

> It is a remarkable fact that American political institutions have survived—indeed flourished—through the strenuous challenges attending the birth of our nation. . . . The constitutional order under which these institutions operate has now remained intact for 175 years, longer than virtually any other government in the world. American political institutions are, by any modern standard, impressively venerable. They are also enormously interesting. (Polsby, 1971, ix)

Polsby affirmed the importance of political institutions and expressed his frustration at those who think otherwise:

> Radicals, in common with many other American intellectuals, betray little interest in how political institutions actually work. They are more concerned with what they conceive to be the outcomes in society than with the complexly interrelated institutions and processes that produce outcomes. The focus here, for better or worse, is on institutions and processes. For the most part, these are real. They exist in time and space, create, spend, and redirect resources, and affect people's lives. They should not be ignored. (Polsby, 1971, vii)

Polsby is certainly an institutionalist.

The pluralists had a time-bound view of the role of law, in the sense that they were reacting to the constitutional and legal study of politics, which might produce compendia of laws and rules without studying how they actually worked in practice. Accordingly, pluralists did not see fit to make statements about the importance of law as ideas influencing the political process; nor did the pluralists give priority to the study of law. Instead, the pluralists were concerned with "the legal process," that is, political aspects of policymaking by the judicial branch and other legal institutions (Eisenstein, 1973). Such study is useful, but soon the discipline moved to study "law and society," that is, legal ideas as a social influence, working within the context of other variables.

Thus pluralism moved from the Truman group theory approach to the Dahl power and policy approach. The Dahl approach regarded political institutions as having a major influence on policy outcomes. It is an extraordinary misreading of this work to say otherwise.

CONCLUSION

The pluralists were criticized for an inadequate treatment of how issues get onto the political agenda and for seeming to legitimate the political status quo. Although the Truman school of group theorists minimized the role of institutions in shaping policy, this was not case with Dahl and his cohort of pluralists, even if Dahl was fuzzy on exactly how institutions fit into the total political picture.

Yet I argue that the pluralists of the 1960s provided a very good start for the evolution of a political process paradigm. The idea of political process as complex causation, the definition of power as causation, the particularity of issue domains, and the subjective definition of interests were four basic assumptions of Dahl's that were implicitly accepted by later generations of political process researchers. Though perhaps adding statistical data analysis, later researchers relied on the research methods of Dahl and his cohort, such as the analysis of case studies of separate issues, the study of press accounts and of documents produced by participants, interviews of participants, sample surveys, and direct observation of events. Such work can be applied to many arenas of politics, not only to hundreds of issue areas but also to events within various institutions, such as legislatures and state and local governments.

However, Dahl and the 1960s pluralists in general did not study interest groups and lobbying because, in their view, too much emphasis had been given to these topics by the group theorists. Therefore, the 1960s pluralists did not do research directed toward another major criticism of their work: their lack of consideration of oligarchical control tendencies in particular issue areas, sometimes called subgovernments or policy subsystems. Nor did these pluralists consider a major reason for such oligarchical control: the logic of collective action. However, much research shortly appeared to fill this lacuna left by the pluralists. I refer to the research focusing on subgovernments and the logic of collective action as "multiple-elite theory," which is treated in the next chapter.

3
The Multiple-Elite Theory

The pluralists may have stopped studying interest groups by 1963, but of course other scholars had been studying groups and continued to study them during the 1960s. Such scholars rejected the idea of a single power elite in America and documented the control of specific policymaking processes by narrowly based elites. In particular, Grant McConnell (1966) and Philip Selznick (1953) argued that various aspects of agricultural policy and public lands management were so controlled. Henry Kariel (1961) made the same argument about agricultural labor policy. Emmette Redford (1969) and Marver Bernstein (1955) studied the capture of federal regulatory agencies. Murray Edelman (1964) argued that such elites could mislead the public through the control of information and symbols. E. E. Schattschneider (1960) provided a theory for the possible dynamics of elite control of a single area, arguing that controlling the range of participants was central to political power. If viewed in combination, Edelman and Schattschneider produced an argument that an issue-area elite could misinform the public, so that it would not be interested in political action to change some particular policy.

Such scholars actually accepted many of the pluralists' theoretical assumptions and research procedures. They studied particular political processes and rejected the power elite idea as it applied to the American polity as a whole. They were concerned about causation in the political process. Furthermore, they viewed American politics in terms of discrete issue areas of policymaking. But these alternative writers did not take as strong a position as the pluralists in eliminating from empirical study all interests that were not known to the participants themselves.

The alternative interest group theorists generally used "fuzzy" versions of the pluralists' research procedures. These scholars accepted the idea of doing case studies within particular policy areas. More than the pluralists, they tended to use the methods of historians, reading histories and commentary by other scholars and gathering documents. Some interviewed participants and observed meetings and governmental decision-making. These scholars were also concerned with who caused what to happen in a policy area, but they were less likely to list participants and specifically enumerate the victories of participants in the manner of behavioral science. Often such writers took themselves out of the theoretical traditions of social science and coined their own concepts for describing oligarchical control of a policy area: subgovernments, little governments, clientelism, interest group liberalism, interest group capture, whirlpools of power, even sometimes using the popular term *iron triangles* (Cater, 1964; Griffith, 1939; Lowi, 1979; Walker, 1991).

The difference between pluralism and multiple elitism can be seen by comparing two research efforts emanating from Yale in the 1950s, when it seems that Yale had the most influential political science department. Robert Dahl's study of power in New Haven, *Who Governs?* (1961b), found that that city's policymaking power was generally dispersed but somewhat concentrated in the hands of the mayor, though he was constrained by the need to please voters to obtain reelection. Herbert Kaufman of Yale joined Wallace Sayre of Columbia, along with research assistant Theodore Lowi, to study policymaking in New York City, publishing *Governing New York City* in 1960. These authors observed islands of power within the city's policy processes, meaning that the Board of Education and the Port Authority had great power within their respective issue areas and that the mayor had little control over these semiautonomous bodies. Sayre, Kaufman, and Lowi (1964b), however, used the same research procedures as the pluralists.

In a classic article, Lowi (1964a) argued that pluralism-elitism varied with the type of policy process in a discrete area. Pluralism might indeed be descriptive, Lowi argued, in policy areas focused on regulation, such as when the federal government regulates working conditions, producing an interest group politics of countervailing business and labor groups. But, Lowi argued, other policy areas might ordinarily be controlled by a narrow coalition seeking to control the distribution of discrete benefits by government, such as the purchase of expensive military aircraft.

Alternative interest group theorists emphasized the finding that oligarchical coalitions tend to control a particular area of policymaking. For instance, one might say that a coalition of trucking companies, the teamsters' union, and sympathetic Interstate Commerce Commission personnel controlled the regulation of interstate trucking. This is an example of what is here termed an "island of oligarchy." Rule by the few exists, but it is limited to an "island," a single policy area consisting of the regulation of trucking.

Such alternative interest group writers found islands of oligarchy in many areas: federal public works construction (pork barrel); the Port Authority in New York City; the anti-monopoly policy of the Federal Trade Commission; and the regulation of airlines, trucking, local and long-distance telephone carriers, nuclear power plants, and railroads before their defeat by trucking interests (Bernstein, 1955; Maass, 1951; Redford, 1969; Sayre and Kaufman, 1960; Stigler, 1975). Defense contracting was another area in which collaboration among defense industries, the Pentagon, and members of Congress with relevant constituencies seemed to be common. Agriculture was seen as rife with islands of oligarchy: the Farm Bureau (the center of many little governments), tobacco production, sugar production, orange production by the Sunkist cooperative, peanut production, the distribution of cheap grazing rights on federal lands, the distribution of subsidies for conservation projects such as farm ponds, the regulation of water sales from federal irrigation projects, and the distribution of the benefits of the multipurpose Tennessee Valley Authority's economic development program (Cater, 1964; Foss, 1960; Lowi, 1969; McConnell, 1966; Selznick, 1953). The regulation of the insurance industry by state-level governments was seen as another example (Orren, 1974).

At the time, most political scientists did not realize that a group of economists, influenced by Milton Friedman and George Stigler, was making a parallel argument, bolstered by quantitative analysis. Such economists argued that government regulation led to the formation of business interest groups, which subsequently captured the government regulatory agencies, thereby controlling the regulations themselves and leading to a form of policy ownership in which "rents" were charged to the general public (Stigler, 1975).

The multiple-elite theorists were not interested in making elaborate arguments about hegemonic domination (an exception being Edelman's [1964] theory of dominance through the manipulation of symbols). They simply dropped the extreme insistence on the self-knowledge of interests. They needed only weak assumptions about the lack of benefits in price fixing and the elimination of competition. Or if a clique of local, wealthy farmers distributed agricultural subsidies among themselves, alternative researchers saw no need to observe the clique defeating the larger number of farmers to prove oligarchy. As realized by most political scientists by 1980, the assumptions of the alternative interest group researchers were similar to the assumptions generally held by economists. Thus, economists might analyze oligopoly or monopolistic competition in terms of raising prices and leading to economic inefficiencies and not worry about whether it was the subjectively understood interest of everyone to use scarce resources most productively.

Economists might talk about the capture of regulatory agencies leading to "deadweight losses," that is, economic waste detrimental to almost everyone. An economist could refer to "market failure" leading to the imposition of costs on those external to the production process, as in the case of severe pollution from factory emissions. The economist does not worry that some of the citizenry might have no opinion about instituting government policies to "internalize" the externalized costs of production (Becker, 1985).

Besides islands of oligarchy, another major new idea put forth by multiple-elite theory was Olson's (1965) logic of collective action. Olson's theory was the best single theory to explain the existence of islands of oligarchy. Olson based collective action theory on the sort of economic theory just considered. Oligopolies produce a collective benefit for constituent units (although not for the public), as a few units cooperate to restrict production and raise prices. But as the number of producer units increases, it becomes more difficult to collude to restrict production, because some firms will leave production restriction to others and produce more to obtain higher profits for themselves in the short run. Similarly, Olson reasoned, a few units will contribute to support a political lobby, but as the number of units increases, they will all try to be free-riders, and the lobby will get no contributions. Olson concluded that a lobby with a large number of units could exist only if an interest group offered selective benefits that were restricted to its members—to make membership worthwhile for the member units—and then put some of the group's resources to work in lobbying.

The logic of collective action therefore predicted that lobbies for consumers, victims of pollution, and other constituencies of perhaps a hundred or more units would not exist unless they provided members with selective benefits worth more than the cost of joining. Collective action theory predicted, in contrast, that small groups of producers would collude to form lobbies to work in their interests, and therefore "the few would defeat the many," in Olson's terminology.

The few would defeat the many by controlling particular policy areas of regulation, for instance, through lobbying and forming a dominant coalition, while the more numerous constituents on the public side would be unable to organize. Such an argument would apply to much government regulation of business, such as the regulation of prices, pollution, service, and safety. It could also be applied to agricultural policy, especially insofar as local farm elites captured policy administration. It could be applied to public works construction, as beneficiaries of construction form political coalitions to maintain spending. The logic of collective action was a persuasive argument on behalf of multiple-elite theory.

Thus, by adhering to weak assumptions about the nature of "interests," similar to those routinely held by economists, the multiple-elite theorists could use pluralist methods and assumptions to develop a policymaking theory that was different in its conclusions about the nature of power and policy.

Unfortunately, the multiple elitists were not conscious of themselves as a school of theory, so that in retrospect, the impact of their work may dwindle. Instead, these writers tended to write separate books about power and policymaking, not citing one another very much, and in general came to be viewed as mainstream critics of pluralism, as opposed to statists (also mainstream) or politically radical critics of pluralism.

SUBGOVERNMENTS AND STASIS

Multiple elitism admitted the absence of a single power elite but viewed public policy as fragmented into hundreds of separate political arenas, many of them under the control of particularistic elites. In this view, in American public administration, the few defeat the many through the mechanism of the *subgovernment*. This is a coalition of interest groups, public administrators, and members of Congress serving on the relevant committees that control the administration of public policy for the benefit of those within the subgovernment. Such policies usually benefit established economic interests. A subgovernment tries to destroy executive agencies working within the same policy area but outside of the subgovernmental coalition. These agencies, which compete with subgovernments, include a disproportionate number that represent the general interests of the poor. Subgovernmental elites normally prevent the implementation of policies set by decision-makers representing widespread constituencies, as when Congress or the president acts in this capacity (McConnell, 1953, 1966; Lowi, 1969, 1979; Cater, 1964).

Multiple-elite politics provides a framework for Schattschneider's (1960) classic dictum that manipulating the scope of conflict is a basic variable in political action. In this sense, the subgovernmental elites seek to act in such a way as to prevent representatives of broad constituencies from acting and exercising power within that elite's area of policy concern.

Multiple-elite theorists do see challenges to the rule of subgovernments. They see that American politics is subject to reform cycles, when the scope of conflict regarding a subgovernmental policy is expanded, in spite of the actions of that area's elite. These theorists tend to think in terms of reform cycles within some area of public policy. At times, general-interest coalitions defeat the subgovernmental coalitions and enact reform legislation in specific areas of public policy, but subgovernments eventually reestablish their control (Lowi, 1971; McConnell, 1966; Edelman, 1964; Bernstein, 1955; see chapters 4, 6, and 8 of this book for further discussion of reform cycles).

Other writers state that even if reformers establish new policy-oriented government institutions, such institutions must compromise major reform goals to fend off the powerful coalition that once constituted a subgovernment, as Selznick (1953) observed about the Tennessee Valley Authority. The more pessimistic McConnell (1953, 1966) seemed to conclude that any reform policy–oriented institution in the agricultural or natural resources domains would be destroyed or captured by powerful subgovernments. Selznick and McConnell argued that many such federal government programs are co-opted by locally oriented subgovernments, which undermine effective policy implementation by diverting the distribution of benefits to local elites (the wealthy farmers get almost everything, the sharecroppers get nothing).

One elite theorist, Murray Edelman, differed from the others in stressing the symbolic element in politics in a work that was widely influential not only in political science but throughout social science: *The Symbolic Uses of Politics* (1964). Edelman stressed that the few defeat the many through the manipulation of political symbols. He saw that widespread but unorganized publics are prone to irrational perceptions of political reality. Such publics confuse symbols with substance—that is, elites manipulate public opinion by creating political forms that give the impression that some problem is being solved or some policy is being followed when this is not the case. In contrast, political groups consisting of a few corporations do not usually confuse symbol with substance. Such small groups, following rational political strategies, frequently defeat the interests of very large publics that are confused by political symbols and following irrational political strategies. Edelman published before Olson and was thus unaware of the logic of collective action, but Edelman provided a very different theory that came to the same conclusion as the logic of collective action: the few defeat the many, and multiple elites rule.

Multiple-elite theorists drew the conclusion that America is subject to economic stasis because of the power of special-interest subgovernments. Congeries of subgovernmental coalitions introduce inefficient policies, which produce economic decay. As Olson (1965, 1982) argued, within pluralistic societies, interest groups are free to organize without significant governmental restriction. But because of the logic of collective action, groups with specific economic interests will defeat groups representing the general public. Over time, this leads to inefficient governmental regulation, subsidies, and oligarchical economic organization, which eventually eliminate economic growth.

Writing before Olson made this argument fully apparent, Lowi (1969, 1979) observed that, beginning in the 1960s, the federal government instituted vast programs of subsidies (especially through subsidized loans) for established interest groups. This, in his view, freezes the political system in the status quo, retards policy innovation, and lessens the influence of newly emerging interests. The pervasive politics of the distribution of benefits renders unattainable other policy goals, such as economic regulation or the redistribution of wealth.

Nobel Prize–winning economist George Stigler (1975) argued in a similar fashion to Olson, but he was more specifically concerned with the effects of lobbying and government regulation on economic policy. Stigler argued that government regulation usually benefits special economic interests. He observed that it is a normal process in industrial society for particularistic businesses or professional lobbies to mobilize political resources to gain legislation or regulations that principally benefit that business or profession. Such regulations typically limit entry into a business or profession, retard the rate of growth of new firms, eliminate substitute products or services, establish protective tariffs, fix prices, and gain subsidies from public funds.

The more conservative version of multiple-elite theory argued that the special-interest politics of governmental expenditures can lead to a continual increase in such spending, which is, in the long run, economically inefficient (Wildavsky, 1980; Niskanen, 1971). These writers viewed overall government spending as the most pressing problem associated with multiple-elite power, more pressing than the long-term economic degradation indicated in the conclusions of Olson and Stigler. The spending theorists argued that if cultural norms restricting governmental spending break down, collusion among interest groups, governmental agencies, and legislators produces spending increases in numerous areas of public policy. A contributing factor is that the size of governmental bureaucracies will continually expand as each governmental agency collaborates with its allies to increase its budget (Wildavsky, 1980; Niskanen, 1971).

CONCLUSION

The general conclusion of multiple elitism can be summarized in the phrase *interest group stasis*. Both political and economic innovation is unstable and quickly dissipates into the relatively simple organization of political-economic oligopoly. The main thrust of politics becomes negotiations among the various policy area elites in a massive system of logrolling. These elites trade political support to maintain one another's subsidies: California defense contractors and their representatives might agree to support subsidies for public housing construction in the Northeast, and vice versa. Dairy farmers trade support for pro-industry trucking regulation for votes for higher milk price supports and so forth. A minority of citizens, aided by well-organized lobbies, gains in the short run, but everyone loses in the long run. Government spends more and more; budget deficits increase as special-interest lobbies gain exceptions in the tax code. The economy deteriorates.

In the real world of political behavior, the "citizens" victimized by interest group stasis would presumably overthrow it, substituting some form of political-economic organization with greater promise for fulfillment of the public interest. One powerful stimulus to such an overthrow would be the maintenance of national political and economic sovereignty in an environment of heightening international economic competition. Indeed, in the real world of American politics, one would expect anti-stasis politics to appear before the whole system came close to economic collapse. This is the politics of countervailing power described in the next chapter.

Multiple-elite theory has contributed the ideas of islands of oligarchy and the logic of collective action to the study of political power, policymaking, and interest groups. The general concepts of the centrality of scope of conflict and the uses of symbolic politics also enhance multiple-elite theory. Multiple-elite theory is further enhanced by such concepts as reform cycles, political and economic stasis, and co-optation. Such ideas are of enduring value and provide guiding questions whenever we study power, policymaking, and interest groups.

Multiple-elite theory should be viewed in a broader context. Much of this theory consists of separate writers, most of whom seem unaware of other writers of this ilk. It is thus incumbent on later scholars to show the relationships among their ideas. Their work can thus be seen as an intermediate point in the development of political process theory. In logic, and usually in research time, the multiple-elite school came after the pluralist school of the 1960s but before the neopluralist school of the 1980s. As the concepts of multiple elitism provide a perspective on the 1960s pluralists, they also provide a perspective on the 1980s neopluralists. The questions posed by multiple-elite theory will always be worth asking. Whether this theory is confirmed or disconfirmed in a particular policy situation depends on a variety of empirical circumstances. In recent years, neopluralist systems of policy have been observed more frequently than the subgovernments of multiple-elite theory (Walker, 1991).

4
Neopluralism

After multiple elitism, four new ideas were added to the policymaking sequence: neopluralism, interest group sustainers, social movement theory (discussed in chapter 5), and state autonomy, emphasizing the state and countervailing power. In this chapter, neopluralism is first discussed as the finding of numerous competing groups in a policy area and as the determination not to equate competing groups with just or fair policymaking in that area. After discussions of interest group sustainers and the state and countervailing power, I return to neopluralism, indicating some of the more recent concepts and research findings that have become part of the neopluralist synthesis. The addition of these ideas produced a theoretical synthesis about policymaking, a sort of stopping point, but one that seemed to be "only halfway there" in terms of a conclusive statement of a policymaking theory within the boundaries of social causation, political process, particular policy sectors, and somewhat relaxed assumptions about the self-knowledge of interests.

During the 1970s and 1980s, political scientists put considerable effort into studies of the American political process, including policymaking and the role of interest groups. Such studies typically did not relate primarily to the elitism versus pluralism controversy, now of less interest to scholars bored with the lack of progress in community power studies of elitism versus pluralism. One such scholar was Charles O. Jones, who later emerged as a disciplinary leader in the study of Congress and the presidency. In his *Introduction to the Study of Public Policy* (1970), a theoretical work, Jones accepts the three pluralist concepts of the political process model, the subjective definition of interests, and the idea of varying research according to issue area, but he shows little interest in pluralism versus elitism or the causal definition of power. Jones affirms that interest groups have importance in the policy process, but not to the degree theorized by David Truman. Accordingly, Jones presumes that Congress and executive branch agencies often have the capability of initiating public policy (C. O. Jones, 1970, 27–32, 56–65, 97). In 1975, Jones published a book that embodies his theoretical conceptions, *Clean Air: The Policies and Politics of Pollution Control*. There, he studies a political process in which many governmental agencies at various levels of federalism and many interest groups all have power, as well as politicians responding to the public. Jones assumes that clean air legislation needs political support, including from interest groups, to be effectively enforced in the implementation phase. Jones recognizes that policy can be captured by industry, but that countervailing political power can forestall this (C. O. Jones, 1975, 272–75).

Other "neopluralist" scholarship was more concerned about criticizing the multiple-elite school than Jones was, but like Jones, it was most interested in certain substantive questions. One of these was the nature of regulation by the federal government, regulation that had greatly increased with new environmental, civil rights, worker health and safety, and other laws, especially in the early 1970s. Other scholars were particularly interested in the nature and impact of new participants in the policymaking process—the public interest groups and new social movements of the time.

In the area of air pollution, for example, in addition to Jones, studies by Bruce Ackerman and William T. Hassler (1981), Norman Ornstein and Shirley Elder (1978), and Lettie M. Wenner (1982) all found that environmentalist groups have significant effects on public policy. Jeffrey M. Berry (1977), Andrew S. McFarland (1976, 1984), Robert C. Mitchell (1984), Mark V. Nadel (1971), and David Vogel (1980–1981), among others, chronicled the significant strength of public interest lobbies. Jo Freeman (1975), Anne N. Costain and W. Douglas Costain (1983), Ethel Klein (1984), and Joyce Gelb and Marian Lief Palley (1982), among others, found women's lobbies to be important. John D. McCarthy and Mayer N. Zald (1977) generalized from such observations to develop the *resource mobilization theory of social movements*, which implies that movements frequently create lobbying organizations. Samuel Beer (1976), Donald Haider (1974), and others described the phenomenon of governments lobbying other governments—associations of cities, counties, and so forth lobbying in Washington and elsewhere. Walker (1983) and his collaborators (Gais, Peterson, and Walker, 1984) found a great increase in lobbying by nonprofit organizations (e.g., churches, hospitals, and colleges); by professions, especially groups of government employees; and by ideological cause groups. Kay Lehman Schlozman and John T. Tierney (1986, 55–57) found a great increase in government lobbies since 1960, although they argue that this has not substantially decreased the business domination of other lobbies.

A new picture of interest groups was presented. A complex welter of group participation in policymaking was often observed (Jordan, 1981; Jordan and Maloney, 1996; Gray and Lowery, 2000; Lowery and Brasher, in press). True, this had been the case with Truman's *The Governmental Process* and policy process studies of the 1950s. But after 1961, such studies lost prestige as the pluralists preferred to study community power or American national institutions. Meanwhile, the multiple elitists concentrated their research on cases in which a particular policy area was dominated by a single coalition.

The neopluralists invariably observed that a complexity of interest groups did not imply a fair or effective policymaking process. But they often found a large number of different groups at work in a single issue area. Air pollution regulation is one such instance. To begin with, national environmental groups had influence, particularly through litigation, but also through lobbying Congress and contacting the Environmental Protection Agency (EPA). Such groups included the Sierra Club, the Sierra Club Legal Defense Fund, and the air pollution specialist the Natural Resources Defense Council. In addition, locally based environmentalist groups might initiate litigation and contact political officials, such as members of Congress.

As argued in traditional group theory works by John Kenneth Galbraith (1952) and David Truman (1951), business interests often were not monolithic, but divided. In the case of air pollution, for example, the interests of Appalachian coal mining, producing relatively high-sulfur coal, were different from the interests of Wyoming coal mining, producing lower-sulfur coal. (The question was whether regulations should emphasize the use of low-sulfur coal and give lower priority to equipment to take sulfur out of emissions.) Northeastern vacation and recreational businesses, hurt by pollution drifting in from the Midwest, had different interests from those of power companies in Ohio. Producers of emissions-scrubbing machinery would advance the use of their technology, as opposed to the mandated use of low-sulfur coal. The nuclear power industry, both utilities and producers of nuclear reactors, might advance the position that nuclear power does not emit air pollution. Railroads might advance the cause of low-sulfur coal, which, if mandated for use in the Midwest, would need to be transported by rail.

In the realm of air pollution policy, charitable associations such as the American Lung Association and the American Public Health Association would lobby. Not only the EPA but also units of the Department of Energy would be involved in the lobbying process. The President's Council on Environmental Quality might be heard from, and the Office of Management and Budget would conduct cost studies of proposed regulations, putting it in a position to influence policymaking.

Units of the federal system might lobby Congress or federal agencies. The state of Ohio might lobby for scrubbing systems rather than restricting the use of Ohio-mined coal. The state of New York and the city of New York might lobby for tight controls on the use of sulfur, which otherwise is wind-borne to the Northeast. The National Governors' Association, backed by state environmental protection agencies, might lobby for significant state government participation in air pollution policymaking. And the list goes on.

We see that citizens groups, a welter of different types of business groups, charitable organizations, state and local governments, and national associations of state and local governments are frequently involved in air pollution policymaking. Because public health is involved, medical doctors and public health officials have some appreciable role, as do various professional groups in most areas of public policymaking. Different units of the federal government may become involved, sometimes with opposing viewpoints; the Department of

Energy may seek to keep energy prices down, while the EPA emphasizes the restriction of pollution.

In this example, we see that units of the state might participate in policymaking as autonomous actors, not largely controlled by some particular interest group. We see that the existence of a social movement—environmentalism—has spun off interest groups that participate in policymaking. And, in general, we see a complex variety of interest groups at work (Ackerman and Hassler, 1981; C. O. Jones, 1975).

INTEREST GROUP SUSTAINERS

Political process research before 1960 usually assumed that persons or organizations would pursue their political interests by forming interest groups, but the traditional research did not pay systematic attention to barriers to organizing groups. The multiple-elite school concentrated its attention on situations in which interest group organization was almost entirely on one side of a policy issue. When Olson published his work on collective action, the multiple-elite writers could then bolster their case by referring to an impressive theory based on rational choice assumptions. But when researchers began finding numerous organized groups active in the policymaking process, they were at a loss to explain why such groups existed in light of collective action theory.

A scholar outside the social sciences might simply object: if Olson's theory does not work, then throw it out. But Olson's theory could not be easily dispensed with. First, it was a general statement based on rational choice assumptions, the very type of theory becoming increasingly popular in political science. Second, it provided the best explanation of why persons did not join interest groups, or why previous members quit. In a number of areas, such as support for environmental policy or regulation of money in elections, surveys showed a much greater support for the platforms of citizens groups than the number actually contributing (Shaiko, 1999, 30). Third, Olson explained the lack of group countervailing power in situations of islands of oligarchy, which even neopluralists agreed sometimes existed. Fourth, Olson's focus on the utility of offering selective benefits to only contributing members proved useful in understanding the dynamics of many interest groups. (For instance, the benefits offered to members of the American Association of Retired Persons are so useful that the majority of persons over age fifty have joined.) In particular, the closed shop is beneficial to unions, since the job becomes a selective benefit to union members. In addition, the selective benefits offered by many professional associations go a long way toward explaining the existence of more than a thousand groups of this nature.

In the mid-1980s, interest group theory faced a puzzle of almost amusing irony. Researchers had an excellent theory to explain why groups should not exist, but there was no widespread agreement on a theory to explain why groups do exist, especially in light of the occurrence of a multitude of groups. By the year 2004, there is still no single textbook answer to this question, although by now, many researchers would point to the action of one or several interest group sustainers, as cited later. Indeed, perhaps social science is such that one cannot develop a single theory to respond to Olson's logic of collective action. Perhaps it is possible only to cite one or a few of the several dozen theories responding to Olson and to indicate a few concepts that have wide usefulness for research (Lichbach, 1995).

First, some groups are started or maintained by political entrepreneurs, to use the rational choice language. One or more individuals take it upon themselves to start a group and to bear the time costs of organizing and doing the necessary fund-raising. There is evidence from Walker's surveys that about half the interest groups responding had been organized by such political entrepreneurs. The general public is aware of the careers of Ralph Nader, John Gardner of Common Cause, Ethel Andrus of the Retired Teachers Association, and Samuel Gompers and others in the labor movement (Berry, 1978; Walker, 1991).

The idea of the political entrepreneur was adopted by sociological theorists John McCarthy and Mayer Zald (1977), who took a new look at the phenomenon of social movement behavior and organizations in light of collective action theory. They then took the idea one step further by concentrating their analysis on the nature of the resources used by movement leaders to start and maintain a movement. What institutions helped the movement? Where did the money come from? This approach was then adopted by Walker (1991) for the study of political interest groups and lobbies. Surveys found that political entrepreneurs often did the organizing, but where did such entrepreneurs get the money and other resources for organizing? Were there outside sources?

Walker argued that *patrons* played a key role in organizing interest groups and were particularly helpful in understanding the organizing of citizens groups, in which members pursued public policy issues even when such policies did not have a great impact on the members' own pocketbooks. Patrons included wealthy individuals, foundations, other organizations (which might offer management knowledge, for instance), and governments, particularly the federal government. Walker observed that many nonprofit groups, oriented to influencing policy, received grants for research and other activities from the federal government. Walker also focused on the history of group organizing, in which federally sponsored conferences, committees, and organizations provided the impetus for organizing the National Association of Manufacturers, the U.S. Chambers of Commerce, the Farm Bureau, the Business Roundtable, and the National Organization of Women. In addition, there are the various associations of governments themselves: the National Governors' Association, the Mayors' Roundtable, the League of Cities, the National Association of Counties, and so forth. Government provides employees with jobs, which then become the basis for organizing groups: police and firefighters at the local level; the National Education Association; the American Federation of Teachers; the American Federation of State, County, and Municipal Employees; associations of prison guards; and so forth. The national association of state attorneys general recently played a prominent political role in attacking the tobacco industry.

Walker emphasized government as a patron because, in American society, it is probably the most important group patron, and also because it contradicts the conventional image of groups organizing to lobby government. Instead, government organizes groups to lobby itself.

In addition to government, foundations were important patrons to environmental lobbies during their great upsurge from 1968 to 1975. The most important of these, the Ford Foundation, backed off from large-scale funding of environmental protest groups in the mid-1970s, but such efforts left behind a flourishing lobbying sector. In addition, lobbies occasionally benefit from grants by wealthy individuals. Such grants usually need not be publicly reported and may not be publicized by a lobby, seeking to maintain a public image of independence from its donors (Walker, 1991).

Another source of the proliferation of groups is social movements (Costain and McFarland, 1998). In America, movements against established institutions and policies use noninstitutionalized tactics, almost by definition. But eventually, movements develop a lobbying arm, using established influence tactics. There was an upsurge of social movements in the 1960s and early 1970s, producing a number of new interest groups, such as those in the environmental, civil rights, women's, government reform, and, later, Christian fundamentalist areas. Social movements and their relationship to interest groups and public policy are the topic of chapter 5.

Another theory addressing the proliferation of interest groups was provided by policy theorist Hugh Heclo, whose concept of "issue networks" found immediate, widespread acceptance among political scientists. Heclo observed that although the structures of multiple-elite theory could be observed in a study, they were frequently countermanded by communications and ad hoc organizing by others in an issue area. For instance, in the case of air pollution policy, there is a tendency for eastern coal mining businesses; eastern miners; legislators representing Ohio, Kentucky, and West Virginia; and the Department of Energy to favor the use of high-sulfur coal scrubbed with expensive equipment. But there are also coal mining, air pollution, and electric utility issue networks filled with persons who communicate about politics and economics. For instance, the air pollution network contains leaders of the EPA and state agencies concerned with the issue. In addition, university researchers, environmental group personnel, recreation industry organization personnel, Lung Association staff, and journalists regularly communicate about policy in this area. Federal and state legislators specializing in environmental legislation, and the staffs of such legislators, are part of the issue network as well. Constant professional communication thus provides sources of policy information different from that provided by the potential "iron triangle" of coal-burning electric utilities, pro-utility state regulatory commissioners, and allied state legislators. The links among the issue network lower the costs of contacting persons and groups to organize a lobby to countervail the power of the high-sulfur coal producers and users (Berry, 1989b; Heclo, 1978).

The concept of issue networks provided another reason why interest groups and coalitions of groups might organize. It also led observers to note communications among agents in a policy area, and how such communications might lessen the tendency to develop oligarchical control of the policy area. The idea of issue networks applies to almost all the separate areas of public policy. With the increasing technical complexity of many public areas, issue networks become more extensive and complex, embodying various types of interests and experts. Professionals, researchers, and publicists become part of the network, as in the case of air pollution. Executive and legislative staffs expand, including many with professional expertise who are incorporated into the network. The groups sustained by entrepreneurs, patrons, and social movements become part of the issue network.

The logic of collective action implies the absence of many large groups having many members. But this is not the case. Entrepreneurs, patrons, social movements, and issue network collectivities organize and maintain such groups. The students of policymaking understand some of the reasons for the proliferation of interest groups in America, so they have turned to other questions.

THE STATE AND COUNTERVAILING POWER

In chapter 2, we noted that Bentley and Truman's pluralist model centered on political groups controlling political institutions, but this view was clearly rejected by Dahl and others of the next generation of pluralist theorists. Such scholars as Dahl, Lindblom, Polsby, and Wildavsky described political institutions as frequently acting autonomously, not controlled by political groups or by some extragovernmental power elite. Such pluralists preferred to refer to separate institutions, such as the Senate, the House of Representatives, the New Haven urban renewal authority, and so forth. Analogous to their preference for studying policy areas separately, these scholars referred to political institutions separately and did not aggregate institutions into a theoretical construct of "the state." This term appears almost nowhere in the writings of this school of pluralists.

This has led to confusion. Pluralists are frequently thought to believe either that the state has next to no power in policymaking, because interest groups control everything, or that the state is only equivalent to the rules of the game of governmental decision-making. For instance, in the fourth and fifth sentences of an important book, sentences not footnoted and apparently judged to represent a scholarly consensus, Stephen Krasner (1978, 5) states: "The governing liberal paradigm does not view the state as an independent entity. At best it is seen as a referee among competing social groups, at worst as a cipher." (Krasner regards pluralist political science as part of the paradigm of liberalism.) The point is that Dahl's generation described political institutions as "independent" entities but did not generalize to descriptions of "the state."

Another confusing factor is that the term *pluralism* was originally descriptive of an early-twentieth-century political philosophy that took the position that others had placed too much value in the concept of sovereignty and the state instead of in social groups and organizations (Laski, 1921). Thus, *pluralism* originally denoted beliefs about the importance of groups in relation to the state and was thus applicable to Bentley and Truman, but not especially applicable to Dahl. To confuse matters further, during the heyday of the pluralist study of American politics, many accepted the conclusion of *American Business and Public Policy* that interest groups did not play an important role in the policy process of the federal government (Bauer, Pool, and Dexter, 1963; Goldstein, 1993).

The bottom line is that the pluralists assumed that political institutions (state agencies) had autonomy, but they never addressed the questions posed by the multiple-elite theorists: the question of subgovernments controlling the state piece by piece, and the question of collective action paradoxes leading to the existence of subgovernments, or the few controlling the many. Thus, another group of writers had to come along to deal with these questions and to show why the institutional independence assumed by the Dahl generation of pluralists was often the case.

The research of the multiple-elite scholars showed numerous cases in which groups controlled state agencies or, more precisely, in which administrative agencies broke off from central control to join in an "iron triangle" coalition with interest groups and legislators to control some particular area of public policy. Some multiple-elite writers implied that administrative agencies and the state could be autonomous, not much influenced by interest groups, if major reforms were enacted. Thus, Lowi's (1969) juridical democracy would put agencies under the control of Congress and remove the control of interest groups. McConnell (1966), in effect, proposed to revive and strengthen the New Deal state, with a powerful president and a supportive Supreme Court and national political party. Schattschneider (1960) proposed to expand conflict, taking it out of narrow interest definitions in particular policy areas and making it the subject of national debates between centralized national political parties that would clearly take different positions on the issues. Schattschneider saw interest groups as having too much power and proposed to strengthen political parties to centralize decision-making in the federal government. As it turned out, it was the multiple-elite school, more than Dahl and Polsby, that argued that interest groups dominated government.

A new step was taken, however, by James Q. Wilson and other neopluralist researchers. Such research found that political processes led to a proliferation of interest groups on two or more sides of an issue. In addition, such research almost always found that administrative agencies sometimes acted in a relatively autonomous fashion, with control by interest groups largely lacking (J. Q. Wilson, 1980). Another strand of research, what might be called the "realist" school of the study of public policy, had already emphasized the basic importance of interest group support for the effective implementation of legislative policy by an agency and had observed that such support enabled agencies to act autonomously (C. O. Jones, 1970, 89–106, 124–32; Rourke, 1968).

In terms of the policymaking theory, why would state agencies act autonomously? The answer was clear. Unlike situations described by the multiple-elite model, no single interest group or type of interest group was observed to dominate the policymaking process in an area. Instead, a variety of groups with different interests was observed. Such groups did not have equal resources or power, and the power of business groups would probably exceed that of citizens groups, such as environmentalists. Still, the power of producer groups (business or professional groups) was often checked, at least somewhat, by the power of *countervailing* groups, such as citizens groups or business groups with different interests. The power of producer groups was thereby lessened, so that a producer group could not form a subgovernment, that is, a controlling coalition in some policy area (J. Q. Wilson, 1980).

I call this situation a *power triad,* in which the producer groups are checked by the countervailing power groups in a policy area, leading to the possibility of autonomous actions by governmental agencies. Groups on both sides of the environmental issue let the EPA act independently, opposing coalitions of the cable industry versus the telephone industry eliminate the possibility of capture of the Federal Communications Commission; civil rights lobbies oppose the pressures of local governments in the administration of voting rights legislation by the Department of Justice. Thus, within the unfolding logic of the policymaking paradigm, because there are interest group sustainers, there is a proliferation of groups acting in a policy area. And with a proliferation of groups comes the possibility of relatively autonomous actions by governmental agencies (McFarland, 1992).

This conclusion is straightforward, but its acceptance is somewhat obfuscated by the connotations of the idea of *countervailing power.* This term became associated with the naive assumption that when one type of interest is mobilized in the political system, opposing interests can be expected to mobilize in opposition to protect their own interests, thereby providing countervailing power to the earlier mobilized interests. To many, this seemed to imply that all interests were equally capable of effective political organization and that the results of the struggle among interest groups to control policy might seem relatively fair—a conclusion supportive of the political status quo. However, the neopluralist writers who found a multitude of active groups and governmental agencies certainly did not subscribe to the idea that such observed mobilization implied an equality of mobilization on all sides of an issue. Nor do neopluralist writers ever argue that all interests pertaining to an issue are organized; it is impossible to argue this after *The Logic of Collective Action.* Political scientists no longer publish models that affirm the old idea of the equality of countervailing power. So, since the term is useful and descriptive, perhaps it can be used again in the context of the power triad, indicating an observation of active groups countermanding the influence of leading producer groups (McFarland, 1992).

Countervailing power occurs with some frequency because it is not limited to situations in which producer groups are all on one side of an issue and well-organized citizens groups, such as environmentalists, are on the other side. Certain business groups may join public interest groups, professional associations, local property holders, and so on to form countervailing coalitions to producer interests on specific policy issues. For instance, domestic sugar producers have been opposed by a coalition of soft-drink bottlers, cookie manufacturers, and consumer groups on the issue of imposing import quotas for sugar (Berry, 1985; Nadel, 1971; Vogel, 1989; Nadel and Vogel, 1977).

Countervailing power enhances the effect of professional norms on public policy. Countervailing power also enhances agency autonomy, so that professionals within the governmental agency have a greater tendency to influence policy. For instance, scientists in the EPA can have some effect on policy formulation because the EPA has some autonomy, due to the countervailing power among environmentalists and business interests. In some instances, especially at the local level, no interest groups are sufficiently organized to influence executive branch policymaking, leading to a situation of enhanced agency autonomy in which professional values have greater impact (J. Q. Wilson, 1980; Peterson, Rabe, and Wong, 1986).

Countervailing power enhances legality in administration because it provides agency autonomy, increasing the sphere of action for legal professionals. This increases the impact of legal norms, as opposed to decision-making controlled by self-serving interests that reinterpret or ignore statutes and regulations on the books. Countervailing power thus enhances the enforcement of general legal standards. This view, derived from Wilson's research, contradicts the work of Lowi (1969, 1979), who emphasizes multiple elitism and the situation of agencies in alignment with special interests that control the interpretation of the law, much of it based on vaguely written statutes in the first place.

ISSUE NETWORKS AND COUNTERVAILING POWER

Through a series of examples, Heclo indicates how issue networks provide countervailing power to attempts to establish oligarchical control of an issue area: "The overlay of networks and issue politics not only confronts but also seeps down into the formerly well-established politics of particular policies and programs. Social security, which for a generation had been quietly managed by a small circle of insiders, becomes controversial and politicized. The Army Corps of Engineers, once the picture book example of control by subgovernments, is dragged into the brawl on environmental politics" (Heclo, 1978, 105). Further examples indicate that developing issue networks that include many technical experts frequently circulate information contradicting the outlook of the various plural elites. This is an important instance of countervailing power, for a basic strategy of a policy area elite is to restrict public information about that policy. If the decision-makers of high politics do not know what is going on, they will have little incentive to challenge the control of a policy elite, thereby letting routine politics run its course.

Heclo mentions, but does not develop, a second aspect of countervailing power: "Knowledge does not necessarily produce agreement. Issue networks may or may not, therefore, be mobilized into . . . a conventional interest organization" (Heclo, 1978, 104). He neglects an obvious implication here, namely, that portions of issue networks may be mobilized into interest groups if appropriately stimulated. One may hypothesize that governmental agencies or independent political entrepreneurs will organize interests from the newer issue networks. Or previously existing groups will tend to expand into issue networks upon contacting sympathetic persons. Because an issue network, by definition, implies the existence of a communications network, the costs of organizing an interest group are lowered by having access to preexisting information about which participants in the network care about what. An issue network performs the same function for group organizing that a mailing list does and, in the case of some technical policy journals, amounts to much the same thing.

Extending Walker's analysis of patrons, we can expect that patrons and issue networks will act together to facilitate group organization. The meetings, journals, and mailing lists of issue networks cut the costs of organizing. The patron is likely to finance one or more political entrepreneurs arising out of an issue network to organize the group. Such entrepreneurs are likely to have acquired years of experience with the personalities and opinions of those within an issue network.

Most of those in an issue network are in that position because of jobs financed by business, government, academic institutions, nonprofit organizations, and newspapers. The network facilitates group organization, and other institutions finance the network. In addition, patrons finance the entrepreneurs, who organize portions of the network into an interest group.

Social movements, upon achieving success in public policy, can lead to the creation or enhancement of an issue network, which in turn may become a foundation for additional interest group organization. For instance, the women's movement led to the creation of a policy network concerned with health issues pertaining to women, and this network could serve as a resource for organizing women's lobbies.

The issue network is not a panacea for the problems of plural elitism. Issue networks are diverse. They contain persons critical of a policy, such as laissez-faire conservatives or personnel of regulated businesses. Some people in an issue network are supportive of emergent subgovernments. Further, top policymakers may ignore issue networks, out of either principle or ideology, depending on one's point of view. During the Reagan administration, for instance, most members of issue networks in arms control, acid rain, and toxic waste disposal were ignored.

SUBSYSTEM CYCLES

Neopluralist theory describes policy systems as going through cycles, from routine politics to high politics and back to routine politics. *Routine politics* is defined as normal, day-to-day decision-making and administration in a policy area. *High politics* is defined as the politics of making general decisions that have an impact on changing policies or the structure of participation in a policy area. Congressional committee or subcommittee members are frequent participants in routine decisions and are then added to the structure of the triad. High politics involves one or more of these participants: presidential policymakers, major sectors of Congress in addition to routine participants, federal appeals courts, and the Supreme Court (Redford, 1969; Selznick, 1957; Ripley and Franklin, 1984).

During high politics, presidential policymakers (most commonly), Congress, or the courts may significantly reduce agency autonomy. Presidential policymakers may side with either producers or countervailing power holders. During high politics, then, the president, in coalition with either producers or countervailing power holders, attempts to restructure policy and participation.

James Q. Wilson (1980, 389–90) argued that the president ordinarily is not part of the politics of regulation. This accurately described the 1970s but does not describe Ronald Reagan's effective intervention into the policymaking of the Federal Trade Commission, the EPA, the Occupational Safety and Health Administration (OSHA), and the Equal Employment Opportunity Commission. One hallmark of the Reagan administration was the conversion of routine regulation and administration into high politics. Congress may be the initiator of high politics in some particular policy area when it takes the initiative to pass legislation, as was frequently the case in the early 1970s (Orfield, 1975). The federal courts also have the capacity to initiate high politics in a policy area, such as by abolishing agencies for their unconstitutional abridgment of the separation of powers and by limiting affirmative action policies in the civil rights area. Consequently, "split high politics coalitions" may form, for example, when Congress, with countervailing power groups, opposes the president and producer groups, as sometimes happened during Reagan's first term.

A policy system may go through cycles from the triad stage to the subgovernment stage. Thus, a space may be defined between triadic and subgovernmental power. The position of the policy area in this space changes with time. As countervailing power, agency autonomy, or both diminish, the policy area approaches the subgovernmental model; as they increase, policy approaches the triadic model. High politics may intervene to move policy through the definitional space.

For instance, A. Lee Fritschler's (1983) account of smoking and politics in America shows the movement away from agency co-optation by the industry and toward triadic power. As the Reagan administration attacked the autonomy of such agencies as the EPA, OSHA, and the Civil Rights Commission, there was movement away from triadic power toward the model of co-optation by business. Paul J. Culhane (1981) found movement away from the co-optation model in Bureau of Land Management policy in the 1970s, but this did not preclude movement back toward the co-optation model in the 1980s (see Clarke and McCool, 1985, 107–22; Miller, 1985; Davis and Davis, 1986). Policy need not be described as fully co-opted or fully triadic; there are obviously gradations. Similarly, it is a mistake to assume that policy always remains at some point; high politics may intervene to restructure any given policy area.

The reform cycle of plural elitist theory can be described as the movement of a policy area from subgovernment to triad and back to subgovernment. The reform cycles of plural elitism sometimes occur, but agency autonomy and countervailing power usually remain present to a lesser degree as the policy area moves back to subgovernmental relationships. One factor in the maintenance of some countervailing power in a policy area is the presence of advocacy coalitions within policy networks.

POLICY NETWORKS AND ADVOCACY COALITIONS

After considering a score of studies of policymaking in particular issue areas, we can conclude that countervailing power to producers frequently exists. Such power in policy systems can be referred to as triadic, as exhibiting a stable pattern of conflict and cooperation among producer groups, countervailing power groups, and agencies acting autonomously. But a more general and exact formulation of policy coalitions is needed, and this was framed by Paul Sabatier and Hank Jenkins-Smith (1993, 1999) as the *advocacy coalition*. This concept has proved useful in dozens of studies of policymaking, particularly in American energy and environmental policymaking. Many researchers have a similar formulation of this idea, even if they do not use the specific advocacy coalition concept.

Sabatier and Jenkins-Smith start with Heclo's idea of the issue network, a system of communications that includes interest group personnel, government administrators, legislators, academic policy specialists, and journalists. (In the following, I use the term *policy network,* since Heclo's *issue network* seems to imply the existence of political conflict.) A policy network is not an interest group but a system of communications among those interested in a specific policy. A definition of political actors can be built from the idea of a policy network, however. An advocacy coalition thus consists of a stable political coalition among the various types of constituents in a policy network. Of most significance are coalitions that are stable, existing for at least ten years. A policy network may have two or more advocacy coalitions, as in the case of a stable environmentalist coalition opposed by a stable coalition of developers and free-market advocates. Clearly, not all the participants in a policy network need be part of an advocacy coalition springing from the network; some persons just are not active in politics and lobbying (Sabatier and Jenkins-Smith, 1993, 1999).

The policy advocate idea seems quite simple and basic, but it states bluntly what hundreds of policy researches have been assuming. The Sabatier and Jenkins-Smith formulation stresses that advocacy coalition members represent both the executive and legislative branches of government and represent all levels of government. Their formulation also emphasizes that advocacy coalitions do not form only around material interests but are often based on agreement on core social and political values or on shared cognitive understandings of some public policy situation (e.g., cognitive views about the probability of global warming).

The Sabatier and Jenkins-Smith framework addresses a major stream of research in the fields of policy analysis, policy process, and public administration. Some leading studies of the policymaking process, addressing research in the areas of regulation, interest groups, and policymaking, implicitly include the idea of advocacy coalition. Martha Derthick and Paul Quirk's influential study, *The Politics of Deregulation* (1985), stresses the role of economists and the cognitive appeal of the deregulation idea as the basis of an advocacy coalition including presidents, legislators, agency leaders and independent commissioners, and interest groups. Gary Mucciaroni, in a parallel work, *Reversals of Fortune* (1995), shows that in certain contexts, advocacy coalitions that include executive branch leaders, legislators, and interest groups can defeat particularistic interests in the areas of regulation, international trade, and agriculture. Like Sabatier, Jenkins-Smith, Derthick, and Quirk, Mucciaroni finds that the general-interest coalitions are based in shared beliefs, as well as in common material interests.

Kevin Hula (1999), as well as Sabatier and Jenkins-Smith (1999), stresses that support for an advocacy coalition varies in depth, from support arising from commitment to a fundamental value to that arising from a relatively superficial congruence of common material interest. Hula divides supporters of coalitions into three categories, depending on depth of commitment, as do Sabatier and Jenkins-Smith, who are interested only in coalitions lasting for ten years or more.

Network theory seems to be a promising tool for the analysis of policymaking, power, and interest groups. Advocacy coalitions spring from policy networks but are not equivalent to the policy network. There may be two or more advocacy coalitions in the same network; not all network participants reliably advocate some particular policy position, as would be the frequent case with researchers and journalists.

A policy network is defined in terms of those regularly communicating about the same set of policy events. *The Hollow Core,* a major research project published by John P. Heinz, Edward O. Laumann, Robert L. Nelson, and Robert H. Salisbury (1993), was based on a network analysis of interest groups and policymaking in the national agriculture, energy, health, and labor policy areas. This study is known for its demonstration that within each of these areas, virtually no group or person regularly communicates with others over the entire range of a policy area, such as agriculture or energy. Thus, a graphing of the communications network has a "hollow core"; no one is in the middle communicating with all those in the various sectors of the policy area. Initially, then, the network analysis indicates a fragmentation of action in such general policy areas. But hundreds of interviews with lobbyists and government officials do not demonstrate the pattern of multiple elitism. Instead, network theory finds that policymaking is fragmented into complex coalitions, with actors normally uncertain about whether the communications process might shift with changes in issues. Jeffrey Berry (1989b) found a similar pattern in the policymaking process in the telecommunications area.

Network theory is now a significant part of the study of sociology, a field committed to depicting the nature of social structure. Political scientists, however, are most concerned about relating social structure to the exercise of influence over public policy and have generally not followed up on *The Hollow Core* study. However, it seems that network theory might be useful in predicting the formation and stability of advocacy coalitions, as well as indicating strains within a single coalition. For instance, even a stable lobbying coalition in the area of national disabilities policy tends to have a bifurcated network structure, accompanying internal conflict over the coalition's lobbying goals (Shapiro, forthcoming).

A second use of network theory might be to explore the function of a "filled-in" core, or what might be called the hub-and-spokes model of networks within a policy system. Two studies have found hubs within two different higher education policy systems. However, the peak association of higher education lobbies, the American Council of Education, though serving as a hub, was unable to broker agreement among such interest groups, except at a level too general to have much effect (Cook, 1998). In contrast, the Illinois Board of

Higher Education served as a hub within its policymaking network and was viewed by the governor and others as being influential in its coordination efforts (Knorowski, 2000). This situation indicates a link between neopluralist theory and the analysis of policy planning, in that organizations at the hub of a system of networks might design plans for public policy and be effective in coordinating the system of networks in the formulation and enactment of such plans (see chapter 7).

Analysis of political process into networks of interaction is a type of research that is likely to go much further. Networks indicate communication, and the substance of communication is information. Scott Ainsworth (1993) and Kenneth Kollman (1998) demonstrated the usefulness of defining lobbying in high politics situations as a process of signaling, communicating information to the subjects of lobbying. Such signals often include the intensity of a group's concern about some issue or whether an entire advocacy coalition of groups is concerned, and if not, which components of the group are intensely concerned. A basic choice in lobbying is whether to extend "insider lobbying" among Washingtonians to "outsider lobbying," whereby an advocacy coalition activates its networks to signal to decision-makers its intensity of concern. Outsider lobbying can involve significant organizational costs, but it can also clearly signal widespread opinion about some issue, and if that opinion is intense, it can have an impact on voting (Ainsworth, 1993; Kollman, 1998; McFarland, 1984).

Control of information is central to the maintenance of subgovernmental control. Narrowly based elites seek to block information about their pattern of control, but this strategy can be defeated by the appearance of scandal. A scandal within some public policy area indicates that a great deal of negative information is circulating about the situation in that policy area. Circulation of such negative information is at the core of the reform cycle, or of the punctuation of an equilibrium, when routine politics is redefined into high politics and reform measures may be passed. In general, countervailing advocacy coalitions and citizens groups seek to act as "watchdogs," which "bark" to signal the existence of some situation requiring the attention of the greater public and possible intervention in high politics.

PUNCTUATED EQUILIBRIUM AND POLICY IMPLEMENTATION

A major neopluralist theory, in contrast to the multiple-elite reform cycle, is punctuated equilibrium, as stated by Baumgartner and Jones in *Agendas and Instability in American Politics* (1993). Instead of the reform cycle, Baumgartner and Jones's theory of punctuated change in policy systems emphasizes that, most of the time, politics and policy do not change to a great extent, but such incrementalism is often followed by shorter periods of rapid policy change, which becomes institutionalized in laws and procedures (and presumably is supported by an advocacy coalition), so that the policy system becomes qualitatively different. A major cause of rapid policy change is exogenous shocks to the system: war and other national security events, domestic riots, corruption, scandals, and so forth. Such exogenous factors hugely increase the amount of public attention to some policy area; who cared about the regulation of accounting before the Enron scandal? Like the reform cycle theorists cited earlier, Baumgartner and Jones see the degree of public attention toward a policy area as a major factor in the study of the political process. Broadcasting and focusing such public attention are major roles of the media in the policymaking process, and there is certainly a great increase in media attention accompanying major policy changes (McAdam, 1982; Costain, 1992; Baumgartner and Jones, 1993).

The theory of punctuated change incorporates the first part of reform cycle theory and is more specific in formulating the role of public attention, the media, and exogenous shocks in instigating relatively rapid changes in the system. But unlike reform cycle theory, punctuated change finds significant and lasting qualitative system change, as opposed to a reversion to subgovernmental control or some other preexisting state. Punctuated change also is opposed to Lindblom's systems theory of partisan mutual adjustment among actors leading to incremental policy changes. According to Baumgartner and Jones (1993), research indicates that most American policy systems are incremental most of the time, but the researcher may be more interested in events that occur during the rapid changes that punctuate most policy systems (Hochschild, 1984). The main policy application of incrementalist theory is that of Aaron Wildavsky to the study of budgeting, but extended research indicates that although agency budgets normally exhibit incremental change, there are times when they change rapidly and nonincrementally, as in the case of national defense budgets (Wildavsky, 1964b; Davis, Dempster, and Wildavsky, 1966; True, Jones, and Baumgartner, 1999). The theory of punctuated change has a focus on agenda change and issue formation and is discussed further in chapter 9.

But what does it mean to say that policy change is stabilized by institutionalization? Does this mean that the problem of subgovernment formation no longer exists, because all subgovernments experience punctuated change and become neopluralistic? That is unlikely.

This is an area in which the policy process and interest group activity supplement institutional considerations. Here is where the considerable research on policy implementation is linked to neopluralist theory. Mazmanian and Sabatier (1989), among others, argue that the formation of advocacy coalitions is central if laws and rules are to be implemented in a fashion congruent with the original intentions of legislators and other decision-makers. According to such research, just because Congress and executive branch leaders set forth civil rights laws in the 1960s, that did not mean that such laws would be enforced as originally intended. A national advocacy coalition, led by the NAACP and liberal legislators, likely was a necessary condition for such enforcement, which, for the most part, did occur. But here is where I wish to amend the punctuated change theory. Particularly in the area of regulating powerful businesses, unless a strong advocacy coalition is active in a policy system, change will be followed by backsliding. An example might be found in the regulation of accounting practices. At any rate, this aspect of the study of policy change will be clarified when researchers finish a thorough job of linking the implementation research with policy change research, as Sabatier has been doing.

The concepts of the reform cycle and that of punctuated change call attention to a different perspective on interest group activity. Is not interest group activity directed toward policy implementation roughly as important as interest group activity directed toward the passage of new laws and rules? New laws and institutions mean little if they come under the control of policy elites who control things both before and after the supposed policy change. True policy change is sometimes impossible unless it is supported by an advocacy coalition. This issue is inherent in the work of Virginia Gray and David Lowery (1996) and is implicit in their recent paper on neopluralist theory (2000). Sabatier and Jenkins-Smith (1999) have led a research effort encompassing thirty-four studies that shows the importance of advocacy coalitions in implementing policy, particularly in the environment and energy fields.

The theory of punctuated policy change is an important aspect of neopluralist theory. However, I would give greater emphasis to processes in which a system tends to revert to a former system of control. To me, it seems that reform or policy change frequently takes three steps forward and two steps backward in relation to the original state of the policy system. I do agree, however, that the professionalization and institutionalization of governmental agencies fluctuate but, on average, increase in the long run (Skowronek, 1982).

In any event, we see that the neopluralist theory of political process incorporates research that emphasizes the role of advocacy coalitions in policy implementation.

POLICY NICHES

Current researchers using the neopluralist model have discovered the "policy niche," a concept likely to make a big difference in the way political scientists view the policymaking process. In the 1990s, William Browne (1990) and Gray and Lowery (1996) began using the term *policy niche* to refer to a highly specific forum or type of public policy. Although a specific policy niche, such as the regulation of cesium waste or subsidies for honey production, might seem unimportant, the total of such policy niches apparently numbers in the thousands at the federal level. Since the 1950s, policy experts had been telling us that agriculture is fragmented into separate policy systems for major commodities: wheat, corn, soybeans, beef, pork, tobacco, and so forth, and even separate systems for smaller sectors such as walnuts or almonds. Browne (1990), the leading academic expert on agricultural policymaking, states that there are more than 400 policy niches in national agricultural policymaking. I had previously thought that there might be about 40 such systems.

At about the same time, Gray and Lowery (1996) stressed the idea of "interest group niches" and "group niche behavior" in their data-rich study of interest group systems and lobbying at the level of fifty state governments. They put forth the ecological model of interest group systems. Because groups compete with one another in their mobilization of resources, it is rational, and "ecological," for interest groups to occupy a piece of the policymaking turf that has little or no competition from other groups trying to mobilize resources in the same policymaking space. In other words, rather than defining itself generally as an agricultural lobby or even as a fruit producers lobby, it will organize itself specifically as the kiwi-fruit producers lobby, an area with no competition. When the constituency becomes small, it can contribute to the maintenance of the interest group in a fashion that is stable and predictable. The research of Gray and Lowery is particularly stimulating in its finding, derived from ecological theory, that interest groups frequently disband or otherwise stop their activity. This is especially important in light of Salisbury's (1984) observation that much lobbying activity consists of the governmental relations function of organizations whose main goal is the achievement of some purpose other than political influence: corporations seeking profits, colleges and hospitals pursuing a nonprofit public service, or local governmental institutions lobbying higher-level governmental institutions on a particular issue. Such organizations may lobby only occasionally and may terminate their lobbying activity for years at a time.

Accordingly, Gray and Lowery (1996) found that much interest group behavior is niche behavior—groups defining relatively specific policies as their own areas of activity, or groups simply jumping in and out of politics due to the specificity and short-lived nature of their public policy concerns.

The broadest study of policy niches is one by Baumgartner and Leech (2000, 2001), who organized the most thorough study of lobbying of the U.S. Congress to date. In 1995, Congress passed the Lobbying Disclosure Act, which, for the first time, mandated that those lobbying Congress file full reports of their lobbying activity. (The previous law was so full of loopholes that lobbies did not file accurate financial information or a true record of the issues they lobbied.) Baumgartner and Leech assembled all the reports filed for 1996, coded them to list all the issues lobbied, and then took a sample of the issue list, which included each mention of an issue, thereby weighting the list to measure multiple lobbying activity on the same issue. The 19,692 reports contained 49,518 mentions of issues (including the multiple mentions), from which Baumgartner and Leech sampled 137 issues. This research provides a clear-cut finding: on a few issues, there is a great amount of lobbying, but on many issues, only a handful of groups lobby. Thus, on each of four issues, at least 500 interest groups lobbied: the Omnibus Consolidated Appropriations; the Small Business Job Protection Act; the Budget Reconciliation Act, which included the welfare reform of 1996; and Defense Department appropriations. "Similarly, an additional 13 issues attracted more than 200 interest groups, and nine more issues were of interest to 100 or more interest groups" (Baumgartner and Leech, 2001, 1200). There were 10,434 instances of group activity on the 137 issues in the sample, but the "top four issues accounted for more than a third of all interest group activity," or 34 percent (Baumgartner and Leech, 2001, 1200); the 26 issues involving more than 100 interest groups accounted for 81 percent of interest group activity. "Of course, the logical counterpart . . . is that a large number of issues saw only a few interest groups involved. The median issue was the object of lobbying by 15 interest groups. Only 2.6 percent of the interest groups were active in the 68 issues with fewer than the median number of interest groups involved. . . . Twenty-three cases were mentioned only by a single interest group" (Baumgartner and Leech, 2001, 1201). Sixteen of these had some significant breadth, such as the regulation of cesium waste and the establishment of wildlife refuges for non-game animals.

Baumgartner and Leech (2001, 1204) state that their data "show that business advantage, while great overall, is even more striking in the cases where the fewest interest groups are active. In the 32 cases where only one or two interest groups were involved in the issue, participation was almost wholly limited to business, trade associations, and the intergovernmental lobby. These data paint a striking picture of the lack of conflict that can often accompany the relatively secretive lobbying processes where few are involved." In contrast, participation by unions, nonprofits, and citizens groups tends to be limited to more conflictual issues with many groups involved. Because the research is just now being reported, Baumgartner, Leech, and other political scientists have yet to give a fully considered theoretical response to these findings.

But a first conclusion seems likely. The multiple elitists applied their findings to a middle level of policymaking; subgovernments controlled such issues as railroad regulation (before 1950), interstate trucking regulation, nuclear power plant regulation, the allocation of soil conservation money among farmers, the allocation of cheap grazing rights on federal land, and the more pecuniary policy toward the production of jet fighter aircraft. On many such issues, case studies indicated a neopluralist pattern of policymaking rather than subgovernmental control. But the issues chosen for such case studies were those seen to be important from the standpoint of either allocation of resources or democratic theory. However, Baumgartner and Leech have come up with a much broader sample of policy issues, extending Browne's (1990, 1995) extremely detailed observations of agricultural policy. And consideration of the whole population of issues shows that there are many more relatively specific issues than heretofore considered by researchers. These newly discovered issues, so to speak, are characterized by low interest group participation and producer group dominance.

The issue areas having restricted interest group participation conform to Gray and Lowery's observations about the tendency to create policy niches. Niche behavior is likely to be explained by derivations from multiple-elite theory. Producer groups are likely to dominate. Olson's logic of collective action is likely to apply as a few producer groups organize, while a much broader constituency fails to organize. The interest group sustainers—policy networks, patrons, and social movements—would tend to be inactive in forming groups. There would certainly be a role in democratic representation for professionalized agencies of the state to enforce laws and rules in the general interest, but one might be pessimistic about the degree of agency independence from producer groups that were not offset by advocacy coalitions representing broader interests. Still, there might be punctuated change at a more specific level of policy formation than envisioned by the earlier publication of Baumgartner and Jones (1993). Nevertheless, policy niches are probably rife with subgovernmental control, accounting for the widespread intuition that multiple-elite theory is still relevant, in spite of case studies showing neopluralism.

Berry (1999) showed a high degree of political success by environmental groups and other citizens groups in lobbying Congress in recent years (see also Shaiko, 1999). But one limitation of such success is that citizens groups are not likely to be active in niche politics. Preliminary evidence indicates that business groups and other producer groups (professions, agriculture) dominate the limited organization of groups in policy niches. Although more research is needed, it is likely that the sum total of such policy niches, characterized by a low level of group organization, may represent a great proportion of public policy. Schattschneider (1960) and Schlozman and Tierney (1983, 1986), among others, argued that business groups dominate the "pluralist heaven" of group organization, and this may be true for policy niches, the "business group heaven" (Berry, 1999; Baumgartner and Leech, 2000, 2001).

CONCLUSION

Neopluralism builds on multiple elitism by adding four elements. The first is neopluralist findings: observing numerous competing interest groups in policy processes. However, such findings and the existence of some countervailing power are not equated with justice in public policy; nor does the existence of a multiplicity of groups mean that all interests are adequately represented. Neopluralism does not necessarily imply policy justice.

A second new element is the observation of interest group sustainers—policy networks, entrepreneurs, and patrons. Social movements, a third element added to political process theory, are also sustainers of interest groups, and they affect the political process in other ways (see chapter 5). Because there is often a multiplicity of interest groups in a policy area, they sometimes provide countervailing power to the producer groups. Groups on both sides of an issue provide leeway for governmental agency autonomy or "statism," a fourth contribution of neopluralist studies.

Neopluralism supersedes multiple elitism. Nevertheless, the multiple-elite theories provide the best interpretation of some policy situations, whether existing at present or before 1975, when such elitism seems to have been more common. In particular, multiple-elite theory may better describe policy niches, which are just now being analyzed and may be rather common.

Neopluralism finds that the concepts of islands of oligarchy and the logic of collective action are superseded in observations of policy processes. Neopluralists observe a plethora of organized groups. Power triads are observed, consisting of producer groups, countervailing power groups, and agencies with some autonomy. Policy networks provide an important check on policy elites. Neopluralists sometimes observe a reform cycle, in which subgovernmental control during routine politics is altered by countervailing power coalitions during times of high politics some issue area. However, the power of producer groups tends to be reasserted, leading to a shift in control of the policy area, according to the reform cycle. Other neopluralists subscribe to the punctuated equilibrium theory, in which periods of high politics lead to a qualitative change, based on new institutions and policies, so that the area does not revert to its former condition.

Neopluralism incorporates concepts such as the advocacy coalition, spanning the boundaries of groups and institutions. Advocacy coalitions that are active in implementation politics can act as a brake on the reform cycle. Further attention is likely to be paid to network theory and its applications to politics and policy, such as delineating the meaning of planning in complex, pluralist politics or understanding the signaling of information by groups active in lobbying. The delineation of policy niches in the 1990s indicates a limitation of the neopluralist model.

5
Social Movements

Neopluralism is a general theory of power, policymaking, and interest groups. But such a general theory needs more specific statement as types of neopluralism are differentiated. One such mode of analysis is to contrast different aspects of social movements within different policy systems.

We have seen that social movements are centrally linked to power and the policy process. Social movements create and sustain interest groups, which provide countervailing power to producer groups.

Social movement theory is similar to political process theory, even by definition. Social movements are ordinarily defined as "noninstitutional." One definitional trend emphasizes the noninstitutional tactics used by social movements (McAdam, 1982). A second definitional trend emphasizes a basic challenge to established institutions (Gamson, 1975; Melucci, 1996). Sociologists thus ordinarily regard a movement as a type of social action process that is not institutionalized or that challenges basic social institutions.

Social movement theory is a social process theory, not a social structure theory. Social movement theory, particularly with the advent of the resource mobilization, political process, and identity formation theories of movements (see below), refers to processes of action. As such, it might be contrasted to studies of revolution, which are normally grounded in some structural analysis of society based on class, hegemonic values, the role of the state, or some combination of these (Skocpol, 1979). Social movement theory in sociology thus has much in common with the developing political process theory in political science.

Social movement theory may be related to the basic concepts of political process theory and is similar to the punctuated change theory of policy systems. As noted, social movement theorists focus on a process of interaction among movement leaders, supporters, organizations, and social control agencies. In analyzing events, such as the American civil rights movement, social movement theory looks for influence and power—which persons and organizations caused what changes in a social situation. Movement theorists since 1970 have focused on the subjective definition of goals and interests, and movements are not predicted on the basis of some "objective" theory of deprivation. In fact, social movement theory is the home of the subjectively defined "relative deprivation" and of a concern with identity formation and self-definition in the process of social action. Social movement theory is specific; it refers to particular movements: civil rights, women's, environmental, Christian fundamentalism, Klanism, and so forth. This is similar to the use of separate policy areas as a unit of analysis (McAdam, 1982; McAdam, McCarthy, and Zald, 1996).

We see, then, that social movement theory is a sociological enterprise sharing the four basic concepts of political process theory. As such, movement theory has much to add to political process theory. However, movement theory does not assume partisan mutual adjustment or incremental social action. The appearance of a movement is a type of "punctuation" in social action (Baumgartner and Jones, 1993) and, if effective, may bring punctuated change in public policy, at least partially through an effect on the issue agenda of policy (see chapter 9).

THE DEVELOPMENT OF SOCIAL MOVEMENT THEORY

Few would deny that social movements have a major impact on the American policymaking process. Yet due to the history of theory construction in this area, there is still a need to consolidate social movement theory with the study of politics and policymaking. In the years 1945 to 1970, social movement theory was the province of sociology and was not something that scholars of American politics thought much about. Social movements had become identified with extraordinary political events, usually threatening to democracy. The example of most concern was the rise of Nazism in Germany; the second and third examples were postwar communism in Western countries and McCarthyism in the United States (Heberle, 1951). Social movements did not have much to do with the operations of American institutions, and when they were relevant, the country was in trouble, according to this view. Social movements were seen as caused by social changes that threatened the values of a large number of people, causing psychological turmoil, anxiety, and the search for a new definition of political events that would alleviate personal alienation and anxiety (Hoffer, 1951). For a while, scholarship emphasized that certain personality types might suffer disturbances, particularly inclining them to a need for stability and certainty, a need for authoritarian direction from above, and a need to displace inner hostility onto those with lower social status (Adorno, Frenkel-Brunswik, Levinson, and Nevitt, 1950). Such theories might be termed the social psychological theories for the origins of social movements (McAdam, 1982).

The American civil rights movement led to a reevaluation of such theories. Virtually all the social movement scholars supported the struggle of African Americans for equal rights, and it became obvious that civil rights supporters were not suffering from undue inner turmoil and stress but were actually more mature and educated than the passive nonactivists (Orum, 1972). This new perspective led to a search for a new theory.

The first new theory was resource mobilization theory, an outlook much more congenial to the style of thinking of political scientists. In fact, the need to explain the existence of the American civil rights movement in combination with Olson's logic of collective action, which implied that the movement should not exist, led to a new theoretical mode that largely paralleled that of interest group theorists trying to explain the existence of groups in spite of collective action theory. In fact, it seems likely that Walker's concept of *patron* was influenced by resource mobilization theory in sociology.

Such writers as Anthony Oberschall (1973), Maurice Pinard (1975), and Jo Freeman (1975) stressed the role of preexisting communications networks in spreading social movements. To them, this meant the existence of organized groups that were susceptible to new social outlooks and perceptions, such as pre-movement women's groups—the League of Women Voters or the American Association of University Women, for example. Doug McAdam (1982), Aldon Morris (1984), and other writers stressed the role of established African American institutions, such as churches or colleges, as communications centers for organizing civil rights protests. In this way, analysis of social movements was linked to an understanding of established social and political institutions. One could say that institutions helped mobilize resources for movements.

At this point, political sociologists John McCarthy and Mayer Zald (1977) developed the resource mobilization theory of social movements to deal with the problems posed by the inadequacies of the social psychological paradigm and Olson's logic of collective action. The two scholars posited a constancy in social dissatisfaction (in contrast to the social psychological theory) and argued that the main variables in treating social movements concerned the compilation of resources necessary to a movement (see also Tilly, 1978). Using economic analogies, they referred to social movement "firms," or social movement organizations, and social movement industries (issue areas). They argued that entrepreneurs might be important in organizing movements; these individuals would be willing to bear time and money costs in pursuit of their own individual goals. Resource mobilization theory asked, where did the resources necessary for the movement come from? Among such resources were money, time, and access to communications, and the source of such resources might be the communications networks and favorable institutions designated by theorists such as Oberschall (1973), Pinard (1975), and Freeman (1975). Of course, another source of resources might be patrons, the concept later adapted by political scientist Jack Walker Jr. Rich individuals, middle-class members with some dispensable resources, previously existing groups in civil society, and even political parties and governmental agencies might provide resources to mobilize and maintain social movements (Walker, 1991).

Another type of movement resource is strategy and tactics (Gamson, 1975). The use of civil disobedience tactics by the civil rights movement maintained the commitment of movement participants, gained support from hitherto uncommitted northern whites, and frequently confused and demoralized the southern white opposition. As Charles Tilly (1978) pointed out in his study of movements among medieval peasants, social movements have action repertoires, a shared understanding of what tactics are effective. The development of repertoires was viewed by theorists as another important movement resource. In general, then, resource mobilization theorists asked: who organized the movement; with what resources in terms of time, money, and tactics; and where did these resources come from (Zald and McCarthy, 1987)? Using such a vocabulary, the political sociologists of movements resembled political scientists (McCarthy and Zald, 1977; Tilly, 1978).

A few years after the onset of resource mobilization theory, McAdam (1982), Sidney Tarrow (1989, 1995), and other scholars developed the political opportunities theory for understanding social movements. Essentially, this outlook rejected social psychological theory, accepted resource mobilization theory, but argued that the latter theory should be viewed within the context of the politics of a society. At times, the regular political system might be conducive to the appearance of movements; at other times, it might repress the origin of movements. In the paradigmatic case of the American civil rights movement, black voting power in presidential elections and changing doctrines in the federal courts were seen as encouraging the development of protest under Martin Luther King Jr. Anne Costain (1992) and others have argued that vote-seeking by presidents and members of Congress was a major factor in encouraging the reappearance of the women's movement of the 1960s. Conservative political elites' support for traditional values encourages the mobilization of fundamentalist Christian movements, according to the political opportunity theory. In terms of voting, the presidency, the federal court system, Congress, and political parties, political opportunity theory can be considered a form of political science (McAdam, 1982; Costain, 1992).

By the early 1990s, political sociologists added identity-formation variables to the combination of resource mobilization and political opportunity theories. Such scholars maintained that even though one might reject the traditional theories of psychological strain as the base of social movements, one needed to add the variable of identity formation to properly understand the appearance of many movements. Thus, following the example of African Americans, the United States saw the appearance of the women's movement, movements for Latinos and Native Americans, the gay rights movement, the disabled movement, and so forth. In each case, after asking the question "who am I within this society?" a social movement developed to gain the social recognition of equality. The development of such movements can be analyzed in terms of resource mobilization and political opportunity factors. Consequently, by the mid-1990s, a synthetic theory of social movements was widely accepted (Morris and Mueller, 1992).

The new social movement theory shows political science that movements are not an aberration but a regular part of the political process, although there may be cycles for different types of movements (e.g., reform decades, conservative decades). There are systematic theories, concepts, hypotheses, and data that can be used to account for the mobilization and maintenance of social movements (Snow, Rochford, Worden, and Benford, 1986; Tarrow, 1995; Melucci, 1996; Orum, 2001, chap. 9). Further, these theories use concepts and methods that are congenial to political scientists, who can therefore adopt them for their own discipline (Costain and McFarland, 1998).

The new social movement theory instructs that social (hence political) movements are a normal part of the policymaking process. We can expect movements to spin off citizens groups to act in the policymaking process as a countervailing power to producer groups. Therefore, the plurality of political movements is a factor checking the formation of islands of oligarchy. Social movements are a relatively constant interest group sustainer, tending to produce a neopluralist policymaking system rather than a multiple-elitist system.

New social movement theory addresses the logic of collective action, although it may not completely answer Olson's paradoxes. The resource mobilization theory would look for Olson's selective benefits as a source of movement organization, in addition to the other economic motivations, resources, and cost-cutting devices it supposes. Other writers on oligarchy, contributing to multiple-elite theory in the American context, often emphasize misinformation among the general public, consumers, or other large, diffuse groups that are hypothetically manipulated by the oligarchy controlling a policy area. The early oligarchy theorist Robert Michels (1959) stressed the mistaken gratitude of publics for former actions by elites, actions no longer being carried out. Michels also stressed elite manipulation of information as a device to control an organization. Parallel to Michels, political scientist Murray Edelman (1964) stressed the manipulation of political symbols by elites to misinform publics as a device for control. In particular, Edelman noted the passage of legislation but subsequent nonenforcement as a means of misleading the public. Theodore Lowi Jr. (1969) implied that social movement leaders, and presumably much of the public, are misled by an ideology of governance that stresses the superiority of informal bargaining in public administration rather than the application of formal rules. This enables the "little governments" ruling a policy area to co-opt protest groups into a status quo of iron triangle–type control. Political scientist Grant McConnell (1966) saw the public disabling itself by its mistaken adherence to the "grassroots" ideology, the mistaken assumption that rule by local units is more democratic than rule by the federal government, when actually local governmental units are much easier for producer groups to control.

However, the new social movement theorists place more stress on the possibility of protest leaders circulating information not controlled by the multiple elites. The social movement theorists see a proliferation of issue networks, not controlled by anyone, through which anti-elite ideas can circulate. The processes of personal identity movements are not subject to control by status quo elites. And as stated in chapter 8, the line of scholarship following Foucault indicates that wide publics may articulate rebellion and resistance in the form of symbolic resistance (styles of manners and dress), joking behavior, and styles of folk art, such as song and dance, or in subterfuge, such as the destruction of property. Publics may not be passive but may express themselves in ways overlooked by previous generations of scholars (Scott, 1990).

Such recent work focusing on identity formation introduces cultural concepts. Another significant introduction of culture and symbol lies in research attention to the reframing of social issues by movements. *Framing* refers to the structure and symbolic meaning by which a situation is described (Goffman, 1974; Snow, Zurcher, and Ekland-Olson, 1980; Snow et al., 1986; Benford and Snow, 2000). In addition to providing new definitions of identity, movements present issues in new ways, or reframe them, for instance, maintaining in 1940 that the federal government should actively protect the constitutional rights of African Americans against deprivations by state and local governments. As noted in chapters 1 and 8, I argue that frame analysis can assist in analyzing the relationship between political power and issue formation within the political process.

The conclusion is that social movements are here to stay and provide a continuing counterweight to the formation of stable islands of oligarchy. Interest groups, originating in movements, are a bastion of neopluralism in the policy-making process.

PATTERNS OF MOVEMENT GROUPS

An additional research task is to differentiate types of neopluralism in policy areas. One part of this task is to differentiate patterns of social movement groups acting in policy areas. Here I state six types of patterns to indicate how such research might proceed. A definitive statement of such models is not possible at this time.

Is there a rich structure among the social movement groups? There are different types of movement groups, and several types may be found in the same area. First, there is the movement itself, not exactly an actor within the policy process but influencing the process. Are there both legal and illegal elements of a movement (Martin Luther King versus Black Panthers)? Are there interest groups, using institutionalized lobbying tactics, affiliated with the movement? To what extent are such lobbies organized to influence not only the legislative branch but executive agencies and the courts? To what extent is there interest group organization at the state and local levels of government? To what extent are such groups sometimes acting in cooperation with other groups and governmental agencies, even while being in conflict with them? (See chapter 7.)

If there are a number of different types of movement groups acting in a policy area, are they synergistic, or do they tend to undermine one another's influence? This may be difficult to predict. At least some observers thought that the use of violence by black radicals and arson by mobs of blacks in the 1960s legitimized the requests of traditional lobbies for fair-housing laws and federal programs to combat unemployment. Yet National Organization of Women lobbyists were undermined by radical feminists who chained themselves to railings at the Illinois legislature during voting on the Equal Rights Amendment, which was subsequently defeated in the state senate. Statements by Christian fundamentalist leaders at Bob Jones University attacking the pope and advocating racial segregation only undermine the position of lobbyists such as Ralph Reed, who are effectively using traditional political tactics on behalf of fundamentalism.

Are social movement groups continually being co-opted into support for the status quo? This is a hypothesis stressed by multiple-elite writers under the shadow of Michels's theory of oligarchy, in which organizational leaders, such as socialists who once challenged the social system, are bought off with material rewards and intangible status, so that they eventually become part of the traditional ruling order. Labor union leaders with salaries exceeding $200,000 seem unlikely to deplete the union treasury by organizing militant strikes. Lowi (1969) made much of the observation that Lyndon Johnson's antipoverty program established community action councils on which black civil rights leaders might serve; they could thus wind up like machine politicians, giving awards and contracts to their friends, thereby becoming part of the status quo of Lowi's interest group liberalism. Similarly, McConnell (1966) thought that American populists tended to advocate systems of local control in which they might participate but that would eventually be overwhelmed by the participation of local elites.

Of course, if social movement agencies become co-opted and become part of an oligarchical ruling coalition, the situation becomes one of multiple elitism, unless some other groups exercise countervailing power, which might happen in the case of more conventional interest groups (e.g., the American Association of Retired Persons) or business or professional groups having an interest contrary to a dominant producer (e.g., trial lawyers versus insurance companies). Thus, it is possible to have a neopluralist interest area, even if social movement organizations have been co-opted.

Is it possible for social movement organizations to cooperate with established groups, government officials, and corporations in endeavors such as planning? Since movement participation in the regular political process is a frequent occurrence in such areas as environmental and energy policy and civil rights policy, it is interesting to explore whether movement organizations must always challenge the status quo organizations, or whether occasional cooperation can be developed within some framework. If movement organizations do not become co-opted but are capable of maintaining their independence, contrary to popular expectations, movement groups may be capable of cooperating in the development of plans and policy frameworks that seem to benefit preponderant majorities. This question is explored further in chapter 7.

SOCIAL MOVEMENTS   69

Are there cycles of power within an issue area? Is there punctuated change? Or is the area relatively static in terms of power relations? As stated in the discussion of neopluralism, some issue areas, such as the regulation of railroads, may move from control by a subgovernmental elite to a reform era, and then move back toward the former control pattern, although the new legislation and other reforms will probably continue to have some impact. However, in the 1960s and 1970s, there was a great upsurge in the structuring of social movement organizations as organized interest groups. In policy areas in which such groups do not substantially decay over time, the movement toward elite control will be slower. In fact, in some environmental policy areas, this movement may not occur at all. Thus, we can identify policy areas in which social movement organizations have substantial continuing power, such as air pollution, as opposed to areas in which social movement organizations weaken, such as consumer lobbies for the general regulation of consumer product safety. (Other groups push for consumer safety in automobiles or in food.) The changing power of social movement organizations will likely be related to the changing output of a policy area, as it shifts between the poles of reform and producer group control.

The punctuated equilibrium theory maintains that the reform laws jump the policy status quo to a different position, which is maintained by institutional changes, although former controlling elites may work to change that position (Baumgartner and Jones, 1993). In my own work, I refer to "cycles," policy continuing on the same terms but not moving all the way back to the status quo before the enactment of reform legislation (see chapter 6).

There may be policy areas, such as Federal Reserve Bank policy, in which social movement organizations have no influence, and this situation does not change.

Are there no social movement organizations in a policy area, just a few, or many? What are the implications for the political process in that area? As noted, in Federal Reserve policy, there are no such groups. Another area with no social movement groups is the regulation of food supplements, such as herbal remedies. (Apparently, environmentalists and consumerists regard such products as "natural," not controlled by big business, and ignore the potential damage to public health.) However, such policy areas are probably elitist, controlled by a coalition aiming toward a single interest.

An opposite case is that in which social movement organizations are the dominant interest group in a policy area, perhaps a key part of a reform iron triangle. Although it is normally part of the political position of business and conservative ideological groups to claim that this is the case for environmental regulation, civil rights, and so forth, it is difficult to locate a policy system in which social movement organizations are dominant. (If one regarded the National Rifle Association as related to a type of social movement, this would be the case for gun regulation in the 1980s, before police organizations and some gun control groups began to exercise a modest check on the NRA.)

We can distinguish neopluralist policy areas that have no (or almost no) social movement groups, those that have just a few such groups, and those that have quite a lot of them. One area having almost no social movement groups is deregulation of banking, characterized by a neopluralist structure of banks versus insurance companies and brokerages, with federal regulatory agencies on both sides of the issue. Neopluralist areas having just a few social movement organizations include the tort reform area, in which insurance companies contend with trial lawyers, with relatively minuscule participation by Naderite groups (presuming we count the public interest movement as a movement). Another such area is telecommunications reform, typically pitting telephone companies against cable companies, with small participation by public interest groups. But quite a lot of social movement groups are active in abortion policy or air pollution regulation, counting state and local groups as well as national groups.

If there are a number of social movement groups in an issue area, one might ask: Based on the expectation that social movement groups will use the strategy of delaying litigation, does it take longer to reach policy decisions? Because of the commitment of participants in movement organizations, is the level of conflict greater? Can we argue that representation is enhanced by the participation of social movement organizations?

Another question is, *how does federalism affect the presence of social movement organizations,* especially in neopluralist systems? On the one hand, national social movements encourage the presence of local movement organizing, perhaps in the form of demonstrations, litigation, or standard political action. Persons at the local level take cues from national movements about identifying issues and protesting grievances. Many readers would find this process to be positive in the case of the women's movement (Woliver, 1993) but negative in the case of McCarthyism, when local demagogues mimicked the actions of the U.S. senator.

On the other hand, the existence of significant local- and state-level political units can serve as an organizational base for social movements, which may then go on to national-level politics. A good example is the gay and lesbian rights movement, which had early, significant influence in such city governments as San Francisco, Washington, D.C., Chicago, Montreal, and Sydney, Australia (Dufour, 1998). Another case is the influence of Christian fundamentalists over some local- and state-level school boards, which helps enhance the national influence of this movement. Thus, local governments can serve as an organizational base for movements, leading to increased movement participation in neopluralist policymaking.

However, the reverse has been argued by social scientists. McConnell and Lowi are mainly concerned with the tendency of grassroots administrative councils of the federal government to co-opt agents of change. But in *City Trenches,* Ira Katznelson (1981) argues that the strength of working-class socialist movements in the United States was co-opted by the machine form of local political organization, which broke down class solidarity in the mechanisms of patronage distribution to machine supporters. Accordingly, the investigator cannot readily assume that local governmental units enhance social movement organization, but must investigate the particular case.

Finally, in developing generalizations, there is an unavoidable confusion about the definition of *social movement*. First, in political science, we are most interested in political movements, and some social movements may initially be outside the pale of our analysis (nonpolitical religious movements or long-lasting pop culture expressions, for instance). The idea of *political movement,* however, usually connotes the use of noninstitutionalized political tactics such as demonstrations, sit-ins, consciousness-raising groups, and even violence, as opposed to voting or exercising the right of petition. But in American society, we immediately recognize that political movements ordinarily use both noninstitutionalized tactics and regular tactics, such as litigation and lobbying, although there is likely to be a division of labor in this respect. A problem arises, however, to the extent that we try to distinguish movement groups from other groups oriented toward public policy change, not just limited to the group itself. Were Ralph Nader and John Gardner (Common Cause) part of a public interest *movement*? Or were they founders of citizens groups, lobbying organizations for policy change, but not part of a social movement? I would refer to middle-class organizing for government reform as a "movement," in that it seeks to change basic decision-making procedures; by using institutionalized tactics, it seeks to change institutions. This also applies to the term-limits movement, the balance-the-budget amendment movement, and so forth. However, some may prefer to call these "citizens groups" rather than "movement groups." In either case, such groups enhance the diversity of participation within the policymaking process, thereby increasing the degree of neopluralism.

SOCIAL MOVEMENTS IN THE POLITICAL PROCESS

Political sociologist Paul Burstein (1998) argued that social movement organizations and interest groups are equivalent phenomena. This may go a bit far, but in important instances in the analysis of policy processes, power, and interest groups, social movement theory and neopluralist theory merge. Let us refer to such instances as the social movement policy process. The discussion that follows can be readily converted into hypotheses for those who prefer to think in such terms.

Let us take American politics and policy as our referent, and let us regard the American system as broken up into hundreds of separate policy areas. Unfortunately, it is not possible to predict when a social movement will occur and when it will occur in a policy area. At bottom, analysis of the beginnings of a movement is an interpretive enterprise (McAdam, 1999, xxxiii). However, once a social movement appears to some significant extent, theory helps us to understand its spread and its impact on policy. One key element is preexisting communications networks within a policy area; these are central to the spread of a social movement (Pinard, 1975; Oberschall, 1973; Freeman, 1975). In particular, the previous existence of interest groups within the area of the movement is key to the spread of the movement. In other words, interest groups such as the League of Women Voters and the American Association of University Women were preexisting networks spreading the ideas of 1960s feminism. The Sierra Club and the National Wildlife Federation were preexisting networks to communicate the ideas of the post-1968 environmentalism. Even though such groups may seem to be "conservative," they nevertheless spread new ideas.

In America, social movements in a policy area occur in waves, about once a generation. Each social movement wave leaves behind interest groups of a relatively conventional sort. For instance, the Progressive-suffragette generation left behind the League of Women Voters; the Progressives founded the Sierra Club. Such interest groups, deposited by a movement "wave," provide a communications basis for the next wave a generation later.

We can interpret in the past, and we can predict that policy areas that had movements before will have them again in the future, because these areas have the most interest groups prone to spreading new movement ideas. The second-generation movements are characterized by a reframing of the original message: the suffragettes become feminists; the conservationists become environmentalists; nuclear freeze becomes anti-globalism. The reframed message becomes effective and powerful to the extent that it is positively received by the broad middle-class public. The reframed message (e.g., environmentalism) is likely to have the capacity to affect the political process in policy areas different from the message of a preceding generation (e.g., environmentalism affects nuclear power plant construction and regulation, which is not really relevant to the preceding conservationist messages).

A handful of master frames are associated with the appearance of movements affecting public policy (Benford and Snow, 2000). One of these is "the rights of Americans": African American, Latinos, the disabled, gays, and so forth—even animal rights. A second is "environmental protection"—a frame now applied to dozens of policy situations in a way that could not have been foreseen in 1965. The master frames tend to induce specific frames applicable to specific policy areas, leading to the formation of specific interest groups in those areas.

Predictably, countermovements occur. These lead to the formation of interest groups that lobby and engage in influencing public opinion in a direction opposite to the social movement organizations. Countermovements also spread through preceding networks, such as fundamentalist church groups or publics listening to radio talk shows. Analysis of countermovements indicates an overlap between conventional political analysis and movement theory;

countermovement groups may use conventional political tactics almost exclusively to seek their goals, yet they are part of the total picture in the analysis of social movements.

Countermovements also have a handful of master frames. The most important of these is "freedom," which is interpreted to mean freedom from government intervention in "free markets" and freedom from government social regulations. The master frame of freedom can be applied to numerous situations in which social movements are pressing for government action to bring about an important social change. Long battles of strategy then occur between opposing sides; for instance, in the policy area of regulating carbon dioxide emissions, the frame of protecting the natural environment is countered by the frame of freedom from government intervention.

A countermovement is not simply based on groups especially organized for that purpose. Preexisting groups, organized for other purposes, will support the countermovement. Individual corporations and business associations will lobby against new regulations that will lower their profits, as in air pollution policy. Media conglomerates and organized schoolteachers will form the base of a countermovement to fundamentalist proposals to control sinful messages in schools and on the airwaves.

In addition to interest group networks, the mass media spread movement ideas to local areas. Media treatment leads to imitation phenomena at the local level. Feminists protest the decisions of a local judge taking a chauvinist view of rape (Woliver, 1993); learning about the cleanup of rivers elsewhere inspires local environmentalists to organize for that purpose (Lowry, 2003). Local lobbying ensues to influence the city, county, and state governments. Countermovements appear. Nearly dormant interest groups, dating from a previous generation, are reactivated by the new wave of movement activity.

Most policy areas are characterized by long periods of relative equilibrium and incremental change. Presently, most scholars see policy areas as having occasional, relatively short periods of nonincremental or "punctuated" change, with some models posing a direction (McClosky and Zaller, 1984; see chapter 6) and some not doing so (Baumgartner and Jones, 1993).

Some policy areas (the "rights" areas) are hypothesized to be more heavily impacted by social movements, due to the presence of interest groups prone to carrying the message of succeeding waves of movements. Punctuated change occurs more frequently and to a greater extent in such policy areas. In addition, a major source of punctuated change is the reframing of a master frame (such as when conservation becomes environmentalism), which is then specifically framed to define issues in the sense of both specific policies (federal regulation of nuclear power) and specific localities (closing the Indian Point nuclear power plants). Intuitively, I would estimate that about 25 percent of policy change analysis in America today involves the analysis of social movements.

Social movements are generally considered to be sequences of action involving noninstitutionalized behaviors, whether nonviolent sit-ins or violent demonstrations. But we have seen that in the perspective of Olson's logic of collective action, social movements provide incentives for participation in both noninstitutional movement activity and conventional interest group activity. Such groups (e.g., environmental lobbies) then provide countervailing power to producer groups, enabling state institutions to have greater autonomy. In turn, government professionals have greater influence in shaping policy. Ironically, in some policy areas, social movements have the effect of enhancing the power of institutions, that is, government institutions.

Social movements provide an important part of the issue definition in the American political system. Scholars of issues and the agenda apparently agree that many years pass as issues develop to the stage of a major vote in Congress (Kingdon, 1984; Polsby, 1984; Baumgartner and Jones, 1993; Lowry, 1998). Accordingly, in most cases, issue definition for Congress has been modified greatly from the initial expressions by movement leaders. In Kingdon's theory of the agenda, a problem-definition event stream is joined to a solution-definition event stream by a political entrepreneur during a "window of opportunity." Social movements frequently provide both early definitions of problems and definitions of solutions (e.g., Progressive institutional reforms in 1905); in addition, social movements often play a role in creating the political window of opportunity (e.g., demonstrations led by Martin Luther King Jr.).

In addition, countermovements provide important issue definitions in many policy areas. Thus, "right to life" has become a countermovement to the women's movement in the area of abortion regulation policy.

A theory of issue formation overlaps with the theory of social movements. Researchers need to understand the framing of issues by movements and countermovements to understand policy within some particular area (Benford and Snow, 2000). The dynamics of framing and reframing between opposed sides is likely to play an important role in policy outcomes. Environmentalists propose to save nature and protect human health; the countermovement frames issues as preserving economic growth and jobs and opposing "big government." The two compete to persuade both an elite audience and a mass audience by establishing a dominant issue frame. (These ideas are developed further in chapter 8.)

Researchers should note the various theories about the impact of social movements on a specific policy area in American politics. At one time, Lowi (1969, 1979) argued that social movements would be absorbed into the political status quo because the politics of interest group liberalism leads to a distributive politics in which movement personnel become part of the system after receiving some type of material or status benefit (e.g., control of a local action council). Another scholarly position is that although public interest activists and other movement persons might organize interest groups with some influence, their reform goals would inevitably be absorbed by the political system, and real change could be achieved only by participation in an advocacy coalition with a revitalized labor movement (Noble, 1986; McCann, 1986, makes a similar argument). My own position, which might be called "centrist," is that movements do have an effect on policy, even though movements are ordinarily represented by somewhat conventional interest groups. However, times of relatively rapid change sometimes ensue, during which movements' impact is much more than incremental (see chapter 6). As indicated by purchased space on the *New York Times* op-ed page and a multitude of newspaper columns, conservative thinkers and activists do not regard environmentalists and other activists as being co-opted by the system, but they regard movements as having a continuing powerful presence in interest groups and in opinion formation.

Thus, the notion of inevitable co-optation seems to be ruled out. Although researchers are not sure which model to use, it seems that the logic of collective action is sometimes canceled by the appearance of nonmaterial incentives, including "identification" (with African Americans, women, gays, and so forth), "faith" (fundamentalism, anti-abortion), "protection" (the environment, human health, quality of future life), and "justice" (government reform, human rights). These seem to be enough to provide stable support for environmental groups and government reform, among others (Rothenberg, 1992; Shaiko, 1999).

Maintenance of reform goals in movement interest groups seems to be the normal pattern if we apply the niche theory of Gray and Lowery (1996). If a movement group is bought off by the government, status quo foundations, and corporate support, it is likely to lose support from movement supporters to the point that it is no longer seen as a significant movement actor. One or more other groups will enter the particular movement niche and begin to take away membership and donations, as implied by research about public interest groups (Rothenberg, 1992; Shaiko, 1999). This almost never happens, however, because movement group leaders are quite aware of this possibility, and most such leaders today still have some identification with the ideal goals of the movement—enough to resist total co-optation.

Finally, social movement theory reminds the policy researcher about the possibility of violence, as in Tarrow's (1995) social movement cycle. A movement may achieve some success in influencing government policy, and at that time, the majority of movement supporters may become newly active in electoral politics and interest groups or just end their participation on some issue. However, a minority of adherents will define movement goals in absolute, possibly revolutionary, terms and form small underground, cultist organizations prone to the use of violence. This violence is likely to be met by counterviolence from the government. Tarrow's observations were derived from his study of the Italian Left and student movements. However, similar phenomena occurred during the late 1960s in the American civil rights movement and radical student movement. At that time, most observers were surprised at the appearance of the Black Panthers and the Weathermen, but if America experiences another cycle of social movements, we can predict that similar violence will occur toward the end of a period of rapid social change.

I have concluded, then, that most of the time, movement interest groups will continue to be active and will advocate some real reform, enough to provide countervailing power in some cases, as on many environmental issues. During sudden shifts of public policy, such interest groups may briefly become more radical and more active due to the influence of the new wave of movement activism. During such times of "punctuation," new movement frames will redefine issues, much more so than in times of routine politics (Baumgartner, Berry, Hojnacki, Kimball, and Leech, 2000).

CONCLUSION

I have reviewed the types of new theories of social movements, indicating that movements impact the policy process with some frequency. Within the overall picture of neopluralism, I have given an indication of the various patterns of social movement activity within policy areas.

Social movement theory fits closely with political process theory, and the four basic pluralist concepts apply to social movement theory. Social movements are studied as processes of action over time; they include activity intended by actors to change one another's actions. One cannot presume that one movement in a society is representative of all movements in a society; in studying movements, one attends to how the actors themselves frame the issues. With regard to a fifth concept—scope of change in a social policy system—social movement theory takes the punctuated change perspective, a type of process theory. Social movement theory addresses Olson's logic of collective action and discusses reasons for participation in movements. Social movements function as interest group sustainers, which often enhance countervailing power to producer groups, thereby enhancing agency autonomy and somewhat limiting the control of elite coalitions in policy areas. Certainly, without exception, social movement researchers make it plain that they do not believe that the appearance of numerous social movement organizations leads to an equitable balance of power with the preexisting established social institutions.

Social movement theory is closely linked to the succeeding chapters of this book. The historical cycles of chapter 6 provide an outlook on recurring political opportunities for social movements. Chapter 7, regarding cooperative pluralism, indicates the possibility of some social movement organizations participating in planning processes with producer groups and government officials. In chapter 8, I examine the relationship between social movements and political agendas as one aspect of a theory of agenda formation.

Unfortunately, a generation ago, the idea of pluralism was often seen as antithetical to social movements (Rogin, 1967). This was an implication that

William Kornhauser (1959) and others drew from Tocqueville's argument that intermediary groups are necessary to prevent tyranny, which in the 1950s, political sociologists identified with such mass movements as fascism and communism. Such writers believed that organized groups in civil society greatly diminished the impact of social movements, because aggrieved citizens would express their complaints within intermediary groups and organizations instead. But as Tarrow (1998) pointed out, since social movements can be based in intermediary groups and communicated through such groups, the existence of social movements is quite compatible with Tocqueville's observations of abundant associational activity in America. In recent years, we have become aware that social movements can be associated with a pluralism of groups and thus can be studied with political process theory.

6
Policymaking and Political Time

On the one hand, the neopluralist theory of policymaking has much to offer; when applied to an area of public policy, this theory is likely to be very helpful in describing and explaining events. On the other hand, as initially presented by scholars of the contemporary American political process, the neopluralist model lacks a historical dimension, something that is embodied in other models of policymaking such as statism and corporatism. But there is nothing about neopluralism that separates it from historical analysis. In this chapter, then, I present an example of the neopluralist policymaking model, extended through American history. In particular, I show that neopluralist theory has the potential to be expanded into a general theory of American politics.

Later I refer to "political time." Some decades are times of reform politics; others are times of business-dominated traditional politics; still others are transitional. Particular issue areas change from pluralist to elitist and back to pluralist, according to the times. This is an expansion of the reform cycle proposition discussed in chapter 4. To recap, the basic concepts of political process theory are the process of politics, power as causation, analysis by separate policy areas, self-definition of interests, partisan mutual adjustment, islands of oligarchy, the logic of collective action, interest group sustainers, statism, social movement theory, and neopluralism. Theory, aggregating these concepts, can be pushed back in time.

Two types of general theories can be contrasted. These are represented by the arrow or the circle. Arrow theories represent the increase of some concept over time. This may be described by the term *development,* as something is seen to develop from a simple state to a more complex state. Thus we have had stages of economic development and even "political development" in less developed countries. Arrow theories are easy to satirize: how many believe in political development anymore? Yet it makes some sense to observe after the events in Tiananmen Square that it may be another generation before the Chinese system "develops" enough to allow an organized opposition, such as Poland had in the 1980s.

Among the most appealing of the arrow theories are those that point to the greater complexity and differentiation of society with "modernization." We may think of Weber's spread of rational-legal norms, enhancing the proliferation of modern bureaucratic organizations, coordinating structures of human action to attack a problem by breaking it into parts and setting human specialists to work at each of those parts. The spread of bureaucratic organization in government is usually said to be part of "state development," providing experience, norms, and capacities for state structures.

In studying interest groups, early scholars adapted the idea of Durkheimian evolution of complexity to observe that the number and types of interest groups proliferated with modernization and economic development. This idea was stressed by David Truman (1951, 52–55), for instance, and was probably stated at the beginning of most interest group texts and college classes in the field. The more social differentiation and economic development, the more types of interest groups—a concept that seems simple, important, and essentially true. Just as Skowronek (1982) surprised us with a developmental theory of state building in America, perhaps someone will surprise us with a simple but powerful developmental theory of interest groups beyond the straightforward Durkheimian observations.

Another type of theory is represented by the circle. As time passes, things go back to where they were before. A similar type of idea is the linear repetition ABCDABCDABCD. Or, to get away from the simplistic image of the circle, we may refer to a "cycle," in which arrows in time travel through some pattern but eventually go back to point A, or perhaps just swing back and forth between points A and B.

Circle theories seem to be preferred by academicians. Circle theories seem more sophisticated, realistic, worldly-wise. One is almost forced to use French: *déjà vu, plus ca change, plus c'est la meme chose*. It is no surprise that after historians of America rejected the arrow theory of a manifest destiny to spread democracy throughout America and the world, "the model of a thirty-year alternation between public purpose and private interest" has become a simple but appealing generalization (Schlesinger, 1986, 31).

What of the subfields of the study of American government and politics? Here the students of political parties have led the way. It was difficult to create an arrow theory of parties, as this phenomenon seemed to have reached the height of its importance during the 1880s. Perhaps this encouraged V. O. Key Jr. (1955) and then Walter Dean Burnham (1967), James L. Sundquist (1983), and others to create a cyclical theory of parties, the party alignment theory.

Stephen Skowronek (1993) has reinterpreted the study of the presidency in a similar fashion. In *The Politics Presidents Make,* Skowronek proposes a cycle theory for the presidency. Presidents Andrew Jackson, Abraham Lincoln, Franklin Roosevelt, and Ronald Reagan are seen to be in comparable positions. Each created a new national governing coalition and thus was in a position to successfully exercise presidential leadership. Each was in a similar position in the presidential cycle or "political time." Similarly, the unfortunates John Quincy Adams, James Buchanan, Herbert Hoover, and James Earl Carter presided during times of the dissolution of a governing political coalition, leading to great difficulty in the exercise of successful presidential leadership.

This contrasts nicely with the dominant convention in the discussion of the American presidency: organizing books and classes around the arrow theory of "increasing presidential power" exercised over society as a whole and over Congress in particular, and expressed in the Supreme Court's grant of greater power to the federal government and to the president as the leader of that government (see Pious, 1979, for a sophisticated example). When certain presidents and historical periods fell away from the vector of increasing presidential power, this was somehow viewed as an aberration, especially by writers in the 1950s and 1960s. This theory was reexamined during the time of concern about the "imperial presidency," evidently leading to a new cyclical theory of the presidency.

What, then, of the study of interest groups? As noted, a rather unfashioned but effective arrow theory of modernization and group proliferation exists. But a clear-cut theory of groups—one analogous to the party alignment theory or Skowronek's presidential time theory—has not been put forth. But is not a cyclical theory of groups lurking in the back of the mind? The pivotal dates of Schlesinger's cycles of history and party realignment theory are the same—1832, 1860, 1900, and 1932, with the 1960s being the big puzzle for realignment theory (Burnham, 1970; Nie, Verba, and Petrocik, 1976). Skowronek (1993) focuses on 1832, 1860, 1932, and 1980 in his theory of the presidency; though not a good overlap in the twentieth century, his theory is similar in its attention to periods when new coalitions were created. Without being very specific, writers on American interest groups sometimes point to the decades of the 1900s, 1930s, and 1960s as having much in common in the proliferating significance of purposive groups, during Schlesinger's cycles of public action. Similarly, the 1890s, 1920s, 1950s, and 1980s are seen as periods in the resurgent importance of economic interest groups, during Schlesinger's cycles of private action (Vogel, 1989, 3–15, 290–300; J. Q. Wilson, 1973, 201–4; G. K. Wilson, 1985, 25; McFarland, 1983, 324–53).

Actually, Truman's *The Governmental Process* contains something like a circle theory of interest groups in the "wave theory" of interest mobilization. This theory states that mobilization of one type of interest (e.g., business) provokes a countermobilization of related interests (e.g., labor). Thus, interest groups organize in "waves," and in some cases, related events of mobilization and countermobilization occur in cycles over an extended period (Truman, 1951, 59–86).

In his pathbreaking article, Robert Salisbury (1969) takes a similar view of Truman's work in noting that *The Governmental Process* states two types of theories about group origins. The first is the "proliferation" hypothesis—the more functional differentiation in society, the more groups there are (an arrow theory). The second is Truman's "homeostatic" theory—a social system undergoes a "disturbance" that is rectified by the mobilization of groups, perhaps occurring in waves. The system then goes through cycles of rest, disturbance, and rest. The historical theory of interest group cycles herein can be regarded as a specification and extension of Truman's wave theory (see below).

LEVELS OF ANALYSIS

The theory of interest group cycles needs to be viewed in terms of two levels of analysis: first, in relation to theories of American society as a whole; second, in relation to theories of specific political institutions, such as political parties or the presidency.

The first level is that of general descriptions and analyses of American society and politics. There are a number of general descriptions of American history, and they usually focus on some basic factor or process and then relate changes in the basic variable over time. One might recall Tocqueville's democracy, equality, and consensus; Turner's discussion of the American frontier; Boorstin's (1953) views about pragmatism; Hartz's (1955) theory of the liberal consensus; Beardian views of an elite protecting property; Marxists and the class dialectic; and so on. In this chapter, I am most concerned with relating a subdisciplinary generalization, interest group cycles, to Schlesinger's general theory of American history as alternating periods of reform and conservatism.

However, the cycle theory of American politics that is best known to American political scientists is Samuel P. Huntington's *American Politics: The Promise of Disharmony* (1981). Huntington argues that Americans generally believe that their government exists not simply to govern but also to express universal ethical principles of liberty, equality, and freedom, now often called "human rights." At sixty-year intervals in American history, Huntington observes, significant numbers of Americans become angry at "the ideals-versus-institutions gap" and engage in collective behavior to restore the seemingly corrupted institutions to an ethical level, based on the creed that American government represents eternal principles of justice. These reform periods occurred in the 1770s, 1830s, 1900s, and 1960s and are described in a well-known phrase as periods of "creedal passion." Although the 1930s witnessed significant reform, the social movements and rhetoric of creedal passion were largely lacking.

Huntington's theory is a general theory of all American politics and thus differs from the interest group cycle project, which refers to group power balances in issue areas as generally corresponding to overall political trends, but admits that important variables in the general picture are omitted. The sixty-year period is too long for policy cycle theory, which posits relevant phenomena in the 1930s (see below).

Policy cycle theory regards the Progressive movement of the 1900s as a normal phenomenon, corresponding to a rather elemental model of motivation that combined rational self-interest with the occasional desire by some to mobilize politically to gain public goods. It does not seem unusual that the educated, middle-class citizenry responded to the perceived threats of rising prices due to monopoly, adulterated foods and medicines, shoddy urban services due to sweetheart deals between contractors and political machines, and rigged elections by expressing their anger in other elections, organizing reform groups, and turning newly organized occupational associations to social reform goals. Interest group cycle theory does not need creedal passion to explain Progressivism.

Huntington seems more useful in describing the 1960s, which exhibited great creedal passion and references to the violation of fundamental human rights. One need only recall the various rights movements for blacks, women, Hispanics, Native Americans, gays, the disabled, and so on. These movements crossed various issue areas of policies and provided an additional countervailing force against the policies of producer groups in employment. In other words, creedal passion was an important source of the synchronicity of issue area reform movements in the 1960s.

The human rights motivations of the 1960s set a precedent for later participants in reform cycles. During the succeeding traditionalist period, the antiabortion movement for fetal rights flourished. By 1990, the "rights" justification for reform was applied to specific challenges in particular issue areas: the rights of nursing home patients, prisoners in jails, subjects of scientific experiments, and even animals. Over and over again, issue area reformers repeat the logic of the Declaration of Independence by claiming that inalienable human rights are being violated, not by some king, but by corrupt special interests.

Huntington thus promises to be of use in developing policy cycle theory, but in terms of a correspondence to general theories of American politics, the interest group theory is closer to Schlesinger's *The Cycles of American History*. This sets forth "the model of a thirty-year alternation between public purpose and private interest [to] fit the political history of the United States in the twentieth century" (Schlesinger, 1986, 31). Schlesinger notes: "By the later 1970s Americans were once more, as they had been in the 1950s and 1920s, fed up with public action and disenchanted by its consequences. The compass needle now swung toward private interest and fulfillment of self" (32). Schlesinger emphasizes that swing groups of the public eventually tire of new appeals to participate in the public forum. Then a reform era runs its course.

In the field of the study of political attitudes, *The American Ethos: Public Attitudes toward Capitalism and Democracy* by Herbert McClosky and John Zaller (1984) parallels Schlesinger's views and also the idea of interest group cycles. In this work, the senior author concludes, after thirty years of research about American civic and political attitudes, that the tension between capitalist and democratic-egalitarian values is central to the understanding of American political attitudes. Almost all Americans have positive views about both capitalism and democracy, but most emphasize one set of values more than the other, given the basic consensus on views that most Americans share. In their concluding observations, McClosky and Zaller express a cyclical view of pubic policy, based on the "strain that lies at the heart of the American ethos" (292). The authors regard the 1920s, 1950s, and 1980s as characterized by a swing toward "the values of capitalism," while the 1930s and 1960s exhibited a swing toward "democratic values" (291–92). Interest group cycle theory can incorporate such conclusions about American political attitudes by noting that reformers call on widespread, latent democratic attitudes during one cyclical phase, while business groups call on latent anti-government, pro-market attitudes at a later phase.

A second level of analysis is that of general theories pertaining to a subdiscipline, such as the study of political parties and elections. Here we have the theory of party alignment or Skowronek's effort to find cycles in presidential leadership. This chapter seeks to point the public policy field and the interest group field in the same direction.

The subdisciplinary theory can be related to the general level of social description. We can ask, for instance: Is there a relationship between the theory of party alignment and Schlesinger's theory of alternating periods of reform and conservatism? Is there some relation between Skowronek's theory and Schlesinger's theory or some other similarly general theory?

Potentially as important, we can relate the general theories of subdisciplines. It seems apparent, for instance, that there is a linkage between party alignment theory and Skowronek's theory of presidents' building new coalitions in 1832, 1860, and 1932. We can ask similar questions of a general theory of interest groups. Interest group and policy cycles are related below to generalizations about political attitudes and to observations about social movements.

We can regard interest groups as acting in terms of specific issue areas of politics. Though not a precisely defined term, *issue area* as a concept has been standard for the analysis of power, policy, and interest groups since the publication of Robert Dahl's *Who Governs?* (1961b). The term *issue area* was essentially a call to divide politics and policies into component units and to discuss power in terms of individuals or groups that deflected policy in the direction of their own intentions (Dahl, 1958). Theodore Lowi (1964a), who prefers the term *political arena,* added to Dahl by arguing that different issue areas have different patterns of power and that this is largely due to the characteristics of the issue itself (regulatory, distributive, and so forth).

Issue is a subjective term. What people perceive as an issue cannot always be assumed. Nevertheless, there is a convention within political science of using the term to refer to an economic sector (e.g., sugar beet production, motor vehicle production) and to clusters of interaction about some government policy (e.g., pesticide policy, food stamp policy). Heclo (1978) put forth the term *issue network* (Kingdon's [1984] *policy communities* is similar), and the idea that people see themselves as participants in issue networks is verified by Laumann and Knoke (1987).

Much interest group theory is based on observations of the policy process in the separate issue areas (McFarland, 1987). One concludes that an issue area is pluralist, elitist, neopluralist, corporatist, or statist. Such research implies that the general political system can be described as a composite of hundreds of separate issue areas. But there is something unsatisfactory in saying that the political system is a collection of various pluralist, elitist, neopluralist, corporatist, and statist issue areas. Interest group theory needs to posit a different general pattern.

Interest group theory is aggressively expansive in portraying the overall political system as an aggregate of issue areas, with the understanding that interest groups normally play an important role in each area. But by the 1990s, we all became neoinstitutionalists; we all admitted that political institutions act autonomously to affect political outcomes (Almond, 1988). Interest group activity is now seen as just one factor affecting political decisions, interacting with elected decision-makers, administrative officials, the courts, and so on (J. Q. Wilson, 1980).

Nevertheless, interest group theory implies that its subdisciplinary generalizations provide an outline for a general theory of American politics. Politics in terms of issue areas in its aggregate provides a blurred image of the overall political system.

ENDOGENOUS CYCLES

The basic idea of policy cycles was well summarized by Boss Plunkitt of Tammany Hall. The patronage organization chief referred to reformers as morning glories, which "looked lovely in the mornin'" and withered up in a short time, while the regular machines went on "flourishin' forever, like fine old oaks" (Riordan, 1963, 17). The machine politician, motivated by material incentives, is continuously active. A version of this familiar idea was dubbed by Lowi (1971, x) "the reform cycle."

This concept can be applied to interest groups within issue areas, in which the role of the political machine is parallel to the phenomenon variously referred to as subsystems, subgovernments, clientelism, interest group capture, iron triangles, and so forth (see chapter 3). With the aid of administrative and legislative allies, producer groups—businesses, professional associations, agricultural groups—control the specific issue areas in which they are economically active. Such producer control yields public policies that benefit producer interests at the expense of more general interests: tax breaks, subsidies, restrictions on competition, oligopolistic trade practices, the economic externalities of pollution, unsafe products, dangerous labor conditions, and so forth. The producer interests are normally well organized for political domination of an issue area, due to the saliency of their large economic stakes and their greater ability to overcome the paradoxes of collective action (see chapter 3). General interests, such as reformers, are vigorously organized only intermittently, due to the lack of saliency of widely shared but diffuse economic interests and the much greater difficulty in overcoming collective action dilemmas. Or, as J. Q. Wilson (1980) put it, if the costs of a public policy change are concentrated (e.g., regulating pollution), or if the benefits are concentrated (e.g., tax breaks for the insurance industry), these groups are initially more likely to organize effectively than are those sharing a widely diffused but less salient benefit (e.g., breathers of air with 20 percent less sulfur dioxide) or those sharing a widely diffused, less salient cost (e.g., a tiny increase in the government's deficit).

However, such elite control over a specific policy area does not persist indefinitely. As the Constitutional Convention well understood, unchecked elites eventually violate widely shared standards. This might be termed *excess*, a situation viewed by many citizens, journalists, and politicians as corrupt, exploitative, and against the public interest. Examples include the nuclear power industry not reporting safety problems to the public in the 1960s; government contractors concealing problems with nuclear waste disposal in government bomb factories; the behavior of many savings and loans executives in the mid-1980s; motor vehicle manufacturers' attitudes toward safety before 1966; lack of concern for the effects of newly invented financial manipulations on the markets; the classic "capture" syndrome in such areas as aviation and trucking (Stigler, 1975; Derthick and Quirk, 1985); and extraordinary inflation in health care costs and personal insurance. Similar examples can be found in the 1890s and 1920s. They are chronicled in the works of the muckrakers and the writings of New Deal intellectuals.

After the widespread perception of excess, the public, the media, and politicians become involved to correct the problems in the issue area. New legislation and regulations are drawn up. Countervailing power groups and governmental agencies act autonomously to check producer groups in the particular issue area. This might be called "high politics," as opposed to "routine politics" (McFarland, 1987; Redford, 1969; Ripley and Franklin, 1984). High politics in an issue area is characterized by relatively great public attention and publicity. The higher decision-making institutions become involved; the president is interested, bills are passed in Congress, federal courts render decisions, and state governments pass legislation. Such periods of high politics contrast to the more prevalent routine politics of an issue area, when there is no reform pressure and producer groups dominate.

But after the reform period in an issue area, after legislation has been passed and regulations issued, the period of high politics is over: the public loses interest, journalistic coverage ceases, Congress and the president turn to other issues. The activity of countervailing power groups and autonomous governmental agencies declines, but the activity of producer groups remains constant, due to their continuing economic stakes in the issue area. After a few years, another period of producer group power is at hand, eventually leading to new excesses, a new reform period, and so forth. This is the *reform cycle* in an issue area.

It is useful to divide participants in an issue area into three types: producer groups; countervailing power groups, whose interests differ from those of producer groups; and autonomous governmental agencies, acting on public policy in an independent fashion, not controlled by groups. Sometimes one producer group exercises countervailing power to another; for example, bakeries lobby to keep sugar prices down, while sugar producers lobby to keep prices up (see chapter 4).

Obviously, in addition to such endogenous factors, there are exogenous factors in relation to a policy system. Thus, Baumgartner and Jones's theory of punctuated change stresses the notion of exogenous shocks as factors initiating the period of rapid, punctuated change in a policy system. Certainly, policy change factors can be exogenous: the depression of the 1930s and the destruction of the World Trade Center are obvious examples. First, however, I prefer to construct a closed theoretical system in which internal factors go to an extreme level, thereby producing a counterreaction from public opinion, group organization, and various sorts of reform political participation. Clearly, such a closed system cannot account for many events leading to policy change. But as step one, let us construct a coherent outlook that might account for change. After that, we can admit that there are unpredictable, somewhat random exogenous shocks to the policy system that are important change factors.

Events such as the Great Depression, war, or national security events (e.g., threats by al-Qaeda) are clearly exogenous to policy systems. But I also regard events such as the Santa Barbara oil spill (environmental regulation), thalidomide-related birth defects (drug testing), Kentucky mine disasters (mine safety laws), and the Enron–Arthur Andersen scandal (regulation of accounting and corporate pensions) as essentially endogenous, in that they resulted from situations of general business power in some policy area that led to abuses, precipitating widespread political demands for reform. An event such as the election of Ronald Reagan in 1980 and the transfer of power in the Senate to Republicans might be viewed as a combination of exogenous and endogenous factors. Reagan's election led to changes in federal public housing policy, control of illegal drugs, subsidies for alternative energy research and development, and education grants. On the one hand, in policy areas such as public housing or drugs, one might say that many voters were disturbed by the perceived waste of money by public administrators in housing or by an increase in drug addiction, excesses that the voters wanted to bring under control. These might be viewed as endogenous factors. On the other hand, the Reagan administration eliminated some education grants and subsidies for research and development for essentially ideological reasons, with the public showing little concern about these areas. These might be viewed as exogenous shocks to the policy area. At any rate, at this stage of theory development, I prefer to concentrate on endogenous factors within a policy system and their effect on changing that system.

In conclusion, the reform cycle is a general theory of interest group activity within specific issue areas. Activity goes through cyclical phases: producer group control, a transition (likely to be short), a reform period, a second transition, a second period of producer group control, and so on. The cycle is driven by incentives for political participation, and it is assumed that producer groups are normally politically active but that reform groups have only a fluctuating incentive to participate. The issue area also goes through cycles, alternating between phases of private, routine politics and public, high politics with greater participation.

SYNCHRONICITY

A major hypothesis of policy cycle theory is that there is a tendency for reform cycles in the hundreds of issue areas to proceed in phase. In other words, in a given year, the political power of producer groups will be relatively high in many issue areas simultaneously, while in another year, the political power of countervailing groups and autonomous government will be relatively high in many issue areas. In other years, many issue areas will be in transition, especially in the case of declining reform power and increasing producer power. It is hypothesized that the transition from producer power to reform periods is shorter, because public reaction to producer excesses tends to manifest itself suddenly—in elections, outraged responses to scandal, and the like.

If reform cycles in issue areas proceed in phase, then the aggregate of issue area politics (the second level of analysis), probably corresponds in broad outline to general social and political trends (the first level). The policy reform cycles then correspond to Schlesinger's cycles of reform and conservatism, public and private action. Since we are now all neoinstitutionalists, the interest group theorist recognizes that the institutions and behaviors studied by other subdisciplines of political science (level two of analysis) have an important effect on the general state of society. Nevertheless, at least in the case of American society, the correspondence between policy cycles in phase and commonly observed general social trends is a strong statement about the importance of interest groups. The conclusion is that policy cycles have an important impact on general social and political changes. That is, the second level of analysis has a major impact on the first.

Policy cycle theory, then, means that during the 1890s, 1920s, 1950s, and 1980s, the power of economic producers was gaining within hundreds of issue areas at the expense of countervailing power groups (Schlozman and Tierney, 1983, 351–57). As stated here, cycle theory implies that during reform periods—the 1900s, 1930s, and 1960s—business and producer power weakens in hundreds of issue areas. This may be due to an increase in the countervailing power of groups, or it may be due to an increase in the regulatory power of a governmental agency. Possibly, countervailing power groups and autonomous governmental agencies act in coalition to check producer groups.

But why does it seem that reform cycles in separate issue areas tend to proceed in phase? First, major social forces had an impact on many issue areas at the same time in 1900 (the Progressive movement), 1932 (the depression and the New Deal), and 1964–1965 (the civil rights movement and the Vietnam War). The reform cycle clock was simultaneously set for many issue areas, which subsequently went through the phases of reform, transition, and business power. Second, the incentives for reform participation tended to diminish at a generally corresponding rate through many issue areas after the clock had been set in 1900, 1932, and 1964–1965.

The events around 1900 were endogenous to policy reform theory, but the events of 1932 lay outside of policy theory (the election of Franklin D. Roosevelt), and the events of the 1960s seem to have been initiated by forces both inside and outside policy theory.

The Progressive reform era of the 1900s is a case in which most of the reform spirit was directed against specific issue area excesses of business and government (Wiebe, 1967). Most government then was local government. Progressives were critical of "special-interest" collaboration in such matters as licensing of gas and electric utilities, contracting in public construction, state regulation of railroads, working conditions for women and children, and so forth. At the national level, Progressives believed that monopolies in oil and steel had accumulated too much power, that the meatpacking industry needed regulation, that large banks manipulated interest rates, and that senators should be elected directly by the voters rather than by state legislatures. The Progressives believed that special interests had seized control of politics and that civic-minded Americans needed to fight these interests on behalf of the public interest. In short, the nationwide Progressive movement (weaker in the South) was a macrolevel embodiment of policy cycle theory. It sprang from a rapidly spreading revulsion among much of the middle class against the power of business in alliance with patronage-oriented politicians.

The depression and the American two-party system produced the New Deal, which was initiated by the national government; in contrast, Progressivism was initiated largely at the state and local government level (Wiebe, 1967, chap. 7). However, support for New Deal politicians was enhanced by the perception of excesses and scandal in specific policy areas. The widespread belief that business exploited labor resulted in government support for the organization of labor unions as a countervailing force in specific issue areas.

The civil rights movement and the anti-war protests in 1964–1965 had much to do with initiating the general atmosphere of criticism and reform referred to as "the sixties," but they were not a revolt against special-interest power. As David Vogel (1989, chap. 4) described, a later wave of reform criticism occurred in 1969 and afterward, similar to the earlier Progressive movement, in which advocates of environmentalism, consumerism, and government reform once again criticized the special interests as part of a public interest movement. So one might say that reform in the 1960s was caused partially by factors related to policy cycles.

Other factors influencing political participation help to produce an effect of corresponding degrees of reform activities in various issue areas. Policy cycle theory can incorporate Albert Hirschman's stimulating view of human nature. In his book *Shifting Involvements*, Hirschman (1982) argues that people easily become disappointed with engagement in public political action and subsequently become more involved in private economic activity, only to find that disappointing as well. History might be analyzed according to such a theory of shifting involvements, he argues.

My theory differs from Hirschman's in its emphasis on interest group activity and on excesses by producer groups as a cause of shifting involvements. In other words, reform cycles are activated by the widespread perception of spreading "public bads"—negative externalities generated by special-interest cliques that offend values of social justice and perhaps threaten public health or waste the taxpayer's dollar (Mitchell, 1979; Hardin, 1982, 61–66, 120–21; J. M. Hansen, 1985). But for explaining the diminishing involvement of reformers, an outlook such as Hirschman's seems appropriate.

One might assume that perhaps 1 percent of the American adult public remains committed to reform activity on a rather constant basis. Thus, 1 percent pursue their goals, spending their time (in contradiction to Olson's logic of collective action) by contributing to politicians, parties, and interest groups; working in political campaigns; attending political meetings and rallies; and contacting politicians on behalf of public causes. This 1 percent might also participate in social movements for change, doing all these things and also engaging in protest demonstrations, strikes, or consciousness-raising groups, sometimes to a level of extraordinary involvement.

During the reform phases of policy cycles, this 1 percent is joined by another (perhaps) 4 percent of the public, which, on behalf of reform causes, engages in public political activities such as those indicated above. But after participating for a few years, members of this secondary group of reformers tend to become less politically active for a number of reasons. Hirschman seems to be correct: a certain disappointment or boredom with politics sets in. But there are other reasons. Edelman (1964) noted that the passage of reform legislation misleads many persons into thinking that some "public bad" has been rectified, when actually the relevant legislation may be more symbol than substance. In American politics, during times of general reform, a great deal of legislation is enacted by politicians backing new causes to enhance their reelection chances (Walker, 1977, 423–25). The more naive reformers will be misled in the manner described by Edelman; the more sophisticated may be disappointed a few years later when they observe problems with implementation, the reactivation of status quo coalitions, and the like. An associated phenomenon is reform disunity. After a major round of reform legislation is enacted, the reformers themselves split into antagonistic groups: New Freedom versus New Nationalism in 1912, left New Deal versus pragmatic New Deal; AFL versus CIO, NAACP versus black power, McGovern supporters versus Humphrey supporters, and so forth.

Hirschman (1982, chap. 1) takes his shifting involvements theory to the point of tentatively endorsing a dualistic theory of human nature: most people at one time tend to prefer public political activity, but at some point they shift involvements and develop the second aspect of modern human nature, the preference for private economic activity (Margolis, 1984). This aptly describes the enthusiasm for war; however, involvement in war—a very demanding form of public activity—seems to deplete the participatory motivations of many people. Many books, songs, films, and folktales have described the longing for private activity on the part of the warrior returned home. The contingency of war had much to do with the depletion of reform activity in 1919 and in the late 1940s. The Vietnam War was a different case because it stimulated protest participation; the end of the draft and the end of the war were important factors in the relative quiescence of the mid-1970s.

During reform periods, egalitarian social movements eventually produce actions that are viewed as excesses by a great majority of the politically active public. Calls for violence, flag burning, anti-Americanism, radical socialism, or even trumpeting the need for zero economic growth act as a "turnoff" to general public support and participation. Such excesses speed up the process of reform burnout, making it more difficult for countervailing power groups to maintain themselves.

Of course, power is relative, and the countermobilization of business in response to reformers is another factor contributing to the decline of the reform phase in various issue areas. The impact of this factor may be hard to trace in 1919 and in the late 1940s, but Vogel (1989, chaps. 6, 7) showed that business mobilization was very important in the politics of the mid-1970s. Business executives and lobbyists, like most other observers, were taken by surprise by the sudden mobilization of anti-business groups around 1969, and it was not until about 1975 that they were able to check the surge of business regulation.

A factor lowering the relative power of business is the multiplicative effect of the organization of countervailing power groups in an issue area. The appearance of such groups has the additional effect of enhancing the possibility of autonomous action by governmental agencies. During periods of issue area dominance by producer groups, policy is sometimes "captured" by the subgovernmental coalition of producer groups and friendly administrators and legislators. But the emergence of countervailing power groups increases the tendency toward a balance of power within an issue area, so that governmental

Table 1. American Political Cycles

Reform CV, AA higher	Transitional	Business CV, AA lower
		1890s National corporations Issue area laissez-faire Monopolies Jim Crowism
1901–1914 Progressive era Professional groups "Public interest" Muckrakers Anti-trust, etc. Regulatory commissions	1915–1918 World War I	1919–1933 Red scare (1918–1919) "Normalcy" "Dollar decade" Cooperation of progressive government agencies Klan revival
1933–1939 New Deal Unions (Wagner Act) Leftist social movements New federal agencies	1940–1948 World War II and aftermath	1949–1961 McCarthyism Tocquevillean consensus Korean War Eisenhower Heyday of business capture "What's good for General Motors . . ."

1961–1974
The sixties (may begin
  c. 1963)
Civil rights
Public interest groups
Feminism
Vietnam controversy
Issue networks more powerful
New regulation
Environmentalism
Warren Court
	1974–1980
	Presidents Ford and Carter
	Deregulation begins
	Business regroups (see
	  Vogel, 1989)
	Traditionalist movements
	  begin
	Burger Court
		1980–present
		Reagan-Bush presidencies
		Business power, but more
		  checks from CV, AA
		Deregulation
		Markets and entrepreneurs
		Anti-abortion
		Fundamentalists
		Rehnquist Court
		Clinton centrism

CV, countervailing power groups. AA, autonomous agencies of government.

agencies have greater political leeway to initiate policies on their own rather than merely reflecting the goals of a dominant producer group (J. Q. Wilson, 1980).

We can thus speak of microcycles and macrocycles in American politics. Issue area microcycles go from a state of relatively high producer power, through a reform period, and then to a new period of produce power as the incentives for reform participation diminish. At the level of society as a whole, we find that certain events tend to affect different issue areas at the same time, initiating the reform phase at the microlevel. Because the diminishing incentives for reform participation are a phenomenon common to most issue areas, countervailing power declines at a roughly similar rate in the various policy areas. As countervailing power declines, so does the autonomous effect of governmental agencies, and the relative power of producer groups increases. This phenomenon is also general to the various issue areas.

Policy cycle theory in one hundred years of American history is summarized in Table 1. But first, two organizing principles need be mentioned with respect to policy cycle theory. First, it is conventional in American cycle theories to mark the beginning of a reform era (e.g., 1901, 1933, 1961) as the beginning of a cycle. Here, however, because the starting point is business power, it is best to start the cycle when industrialization is in full swing—at about the 1890s. Thus, ten years or more before 1901 is regarded as the starting point of the theory, a time of relative business power (Hays, 1957).

Second, it seems useful to designate a "transition period" between the reform eras and the business eras. The years 1915 to 1919 mark the end of a reform period, as President Wilson became preoccupied with the First World War. A similar phenomenon occurred in the 1940s, with an ambiguous period marked by the election of a conservative Congress in 1946 and the passage of the Taft-Hartley Act in 1947, followed by Truman's surprising election victory in 1948. Although there was no war, the Ford and Carter administrations represent a transition from 1960s reform to 1980s conservatism. And as Orfield (1975) and Vogel (1989) remind us, a great deal of legislation regulating business was passed in the early 1970s.

NEOPLURALISM AND SOCIAL MOVEMENTS

The reform decades of the 1900s, 1930s, and 1960s were characterized by the great impact of egalitarian social movements. Although a movement of the white middle class, the Progressive movement was directed to a reduction of the power of business and political special interests for the sake of equal representation of the people, the public (Mowry, 1962, chap. 4). Although the main source of New Deal egalitarianism was the president and his administration, egalitarian movements were active in the 1930s: organized labor was a movement as well as an interest group; there were farm mortgage strikes and sharecroppers movements, Long's "share the wealth," communism, and so on (Piven and Cloward, 1977, chaps. 1–3). The 1960s need no comment. Such egalitarian movements are part of the interest group cycle, in that they tend to spin off new political interest groups. Or they may influence preexisting conventional interest groups to be more active in search of egalitarian goals. For instance, 1960s feminism led established groups such as the League of Women Voters and the Federation of Business and Professional Women's Clubs to lobby for some of the feminist goals (Freeman, 1975, 67–68, 214–18).

Although reform periods exhibit an increase in egalitarian movement activity, this does not mean that all the major egalitarian movements will have a significant impact during such a period. The 1900s and 1930s were not periods of exceptional activity for black civil rights groups. The women's movement and environmentalism (i.e., conservationism) surged in the 1900s but not in the 1930s, then surged again in the 1960s. Labor scored some gains in the 1900s, made major gains in the 1930s, but was not particularly active in the 1960s.

When such egalitarian movements are successful, they may be organized in groups to provide countervailing power to business in some issue areas. This is clear in the case of labor and environmentalism, for instance. Egalitarian rights movements may not have a day-to-day presence in policy networks but may instead rely on occasional litigation to limit business control over personnel policies.

Business is not the source of social movements, since it is already the most powerful social force, with the possible exception of the federal government. However, during periods of business power, we can expect the appearance of traditionalist social movements and new interest groups to accompany these movements. More significantly, however, the new traditionalist movements will influence preexisting interest groups to become more active in pressing for traditionalist goals that appear on the political agenda. If feminism made the League of Women Voters more militant, so will the rise of ultra-patriotism make veterans organizations more militantly patriotic.

In 1918 and 1949, about twenty years into the thirty-year cycle, the country experienced surges of ultra-patriotism, expressed as punishment of reputed communist sympathizers. No equivalent phenomenon occurred in the early 1980s, perhaps because communism was not so threatening in the era of Brezhnev, and perhaps because President Reagan expressed traditional patriotism without directing hatred against scapegoats.

Starting in the late 1970s, a number of traditionalist movements appeared, spinning off considerable interest group activity. Such movements include fundamentalist Christianity, the anti-abortion movement, and the taxpayers' revolt, which flourished in California's Proposition 13 vote in the 1978 election and in many other areas for a few years. In the 1950s, such traditionalist sentiments were expressed by preexisting groups, although this was also the time of the White Citizens' Councils and the rise of the John Birch Society. The 1920s were the height of Klanism in the twentieth century, including a great deal of activity in the North. This sort of traditionalism may not have been especially strong in the 1890s, however.

Traditionalism here is conceived as a desire to change policy to restore past practices in society. But traditional racism does not typify other movements in this category, which might include the movements to ban abortion or restore prayer in school, goals that have no association with race. Traditionalism is not especially a product of business interest groups, although pro-business conservative politicians sometimes contribute significantly to traditionalist movements.

Such political leaders (usually Republicans) provide a climate of political opportunity for traditionalists (Rogin, 1967; Polsby, 1960). In addition, these traditionalists can be seen as reacting against their perceptions of excesses committed in public policy during the previous reform era.

THEORY OF THE POLITICAL AGENDA

A theory of political cycles is a theory of the political agenda. Once stated, this seems obvious, but the point is seldom made in the political science literature. Schlesinger's cycle theory can be restated as a hypothesis that about every thirty years, a number of public-oriented, egalitarian issues will dominate the political agenda, to be followed fifteen years later by an agenda that is private and market oriented. This is a theory about the content and timing of the political agenda. Schlesinger's theory also contains observations about the factors causing the cycles—exogenous shocks, such as the depression, plus internal factors, such as the waxing and waning of the public's interest in political participation (Schlesinger, 1986, 27–48). McClosky and Zaller (1984, 290–302) provide a theory of the content of the political agenda—emphasizing capitalism or equality—and accept without comment the idea that the cycles are about thirty years long.

The theory of policy cycles herein is similar to that of Schlesinger and McClosky and Zaller, except that agenda setting is viewed more specifically in terms of issue areas, and a major causal factor is dominance by business, which produces excesses that, in turn, lead to high politics and public intervention. In other words, excesses put an issue on the public's political agenda.

This view of political agendas can be combined with Kingdon's influential theory of agenda setting in political science. Applying the "garbage can model" of organizations developed by Cohen, March, and Olsen (1972), Kingdon (1984) views policy in terms of policy communities (Heclo's issue networks), which separately develop concepts of problems and concepts of solutions. As an issue network is affected by exogenous social forces, a window of opportunity may develop in which political entrepreneurs assemble the separate problems and solutions into new legislation and regulations for public policy.

Policy cycle theory accepts the idea of issue networks as part of issue areas. However, rather than viewing the issue area as containing an essentially random collection of problems and solutions, policy cycle theory posits a general tendency for an imbalance of power to lead to insufficient restraint on business or business-dominated iron triangles, leading to unpopular actions or excesses, which, when discovered, set the political agenda for a new reform cycle. Similarly, reformers may be overzealous or make major policy blunders, producing an anti-reform reaction and enhancing the resumption of producer power in an issue area. More significantly, there is a general tendency for reformers' participation to decline, for the reasons summarized by Hirschman's "shifting involvements."

In Kingdon's language, one might say that reform or business periods in the cycle provide windows of opportunity for those social movements and interest groups having a greater appeal during a particular era. Political entrepreneurs help bring issues to the political agenda by locating and publicizing certain excesses out of the total number committed by business during one period or by reformers during another.

Social movements also affect the political agenda. It is suggested here that Progressivism was a movement that could be defined in terms of policy cycles. But most twentieth-century social movements are best viewed as exogenous to policy cycles, although movements produce groups that affect the cycles. But it can be said that different stages of the cycles encourage different types of social movements to become active in order to influence public policy. Egalitarian and public interest movements are encouraged during reform periods, when politicians are gaining popularity by exposing business excesses. Movements for patriotism, fundamentalist values in public policy, and the elimination of abortion are encouraged during the traditionalist periods of business preeminence. As sociologist Doug McAdam (1982, 41–43) put it, "the structure of political opportunities" is central to the appearance and impact of social movements.

TRUMAN'S WAVE THEORY OF GROUPS

As noted, the classic *The Governmental Process* contains a cycle theory, the wave theory of group mobilization. Truman (1951, 59) introduces the wave theory in this manner: "The evolution of associations does not necessarily proceed at a uniform rate. When a single association is formed . . . in the performance of its function it may cause disturbances in the equilibriums of other groups. . . . These are likely to evoke associations in turn to correct the secondary disturbances. The formation of associations, therefore, tends to occur in waves."

Most of his discussion of wave theory is devoted to the history of mobilization and countermobilization between labor and business in the United States. After workingmen's associations organized in the early 1800s, business associations were formed, followed by an attempt to organize a national workingmen's association in the 1830s and other unsuccessful efforts before the creation of the American Federation of Labor in 1886, followed by a countermobilization of business groups after 1901, followed by the union organization drive of the 1930s (Truman, 1951, 66–74). Although Truman (1951, 60) gives a few other examples of his wave theory, he does not develop another example of the theory through an extended period, as he does in the case of labor versus business. Since the wave theory appears in a chapter about "group origins," and since Truman gives only one example of the wave theory extending through time, the reader becomes somewhat confused as to whether the theory is intended to encompass both group formation and group evolution. In the literature, however, scholars normally refer to the wave theory as one describing the formation of groups (J. Q. Wilson, 1973, 198; Salisbury, 1969, 1–8; Schlozman and Tierney, 1986, 122 n. 2; Berry, 1978, 394; Walker, 1983, 390–91; Micheletti, 1993).

But Truman apparently wanted the wave theory to cover not only the initial formation of groups but also their evolution through mobilization and countermobilization across generations. Thus, in the conclusion to his group origins chapter, Truman (1951, 107) states: "The growth of labor and trade associations, and most others as well, exhibits a wavelike pattern; for the very success of one group in stabilizing its relationships creates new problems for others and makes necessary either new organizations or the extension and strengthening of existing ones." Earlier he notes that the "phenomenon of organization in waves" includes "the new practices of established groups" that "invite or compel other groups to utilize the same methods . . ." as 1920s reform groups adopted tactics learned from preceding systematic campaigns of women's suffrage organizations (Truman, 1951, 60). It is a fair conclusion, then, that Truman's wave theory was intended to describe not only the formation of groups but also cycles of mobilization and countermobilization over time.

Policy cycle theory, accordingly, can be regarded as one specification and extension of Truman's wave theory. We might regard Truman as providing valuable insights, but because he was writing in 1951, a relatively early point in the development of systematic political science, he obviously could not encompass a number of later developments in the field. To Truman's wave theory, then, policy cycle theory adds capture theory and subgovernments, Olson's observation that some groups may not mobilize, Hirschman's shifting involvements, the recent rediscovery of the state, and the newer emphasis on business as often being the most powerful interest.

Truman emphasizes the labor-business relationship in wave theory, whereas cycle theory emphasizes the three-sided relationship among producer groups, countervailing power groups, and agencies of the state acting in cycles or waves of mobilization and countermobilization. Truman generalizes on the basis of a type of systems theory, in which equilibriums undergo "disturbances" that result in group mobilization to restore equilibrium. As such, he is not interested in historical generalizations about eras or alignments in American politics that relate cycles of mobilization of one type (business versus labor) to those of another type (producers versus reformers).

Cycle theory, then, brings Truman's theory up-to-date. Truman refers to the restoration of equilibrium in the balance of group power, but he is not specific whether this can bring about an institutionalized change in policy outcomes, punctuated change (Baumgartner and Jones, 1993), or the spiraling change of McClosky and Zaller (1984).

FLATTENING THE CYCLES

The persons actually involved in the policy process have shown some understanding of the issues treated in the interest group cycle theory. Particularly in the last generation, reformers have been concerned that enacted reform policies should not become co-opted or captured by opposing political forces (McCarry, 1972, 173–75, 198–99). Political persons can learn about the policy cycle and act to change it.

This brings us to another theoretical metaphor. If there are arrow theories and circle theories, there are also spiral theories. If "what goes around comes around," spiral theorists say that it does not come around to the same place but reaches a higher point on some dimension. Spiral theories are three-dimensional cycle theories. Schlesinger (1986, 31) states that he is actually a spiral theorist: "because the cycle is not a pendulum swinging between fixed points but a spiral, it admits novelties." Schlesinger cites with approval McClosky and Zaller's conclusion, in which they state that even though American politics goes through cycles between eras of capitalist and democratic dominance, the amount of democracy has been increasing over the course of the last century, somewhat at the expense of capitalism.

> There appears, however, to be a marked asymmetry in these swings: movements in the procapitalist direction have increasingly turned out to be little more than holding actions, efforts that have only temporarily halted a long-term trend toward government efforts to assist the needy, broader individual liberties, and greater popular control over the economy. Thus the gains made by the Coolidge, Hoover, and Eisenhower administrations on behalf of free enterprise capitalism in the 1920s and 1950s were largely undone by the liberal Democratic administrations that followed. National swings in the prodemocratic direction, by contrast, have tended to produce enduring changes in American life. (McClosky and Zaller, 1984, 292)

Schlesinger himself expected another democratic cycle in the 1990s, but he did not see this as inevitable (Schlesinger, 1986, 47).

By the mid–twentieth century, reformers were acting to change the policy cycles, to bring a higher level of countervailing power to issue areas during times of producer dominance. The Progressive reformers did not seem to be aware of policy cycles in their battles to initiate new government policies to counteract the special interests. The Progressives thought that they could combat special interests by establishing a greater amount of direct democracy in elections: primaries, initiatives, referendums, the recall, and so on. In public administration, experts using scientific administration would fend off the special interests in independent regulatory commissions, city manager systems, the urban commission form of government, and so forth. But in fact, the Progressives only intensified the policy cycle, because after their reform impetus waned, special interests captured public administration issue area by issue area.

New Dealers were aware of the problems of capture and knew that the administration of their reforms needed political backup. The major New Deal reaction is exemplified by Louis Brownlow and later by Richard Neustadt (1960) in arguing that the president must guard his power stakes and sometimes use them to keep control over his own administration. The president needs help in doing this; hence the need to create an effective White House staff and Executive Office of the President. A secondary New Deal reaction to the policy cycle was support for labor unions. This is exemplified in John Kenneth Galbraith's *American Capitalism* (1952), in which unions are seen as capable of providing countervailing power to business. Of course, it was Galbraith who made this term famous.

The Wagner Act provided government coercion to enforce the union shop, thereby ensuring continuing union participation in many issue areas for a generation (Olson, 1965, chap. 3). New Dealers tended to assume that the president would represent such diffuse interests as consumers, the public interest in the environment, and the prevention of conflict of interest among government personnel. But as McConnell (1966), Lowi (1969), and other writers point out, such presidential representation did not work out well in the 1950s and 1960s. Countervailing power groups, similar to unions, were needed in many issue areas, and the public interest reformers in the late 1960s organized such groups in the environmental, consumer, and good-government areas (McCann, 1986, 15–121).

Heclo (1978) and other political scientists such as Kingdon (1984) and Gais, Peterson, and Walker (1984) pointed out the phenomenon of issue networks, which have a function similar to that of public interest groups (Laumann and Knoke, 1987). These issue networks—patterns of persons continually concerned with some issue area and constantly communicating about it—mushroomed during the 1960s and 1970s and seemed to have passed some intuitive threshold point of influence. Obviously, issue networks had existed throughout the twentieth century, but the increasing scope and technicality of government by the 1970s made them a continuing source of countervailing power to producer groups. Thus, although an issue network contains affiliates of business and other economic powers, it also contains academics, journalists, and politicians specializing in some policy areas, as well as government officials and members of countervailing power groups. As Heclo (1978) specifically noted, these issue networks can provide an organizational basis for checking the mechanisms of the iron triangle, business-led alliances that control policy in an issue area.

These phenomena of public interest groups and issue networks correspond to a trend in policy case studies in the political science literature. In Culhane's (1981) study of public lands policy, Berry's (1985) study of food policy, Bosso's (1987) study of pesticide policy, and Browne's (1988) study of agricultural policy—all areas in which capture seems possible—public interest groups and governmental agencies provided an important check on the power of producer groups. Culhane's study was conducted in the late 1970s, and perhaps this is what one would expect during the transitional phase of the interest group cycle. But the other three studies encompassed the early and mid-1980s. They provide evidence that politicians have devised new means of exercising countervailing power in a way that survives the business period of the interest group cycle (Berry, 1999).

For a while, it seemed that President Reagan might overreact to the ideas of reformers in the environmental policy area, thereby helping to produce a degree of business excess in this area that would produce a strong reaction, contributing to the onset of the next cycle. However, the accumulated power of environmentalist groups and outraged cries from the affected issue networks checked the Reagan cutbacks on environmental regulation, symbolized by the replacement of Burford with Ruckleshaus in the Environmental Protection Agency. The George H. W. Bush administration seemed to prefer a policy of conciliation in environmental areas, and its incremental policy changes defused public anger at business excesses in this and in other areas. Bush, who claimed to be more committed to environmental policy than his presidential opponent Michael Dukakis, tried to be responsive to the issues placed on the agenda by environmental lobbies.

A significant degree of political learning had taken place. The pro-business George H. W. Bush administration learned to be responsive to some of the issues initiated by public interest groups and countervailing power groups in the issue networks. These countervailing forces could then influence the agenda during a business period, thereby reducing the tendency toward business excesses outraging the public. Autonomous government and countervailing power groups prevent producer groups from going "too far out" in the eyes of the public, thereby "flattening" the reform cycle. This situation, in which producer groups predominate but countervailing power groups and governmental agencies have considerable power, increases the length of the business period of the cycle, because the public has less reason to intervene in an intense fashion.

A NEW REFORM ERA?

By the 1990s, two changes in the policymaking system had occurred. First, presidents and leaders of their administrations became aware that enacting extreme policies can produce a counterreaction, weakening their programs as a whole. Second, the appearance of many more groups and the appearance of issue networks exercising countervailing power to major producer groups changed the policy process in many issue areas. This is not to imply that the countervailing groups were equal in power to the producer groups, but just to say that they had some significant power—enough to induce producer groups to avoid enacting relatively extreme, often the most profit-maximizing policy. For instance, the power of the American Association of Retired Persons is not equivalent to that of the pharmaceutical industry in the policy area of consumer drug price regulation. But the AARP and other countervailing groups can influence the pharmaceutical industry to support some federal government subsidies and regulation of consumer drug prices. This heads off the most angry reaction against industry, as exemplified by the trustbusters of the Progressive and New Deal eras.

Thus, based on previous cycles, we might have expected a reaction to the conservative Reagan era to occur around 1990, bringing another period of aggressive reforms. But this did not happen, because previous trends had been mitigated by political learning and the organization of many countervailing power groups. Certainly few would argue that the Clinton era was comparable to the New Deal or to the Great Society. Voters were not interested in major new reforms, as evidenced by the Republican control of Congress during the last six years of the Clinton administration.

The best possibility of restarting the cycle would come with control of the presidency and both houses of Congress by the Republican party, which, though headed by a president advertising "compassionate conservatism," permits policy area elites to initiate relatively extreme policies. This could happen in various areas, such as the opening of loopholes in air pollution policy, increased restrictions on abortion, failure to act in the face of Enron-type business scandals, corporate lowering of baby-boomer pension expenditures, skyrocketing pharmaceutical prices, global trading with no concern for labor or environmental regulations, tax cutting that disproportionately favors the upper 2 percent of the population, a rollback of affirmative action, and so forth—all happening at the same time.

Such a situation would be enhanced by business and professional groups exploiting loopholes in the 2002 campaign finance reform and spending enormous sums for election campaigns, dwarfing countervailing expenditures by labor, citizens groups, and wealthy liberals. Such sums would have a particular impact on marginal House districts and marginal Senate seats, giving pro-business candidates a great publicity advantage in dealing with swing voters. Upon election, such pro-business candidates would not necessarily be bought, although of course they would spend a disproportionate amount of time communicating with campaign contributors. It is just that such pro-business legislators would not act to prevent the implementation of relatively extreme policies by elites in other policy areas. For instance, such a legislator might have little concern about the increasing lack of enforcement of environmental regulations by an anti-regulation administration, similar to the 1981–1983 Reagan years, when major environmental rollbacks were attempted.

If a Republican president is successful in appointing Supreme Court justices who make the Court even more conservative, this might further the perception of policy excess in the minds of politically moderate, middle-class voters. Repeal of *Roe v. Wade* would likely produce an unprecedented mobilization of the women's movement, as the abortion issue is fought from statehouse to statehouse. A rollback of affirmative action for minorities, women, and the disabled would also lead to new mobilization of these groups. If the leaders of all three branches of government, relying on high campaign spending through election finance loopholes, begin to enact conservative policies that are seen as extreme by a majority, the stage will be set for a new reform era.

Another major source of unpopularity for a Republican regime might be U.S. involvement in a war (or more than one war) involving considerable American casualties (though perhaps not as great as the Korean War or the war in Vietnam) that is being fought for reasons widely regarded as unconvincing, although related to the "war on terrorism." Certainly, the Vietnam War was a major cause (though not the only cause) of the undermining of traditional policies and views during the reform era of the 1960s.

If the scenario of unpopular pro-business traditionalism does not take place by 2008 (perhaps), one would need to rethink the theory of policy cycles. When and how might a new reform era come about? Another possibility is that judicious policies by "compassionate conservatives" or Democratic party moderates, combined with countervailing power lobbies, really do prevent, for a while, the enactment of excesses that would produce a countermobilization of reformers.

The policy cycle theory calls for special attention to an incremental buildup of problems, as seen by middle-class voters. A lessening of investor confidence due to corporate fraud and higher interest rates caused by federal deficits would produce negative effects over a fifteen-year period. Rather than a sudden repeal of *Roe v. Wade,* an accumulation of decisions restricting specific abortion practices, together with a line of decisions restricting affirmative action policies, would produce disaffection, leading to increased tension among races and aggrieved white female swing voters. Air pollution might become worse not just in Texas, as is happening in 2003, but in other areas of the country. Rising medical care costs and pharmaceutical costs might continue to create major problems, even though remedial policies are produced by agreement between compassionate conservatives and moderate Democrats. Tax policies might be such that the top 1 percent of the wealthy increase their share of the wealth, while the median wage slowly decreases. Relatively apolitical baby boomers might find that corporate pensions are cut back or dwindle due to a declining stock market.

Such conditions, seen as negative by political moderates, could then build up over a fifteen- to twenty-year period as government is shepherded by moderate conservatives, checked by the action of countervailing power groups. But such incremental changes could eventually provide the context for an explosive return to progressive reform politics. One proximate cause for a political explosion would be high casualties in a relatively unpopular war. We might call this the "2020 scenario"; that is, the next reform era will appear only after a relatively long period of incremental policy changes by a moderately conservative, pro-business national political leadership that, in the long run, does not satisfy the desires of a national majority. It is interesting that a reform era in 2020 would coincide with the prediction from Huntington's "every-other-generation" theory. According to Huntington, at that time we would expect another outbreak of creedal passion, as a younger generation rejects the moderation and compromise of its elders in the name of an idealist interpretation of American values.

If, by that time, a new reform era does not appear, we might have to pack up the theory of policy cycles. If so, in addition to the stable moderation of a national pro-business political leadership, another change might be that international factors are playing a greater role in determining American domestic policies, and that the policy cycle theory did not accommodate the new factors of globalization. One would need to consider that many policy systems are becoming more international and include a degree of influence from foreign corporations, multinational corporations, foreign governments, the European Union, and transnational nongovernmental organizations overlapping with transnational social movements such as environmentalism or human rights and other transnational behaviors such as immigration or criminal activity. As a policy system becomes international, it is less subject to fluctuations of domestic, endogenous variables (Keck and Sikkink, 1998; Klotz, 1995; Layton, 2000; McAdam, 1999, xix–xxi; Thomas, 2000). Perhaps such variation has become international, but no one has formulated a theory of international policy cycles. From these observations, it follows that current reform movements, and movements protesting business activity, will become transnational, as indicated by the growth of the anti-globalization movement, evidenced in demonstrations in Seattle and elsewhere.

CONCLUSION

There are several models of policy system change. The policy model stated herein, as well as the McClosky-Zaller model referred to, is a spiral model: the system changes but returns to a position parallel to its previous position (McClosky and Zaller, 1984). In other words, after the reform cycle, some change is institutionalized, but there is an expectation that producer groups in the system once more have the most power. In addition to being endogenously driven, the reform cycle model contrasts to the punctuated change model, in that the Baumgartner-Jones model incorporates such a change, much of which is institutionalized, and does not specify a direction, such as a return to producer group power (Baumgartner and Jones, 1993).

This depiction of the political process in political time and policy cycles fits with the central concepts of political process theory. One set of observations begins by treating the political system not as a whole but as divided into policy systems, each one a separate policy process of interacting persons and organizations. Power and influence are seen as causing others to change policy outputs; interest is defined subjectively, as in the idea of middle-class citizens reacting to the actions of business or reformers as "excesses," not in terms of the observer's criteria but in terms of the thoughts and emotions of the citizens themselves. Along the lines of collective action theory, participation is viewed as costly to individuals; islands of oligarchy are sometimes present, but state agencies may gain autonomy in a policy area if there is countervailing power, including that spun off from social movements. In conclusion, a historical theory can include political process assumptions and concepts.

The policy cycle theory is discussed again in chapter 8 in relation to theories of agenda building. The next chapter explores the possibility for political learning among producer groups and countervailing power groups, which could result in a fair measure of consensus on some policy measures, providing a basis for policy planning.

7
The Political Process and Planning

It is appropriate that neopluralism, as a developing theory of political process, be related to a perspective on planning. Here we need not extensively analyze what is meant by *planning,* other than to remark that the policymaking process has an aspect in which participants state policy designs for the future that purport to be in the interests of almost everyone in some jurisdiction. Statement of such a plan implies activity to gather political support for it, coordinate disparate technical and political factors related to the plan, and initiate enactment of the plan by appropriate authorities. Although traditionally not implied by the concept of planning, activity directed toward effective implementation of the plan seems to be part of the same overall policy process.

Traditionally, pluralism is seen as opposed to effective planning. *Pluralism* in the early twentieth century denoted the devaluation of the norms of state sovereignty, as opposed to the positive evaluation of the activities of groups in civil society (Laski, 1921). But such pluralist theory was thereby open to the criticisms of socialists and others: do we not need sovereignty to bolster effective planning for society as a whole? Midcentury models of pluralism, such as Truman's *The Governmental Process,* were open to the criticism that policy must result from something other than the proliferation of groups, especially in the decentralized American system of institutions, in which numerous groups could each be expected to locate a strategic decision-making point by which it could veto part or all of a new policy initiative. In such a system, the general interest is thwarted by multiple "veto groups" (Riesman, 1953, 246–60; Pressman and Wildavsky, 1973). Or the pluralistic difficulty of attaining concerted action in the general interest might be termed "hyperpluralism" (Wirt, 1974).

Strongly influenced by the bounded rationality decision-making theory of Herbert Simon, pluralists such as Charles Lindblom and Aaron Wildavsky in the 1950s and 1960s attacked the necessity of special institutional provisions for planning. In this outlook, referred to as "the science of muddling through" or "incrementalism," attempts to project a comprehensive model of future policy in some area usually do more harm than good, due to the limitations of cognitive capacity and the lack of understanding of the perspectives and interests of the multitude of players in a single policy game. Instead, the model of the incremental system emphasized the value of partisan mutual adjustment, in which policymakers and game players adjusted goals and definitions of interests in light of the evolving politics of the policy system, which would produce incrementally changing policies reflecting an approximately optimal aggregation of the interests of the participants. It should be noted that the main emphasis of incrementalism was on dealing with cognitive limitation in policy situations: if a policy base seemed satisfactory, then bargaining by multiple game players over incremental change would be relatively rational, considering limited cognitive capacity, as opposed to bargaining over big, "punctuating" system changes, which would have many impossible-to-anticipate consequences. Some pluralist research, such as Wildavsky's classic research on the congressional budgetary process, indicated that the incremental model of the decision-making process actually existed, accounting for relatively rational policies, even though there is little planning by the federal government (Simon, 1957; Lindblom, 1959; Wildavsky, 1964b).

In *Who Governs?* Robert Dahl found a sort of planning process in the New Haven urban renewal policies, but this planning was brought about by a "political entrepreneur" looking for popular policies that he could initiate and enact to get credit from voters, who would reelect him. This might be called the entrepreneurial theory of efficiency, and it differs from the incrementalist argument that planning is not necessary. In addition, various pluralist writings argued that explicit planning is of limited usefulness, undemocratic, and less efficient than viewing the political process of groups as a policy market, effectively processing information about participants' interests (Banfield, 1961). (The policy market might or might not be viewed as incremental.)

Olson's logic of collective action destroyed much of the force of the arguments that incrementalism or policy markets of groups are efficient aggregators of policy interests, thereby vitiating the need for planning institutions. If many or most interests are not adequately represented in partisan mutual adjustment or in a policy market, one cannot claim that such pluralistic processes aggregate and coordinate particular views to create policy in the general interest. It is no surprise, then, that both Lindblom and Wildavsky modified their attitudes toward planning. Lindblom eventually advocated national economic plans to set the structure for specific incrementalist policy processes, and both Lindblom and Wildavsky emphasized the need for social science analysis to guide the activities of policy decision-makers (Lindblom, 1977; Lindblom and Cohen, 1979; Wildavsky, 1979, 124).

Theodore Lowi Jr. had an enormous impact on the study of American politics and policymaking during the 1970s. One of Lowi's central arguments was that pluralist theory and reality had made effective planning impossible in American government, although social security and other sectors that were relatively free of pluralist concepts still exhibited effective planning. Lowi also argued that the pluralistic delegation of power to groups, such as in school integration, anti-poverty, and grassroots-administered agricultural programs, had subjected these programs to the whims and self-aggrandizement of special-interest elites. In any event, according to Lowi, the American pluralist system could not plan, and policy needed to be rescued by clarified legal codes administered by a stronger national state, similar to the administrative ideal of French government. In general, multiple-elite critics of American policy subscribed to the view that there needed to be more than incrementalism of a market of groups, but that American institutions failed to produce needed plans for policy in the general interest (Lowi, 1979).

Thus, empirical pluralist theory emphasized the limits of rationality and discredited the possibilities for outright planning in the political process. This contradicted the notion of plans being introduced by executive officeholders to promote their reelection, as Dahl did not theorize on the relationship of such plans to the idea of bounded rationality. Lowi and other multiple-elite theorists argued that pluralism (both in practice and in theory) was incapable of effective planning. I argue below that neopluralism alters this situation, but first it is necessary to consider corporatist theory, believed by both its theorists and its practitioners to be the answer to the deficiencies of pluralism as effective policymaking.

CORPORATISM

A step in the theoretical narrative of political process theory, corporatism is both a political theory and a statement of how policymaking is conducted in various countries. Within American and European political science, corporatist theory was revived and greatly advanced after Philippe Schmitter's pathbreaking article "Still a Century of Corporatism?" (1974). Schmitter observed that the patterns of power and policymaking in America as observed by Dahl and others did not apply to a number of European and Latin American countries that he styled as "corporatist." In such countries, business, labor, and possibly agricultural groups were organized in national federations that embodied all significant associations of a specific nature, such as associations of business in an economic sector or a national trade union. Decision-making on important macroeconomic issues, such as international trade policy, was made by a regular negotiation process among the leaders of such nationally inclusive federations and leading government officials, who, in parliamentary systems, represent a majority of the legislature. The leaders of the national associations exercised enough authority so that members would cooperate with centrally negotiated decisions about wages, price increases, and export priorities (Katzenstein, 1985).

Metaphorically, the groups in such a society constitute a unified body, at least in comparison to Dahl's model of pluralism, in which there are no such centrally directed inclusive group federations, and in which decision-making on macroeconomic issues is more fragmented. One advantage of corporatist policymaking seems to be an increased possibility for planning and executing macroeconomic policies in the general interest, due to the collaboration of government, business, and labor and their authority to implement joint decisions. And for those subscribing to a multiple-elite theory of power and policymaking in America or elsewhere, corporatism provides an alternative model, a possible solution to the problems of subgovernmental control. For instance, Mancur Olson, influenced by Norwegian corporatism, advocated a type of corporatist decision-making to remedy what he saw as an inexorable trend toward subgovernmental groups undermining economic efficiency in societies that allowed freedom of association. Thus, Olson (1982) favored the formation of national group federations, supported by subgroups that understood their own economic interests.

Corporatism does not refer to rule by business elites, but instead refers to the tendency to view society and politics as composed of entities other than small units, entities such as "business," "labor," "the state," and so forth. Corporatism is thus seen as the opposite of atomism, the tendency to view society as basically composed of unconnected individuals. As a view of society and politics, corporatism is a type of political theory that is associated with Catholic writings and has flourished among Italian intellectuals for several centuries. Corporate theory has been used by authoritarian rulers to justify themselves in opposition to individualism. However, another type of corporatism has developed in the institutional practice of Western European democracies and is associated with both democratic socialism and democratic conservatism (Katzenstein, 1985).

Democratic corporatism refers to a type of decision-making for an entire country. Within a country, both the business and the labor sectors are organized into a single organization, which is inclusive of either corporations or unions. That is, there is one business federation and one major labor federation that includes nearly all the unions and the majority of blue-collar workers. The single business or labor federation is centrally directed; the constituent businesses or unions follow direction from federation leadership. The business, labor, and perhaps agricultural federations meet regularly with the leaders of the state, most likely a parliamentary democracy with unified administration under the direction of a prime minister. (Parliamentary government, of course, is frequently coalition government.) Sometimes called a "concertation of interests," these regular meetings of the leaders of the "pillars" of the corporate society result in decisions about macroeconomic issues: policy about a country's exports and imports, ceilings on wage increases, limitations on price rises, tax rates, and so forth. The centralized leadership of the state, business, and labor is able to implement such concerted decisions because these elites have power over subordinate associations, unions, or state agencies. Countries having corporatist decision-making include Germany, Austria, Switzerland, Belgium, the Netherlands, Denmark, Sweden, Finland, and Norway (Katzenstein, 1985).

The corporatist model can be applied to the middle level of government (the states in the United States) and readily to the urban-local level. It makes sense to ask whether some American cities might be essentially corporatist, with many policies decided by regular negotiations among the city government, the chamber of commerce, the local union federation, and perhaps an institutionalized group of African American leaders. Unfortunately, this possibility was not explored by those looking for alternatives to pluralism in the community power debates. Instead, the critics of pluralism concentrated on the possibility of rule by a single elite, the business leadership and the wealthy.

Corporatism is now generally accepted as another model of power and policymaking in the same group as elitism, pluralism, multiple elitism, statism, and neopluralism. Not surprisingly, there is controversy about the true effectiveness of corporatism as a mode for planning and centralized economic direction. Corporatism runs the danger of ratifying the existing distribution of jobs and the distribution of profits among major economic enterprises. And when corporate arrangements break down, there may be a tendency for unions to feel that they must catch up with wage increases and for business to feel pressured to increase prices, leading to an inflationary situation. We need not readily assume that corporatism is preferable to neopluralism for organizing an economy (Gobeyn, 1993).

In the 1980s, with both the corporatist and the neopluralist models on the table, it is clearly the next step in the theory-building sequence to consider the hybrid of the two models and inquire about its relevance to planning and policymaking.

COOPERATIVE PLURALISM

But what about corporatism as applied to power in the political process in a particular policy area? Such a relatively specific usage is somewhat distant from the core definition of corporatism as applying to decision-making for an entire political system. Therefore, I prefer to use the term *cooperative pluralism* to refer to negotiations among the agents of a neopluralist policy system. Various producer groups, countervailing power groups, and state agencies may find that they have common interests within a policy area, as well as conflicting interests. These common interests may be expressed in ad hoc coalitions, something stressed in the pluralist theory of Dahl and his associates. But it is possible that common interests may be expressed in more than an ad hoc fashion. To the extent that such common interests are general and repeated among the various participants in a neopluralist policy area, and to the extent that such common interests are perceived and embodied in political activity in the policy area, we can speak of *cooperative pluralism* within that area (McFarland, 1993).

Thus, cooperative pluralism fits into the neopluralist framework as a concept of the relationships among the producer groups, countervailing power groups, and governmental agencies. To what extent is the policy process other than a struggle among contenders for influence, and to what extent is the process marked by stable, cooperative arrangements? The perspective on cooperation is new to the framework, as elitism, pluralism, and statism emphasize competition; in elitism, however, the competition is latent, and in statism, the point is that the state has more power than groups do. The multiple-elitist theory refers to cooperation among some iron triangle, indicating that cooperative pluralism refers to cooperation within the neopluralist model only.

Accordingly, corporatism, and its derived concept cooperative pluralism, enriches the basic neopluralist model by adding the analytic possibility of stable cooperation within a policy area. And, as indicated in the discussion of the National Coal Policy Project below, stable cooperation can coexist with continuing conflict among the same groups and governmental agencies.

Cooperative pluralism is a term best applied to the situation of stable cooperation within a neopluralist system. However, national corporatism might break down and not be relevant to some policy system that is not much influenced by the centralized group federations and by the hierarchy of government. Such a system might in fact be neopluralistic, and if stable cooperation exists among its elements, it would be an instance of cooperative pluralism.

It is imperative to stress that there is no cooperative pluralism without countervailing power. Cooperative pluralism necessarily implies group organization to counter the organization of producer groups; it implies some degree of successful organization and maintenance of citizens groups and other countervailing power groups. For cooperative pluralism to exist within some policy area, there must be neopluralism within that area, as described in chapter 4. Planning does not involve cooperative pluralism if countervailing power groups are not organized. Lacking such groups, planners attempting to advocate and implement diffuse interests will fall victim to the logic of collective action, as such plans are likely to be blocked by organized producer groups.

As described in chapter 4 on neopluralism, like most political scientists, my first expectation is that producer groups and countervailing power groups will come into conflict—they will fight. In the United States, this is common and important. Less common, but still important, is that producer groups and countervailing power groups sometimes cooperate, and on an autonomous basis, a governmental agency may join in that cooperation.

RESISTANCE TO STUDYING COMMON INTERESTS

In studying power and policymaking, until recently, political scientists have neglected to study the dimension of common interests among groups. This is more a matter of emphasis in the choice of research projects rather than an articulated theoretical statement. Students of the political process around the time of Truman and Dahl reacted against reformers' idealistic views of the breadth of common interests shared among the public. Many writers during the Progressive era were convinced of the existence of a readily recognizable public interest that should be represented in government policy. Such writers regarded the everyday political and policy process as inefficient, if not downright corrupt. The goal of political science, in the view of such reformers, is to suggest institutional changes to enact and implement the public interest. Such Progressive writers thought that the "science of public administration" or other forms of applied science could be used to discover the public interest, and that certain public institutions should embody this scientific process. Reformers thus believed in planning, city managers, departmental commissioners deciding urban policy, scientific experts regulating industries by independent regulatory commissions, theories of scientific public management, and so forth (Waldo, 1948, 1955; Wiebe, 1967).

Reform theories about the need for science and efficiency were widespread in the academic and political environment in the first half of the twentieth century. The Progressive reform views were opposed by Pendleton Herring in the 1920s and by Herbert Simon in the 1940s, among other political scientists, and although such scholars probably enjoyed attacking the "politically correct" ideas of their time, they were also considered to be peddling a casuistry defending the status quo (Herring, 1929, 1940; Simon, Smithburg, and Thompson, 1950). The import of the "behavioral revolution" of the 1950s (as applied to policymaking, more of an affirmation of empiricism and data collection) was to spread the idea that legalistic, formalistic, and reform-oriented public administration was a second-rate form of scholarship in comparison to the new empirical studies (Dahl, 1961a). One by-product of this academic controversy was a disregard for research emphasizing common interests, because it was similar to the work of the discredited reformers, and especially a detestation for any assertions about the "public interest" (Schubert, 1960).

Another reason for the disregard of common interests was simply the logic of the unfolding of the policymaking paradigm, as discussed herein. Pluralism was a theory of competing, conflicting interests, as opposed to the power elite theory. Multiple-elite theory did not emphasize a portrayal of conflicting interests but was based on the premise that there should be competition among interests that was not present. Statist theory portrayed the development of state institutions but did not emphasize the question of whether the state was representing common interests, possibly in distinction to some "uncommon" or factional interests.

Political scientists studying policymaking have neglected the study of the common interests among contending interest groups. This situation is reminiscent of international relations theory, in which the realist school, led by Hans Morgenthau in the 1950s, argued that international politics should emphasize the study of the search for power to serve national interests (Morgenthau, 1964). Many political scientists were trained to accept this outlook, which criticized an "idealism" emphasizing the possibilities of international peace treaties and strong international organizations without considering the conflicts of interest among nations.

A later view modified the realism of Morgenthau. Thomas Schelling (1960) and other writers influenced by game theory argued that international conflict is a "mixed-motive" situation and that even adversaries usually have important interests in common. Game theorists argued that conflict is not always "zero-sum," in which interests are completely opposed, but is also "non-zero-sum," in which both adversaries gain from certain outcomes of an interaction. Schelling extended this idea to analyze the joint interests of the United States and the Soviet Union to prevent Cold War crises from escalating into nuclear war. By now, we realize that the superpower adversaries frequently shared common interests, such as preventing the spread of nuclear weapons to third parties, communicating about military accidents, such as missiles veering off course, and so forth.

The experiment of the National Coal Policy Project (NCPP), discussed below, demonstrates that while we may initially accept Morgenthau's view of power, the study of interest groups also profits from the game theorists' understanding of mixed-motive, non-zero-sum rivalry among adversaries. Such an assumption is not an idealistic assertion that cooperation is more basic than conflict; it is simply a complex realism that finds that common interests are still present in adversarial relationships (Hardin, 1982). This viewpoint characterizes cooperative pluralism. Recognizing the dimension of common interest in the interaction of producer groups, countervailing power groups, and autonomous agencies promotes the design of such institutions as the NCPP to further the discovery of common interests.

NETWORK THEORY AND THE HOLLOW CORE

Network theory is an important theory used by sociologists to understand the structure of relationships among elites (Laumann and Knoke, 1987). As such, it can be applied to the actors in political processes (Schneider, Scholz, Lubell, Mindruta, and Edwardsen, 2003). The language of network theory is not suffused with the connotations of realism versus idealism; thus it may help sidestep prejudices remaining from past intellectual controversies in political science. Network theory was the basis of study for one of the two biggest studies of interest groups in Washington: *The Hollow Core: Private Interests in National Policy Making* (Heinz, Laumann, Nelson, and Salisbury, 1993).

The idea of network theory is to chart, even with graphics, relationships among individuals or organizations to understand the social structure. These relationships are most frequently understood as communications among individuals.

In the political process, such relationships include collaboration on some influence attempt (Hula, 1999).

Heinz et al. interviewed 776 individuals in the policy areas of health, agriculture, labor, and energy policymaking in Washington, D.C. To arrive at this group of individuals, they first made a list of organizations engaged in lobbying by conducting a computer search of newspapers, compiling organizations that testified in congressional hearings, and interviewing twenty to twenty-three officials in each of the four policy areas and asking them to list organizations that contacted them frequently, as well as those that contacted them episodically. Finally, they added organizations listed in a handbook of Washington organizations. Then a sample of 100 organizations was drawn in each of the four domains. These organizations were contacted by the researchers, and their government representatives were interviewed.

The research was extended by asking the interviewees to name their contacts in government. From this list, 301 officials were located, split among the four policy areas; they included those in elected, appointed, and career positions, as well as twenty members of Congress and thirty congressional staff (Heinz et al., 1993, 16–21).

The communication relationships among these 1,077 lobbyists and government officials were determined from the interviews and then expressed through mathematical graphing techniques. In general, the graphs showed that like communicated with like, meaning that producer representatives in some policy area communicated among themselves, and the countervailing power representatives did the same. The four general policy systems of health, agriculture, energy, and labor were split into policy area segments (e.g., oil, coal, electric utilities). Government officials were located within the particular policy segments. Accordingly, the main research finding was that policy areas tended to have "hollow cores," that is, almost no one had relationships with a wide range of actors within one of the four general policy areas. Similarly, very few individuals had communications transactions with individuals on both or all sides of issues in a subsystem. When this does occur, we might refer to the "hub-and-spokes" model, with the centrally placed individuals as the hub of a system, radiating relationships to others as so many spokes.

The fragmented networks of policy relationships are a representation of pluralism. However, the researchers did not find graphic representations of multiple elitism, that is, segments totally unconnected with the larger policy system and representing only a cluster of producers and executive officials. Instead, the graphs are neopluralistic; producers, countervailing power groups, and government officials are represented in segments but are unrelated to some central hub for their policy area. The network research also represents the initial four assumptions of the policy process model: policy as a process of complex interactions among individuals, individuals attempting to exercise power by communicating to change behavior, policy divided into particular systems, and a perspective derived from the individuals' own definitions of their interests as expressed in interviews.

The Heinz et al. study provides strong evidence that the hollow core is the most common form of network structure in the American political process. To the sociologist, this presents a theoretical problem: how is social structure held together? To the researchers, this seems to be answered in their graphs, in which adjacent policy systems communicate with one another, so that the entire circle (or sphere) of policy is held together by communication flowing from one adjacent area to another. To the public administrator and the political scientist, the hollow core poses another problem. To what extent do "nonadjacent" policymakers work at cross-purposes, such as the Department of Energy promoting coal development without regard to sulfur content while the Environmental Protection Agency is trying to reduce the burning of high-sulfur coal, to cite a plausible example. The questions discussed in the next section are: Is it possible to have more communication among producer groups and countervailing power groups? And could such communication be in the general interest?

How does planning relate to the political process, especially the neopluralist political process? Planning can be represented as the effort to insert actors into the hollow core and create a hub, one that initiates policy proposals affecting all those radiating outward in the system, communicates through the system of spokes, builds a coalition through such communication, and then enacts and implements some policy, supported by a preponderance of interests.

NATIONAL COAL POLICY PROJECT

Normally, in a neopluralist system, adversarial groups might also have significant common interests. But such groups frequently act in networks having a hollow core. This means that adversaries do not communicate and thus do not discern such common interests. Such lack of communication undermines the basis for planning for policymaking in the system; such planning needs to be based on agreement among a wide range of political actors. Accordingly, application of network theory implies the insertion of individuals or an organization into the hollow core, which then forms communication links with participants on the "periphery." In other words, planning in the neopluralist process implies creating an institution to provide a hub for some policymaking system.

Sponsored by the Center for Strategic and International Studies of Georgetown University and several foundations, the National Coal Policy Project (1976–1980) was an early attempt to create such a planning institution, although such theoretical terminology was not used a quarter century ago. Research about the history of the NCPP demonstrates that the dimension of common interests among normally adversarial groups can be quite significant (McFarland, 1993). This is not the easy argument that many groups have common interests; this is the argument that groups, normally in bitter political contention, also have common interests.

The NCPP was a project to bring together representatives of coal-mining companies, electric utilities, environmental lobbyists, and litigators to discuss federal policy about strip-mining regulation, air pollution regulation, and some allied topics. The goal was to develop a common agenda and get the common platform enacted. To the surprise of most observers, an elaborate 800-page report was published, containing a number of unexpected and significant agreements. But although the negotiators were, in a sense, "representative," they were not formally representative and could not commit their corporations or groups to lobby for the common platform. Thus, only a relatively small fraction of the report, entitled *Where We Agree,* became federal policy (Murray, 1978; McFarland, 1993, chap. 7). The main problem with enacting the agreements was the definition of the NCPP as a private effort without participants from governmental agencies, but such governmental participation would have greatly facilitated turning those agreements into law.

The NCPP involved 15,000 person-hours of work, $1.4 million (in 1977 dollars), and negotiations among 110 business executives and environmentalist spokespersons. Executives from Dow Chemical, Peabody Coal, Consolidation Coal, Union Carbide, Detroit Edison, Pacific Gas & Electric, and Air Products and Chemicals were among the prominent business participants. Environmentalists were represented by the Sierra Club, the Environmental Defense Fund, the Environmental Law Institute, environmentalist litigators, and some academics. In terms of funding, 86 businesses contributed an average of $9,000 each, for 60 percent of the funding; several foundations contributed $350,000, or 24 percent; and the Department of Energy and other governmental agencies contributed $225,000, or 16 percent. The NCPP was organized by Gerald Decker, an executive with Dow Chemical, whose management was concerned about possible future energy shortages and also felt pressure to show some concern for the environment.

Discussion and negotiation were conducted in committees related to subject areas, such as strip-mining or air pollution. Participants were disciplined to accept a negotiating code, called the "rule of reason," developed by lawyer Milton Wessel (1976). Participants were primarily enjoined to avoid personal attacks and to make arguments by citing evidence. After initial mutual suspicion, participants for the most part enjoyed meeting one another, and the NCPP provided further evidence that business and environmental lobbyists never get to know one another on a personal level. Accordingly, NCPP committee meetings developed a successful process of diplomacy.

The major agreement among the participants was that in return for public or other funding, environmental lobbyists would drop their strategy of delaying new development through multiple litigation and lobbying multiple decision-makers in a government of separated powers to find one willing to block action.

If they had adequate funding for research and legal representation, environmentalists would be willing to make their case in consolidated hearings about issuing permits or regulations. Other agreements included support for cogeneration of electricity (steam from major industrial plants could be used to work generators); changes in electricity pricing to discourage increasing usage; greater attention to regional differences in strip-mining practices, such as water wastage in the West and acid runoff in the East; and support for emissions taxes to regulate air pollution. The NCPP published about 100 regulatory recommendations to limit the numerous problems caused by strip-mining; in general, business participants conceded the need for regulation, but they got agreement from environmentalists that regulation might be flexible. For example, the arid West needed different emphases in regulation from the wetter but often mountainous eastern coalfields (Murray, 1978).

The participants in the NCPP were, loosely speaking, representatives of corporations or lobbies, but they did not have the power to commit their organizations to lobby for the NCPP program. Unfortunately, no one tried to get the support of all the participant businesses and environmental groups for a joint lobbying effort. Indeed, some of the corporations and environmental groups participating in the NCPP might have opposed the platform, even though one or two of their executives had participated in writing it. Accordingly, enactment of the platform was limited to a few smaller measures, and there is evidence that individual lobbying efforts resulted in changes in federal regulations to encourage cogeneration and affected some details of strip-mining regulation. In addition, the example of the NCPP encouraged reformers to experiment with "regulatory negotiation," holding regulation-writing conferences involving the various groups with a stake in a regulation, together with government regulators (McFarland, 1993, 131–50).

The NCPP might be considered a failure, in that only secondary items in its platform were implemented by the government. The NCPP showed that such an institutional experiment to create a hub for policy networks needs to include governmental participants to enact its suggested policies. Yet the NCPP also demonstrated that similar institutional experiments might succeed if they included governmental institutions.

ILLINOIS BOARD OF HIGHER EDUCATION

The Illinois Board of Higher Education (IBHE) is an example of an institution designed to provide a hub for the relationships within a policy system. The IBHE was established in 1961 by the state legislature and Governor Otto Kerner to further the development of higher education in Illinois by acting as a coordination and planning unit. In 1999, Illinois had twelve public universities, one hundred four-year independent colleges and universities, forty-nine community junior colleges, and twenty private profit-making colleges, and these numbers were about the same in 1961. For about two decades, the twelve public universities were organized into four systems, each with its own governing board; since 1995, nine of these universities had their own boards, with the remaining three universities under one board of trustees for the University of Illinois (Knorowski, 2000).

The numerous institutions of higher education have common interests, such as increasing the overall amount of state appropriations for universities and preventing political measures that interfere with academic autonomy. The various institutions also have conflicting interests, in their competition for shares of the overall higher education budget. Another aspect of competition is that separate colleges have an interest in establishing duplicative academic programs that vie for students and resources. If one were to describe the higher education policy system as networks, before the IBHE, there was a hollow core; unlike in Washington, there was no peak association, such as the American Council on Education, that represented all higher education institutions (Cook, 1998). Lobbying activity represented separate associations for the private colleges and universities and another for the junior colleges. In addition, the different boards for the public universities lobbied the state government. Large single institutions, such as the University of Illinois at Urbana-Champaign, University of Chicago, Illinois State University, Southern Illinois University, and Northwestern University, also conducted lobbying efforts. Moreover, presidents or other representatives of smaller institutions lobbied on an ad hoc basis on particular issues, affecting only one or a few institutions.

This policy system differs from others, in that there is no institutionalized opposition to the higher education lobbyists, except for the goal of the legislature and the governor to limit appropriations for higher education. Nevertheless, the policy area could constitute the sort of unpredictable chaos that has been criticized by some opponents of pluralism. The actors consisted of a jumble of associations, institutional governing boards, and institutional lobbyists, with some of the last being active only intermittently. Higher education policy could be plagued by diversion of money to the districts of powerful legislators or in anticipation of the next gubernatorial campaign. In addition, institutions with better political connections might get financing for academically inferior programs, draining money from the better programs.

The IBHE is an institution designed to fill in the hollow core and form relationships with the various higher education institutions, their associations, the executive branch, legislators, and others concerned with this policy area. Acting as a coordinating and planning unit, the IBHE has fifteen members, all of whom are appointed by the governor for six-year terms. Decisions are made by the board after consultations with a research staff, which is very influential, and discussions at regular public meetings attended by representatives of higher education institutions and other concerned groups (Knorowski, 2000).

The IBHE has been considered one of the four most powerful state higher education planning boards, along with California, Michigan, and Tennessee (Lenth, 1997). The IBHE's basic powers are to make annual budgetary recommendations for public colleges and universities to the governor and state legislature; to approve all requests for new units of instruction, teaching, and public service in higher education institutions; to review periodically all existing units of instruction and research and verify their continued educational and economic justification; and to approve operating authority and degree-granting authority for private colleges and universities in Illinois. All this is to be done in accordance with a higher education master plan, which the IBHE is charged to study and amend (Knorowski, 2000).

According to virtually all observers of higher education policymaking in Illinois, the IBHE is not just a paper organization, but actively exercises the powers given to it by statute. As such, higher education institutions, which once tried to contact the governor directly, now work through the IBHE in seeking their goals (Matsler and Hines, 1987; Knorowski, 2000). Research indicates that the IBHE is at the hub of a higher education network; in a survey of sixty-eight presidents of higher education institutions, thirty-five named the IBHE as one of their representatives to the governor and legislature. Governor Jim Edgar (1991–1999) told an interviewer that he wanted all higher education proposals to be considered by the IBHE before they reached his desk; the chair of the assembly's Higher Education Committee had similar regard for the board (Knorowski, 2000).

The IBHE and its staff seek to negotiate consensus on policy proposals among policy area participants, and during 1991–1999, all the board's votes were unanimous, with the exception of two politically charged issues. Obviously, unlike the National Coal Policy Project, the IBHE is a governmental body, and its participation is necessary to achieve such consensus. Probably most would agree that the IBHE is a successful institution, especially in comparison to the alternative of the hollow core situation, with no institution at the hub of the policy network. The IBHE, then, is an example of how pluralist systems can plan public policies, while taking the various views of interest groups into consideration (Knorowski, 2000).

HOW MUCH COOPERATIVE PLURALISM IS THERE?

Political science does not have a clear picture of how much cooperation exists among interest groups or advocacy coalitions in America today. We know that cooperation among groups is important to the understanding of legislative lobbying, and there has been some study of cooperative lobbying, although research so far is insufficient to evaluate the importance of cooperative lobbying in determining legislative outcomes. Still, we can point to the hollow core study's presentation of complex, shifting relationships among interest groups and other actors in Washington lobbying, to Hula's charting of the differential participation rates of groups in more stable lobbying coalitions, and to Shapiro's forthcoming study using network theory to understand the internal dynamics of a permanent lobbying coalition. In large lobbies reflecting the federal character of American government, we need to know how internal bargaining affects the selection of lobbying initiatives from the wider set of possible initiatives (e.g., how does the U.S. Chamber of Commerce or the AFL-CIO decide what type of pharmaceutical benefits plan to lobby for?) (Costain and Costain, 1983; Hula, 1999; Shapiro, forthcoming).

In addition to the cooperative lobbying of legislatures, another phenomenon is represented by the IBHE, in which groups with many common interests and some conflicting interests work among themselves to present common positions to the legislature and the executive. How widespread is this phenomenon within interest group politics and public policymaking, especially with regard to organizing lobbying contacts with all branches of government, and not just lobbying bills already introduced in a legislature? Apparently, at least several other states have organized higher education policymaking in a manner similar to that of Illinois (Lenth, 1997), but how far does this phenomenon extend? Does higher education policymaking at the state level represent, say, 1 percent of the policy made in this fashion? Such policymaking would usually be called "planning," but not everything called planning would correspond to the creation of institutions to become a hub in a hollow core of policy relationships. Political science simply has no idea how widespread such IBHE policymaking might be.

So far, political scientists have not found these cooperative phenomena very interesting, at least in domestic policymaking, as opposed to the study of international relations. Political scientists generally have little interest in mapping out social structure, such as the structure among groups (which would include cooperation), although leading sociologists have shown a great deal of interest in such questions (Laumann and Knoke, 1987). Still, some examples of such political science research can be noted. Clarence Stone's (1989) influential *Regime Politics: Governing Atlanta, 1946–1988* describes Atlanta as being governed in a somewhat corporatist manner, with shifting arrangements among the city government, the organized business community, and African American leadership. These three groups have both conflicting and common interests, and rather than use the term *corporatism,* designated for entire countries, we might refer to cooperative pluralism in Atlanta. Susan Hansen (1989a, 1989b) and others (Gray and Lowery, 1990) have conducted research into whether state-level governments in the United States might be said to have an industrial policy or a policy for economic development, sometimes jointly decided by the state-level government, business, and labor. Political scientist Edward P. Weber (1998) found that the Environmental Protection Agency, environmental lobbies, and affected business groups have common interests in propounding environmental regulations in the areas of acid rain and reformulation of gasoline. Another political scientist, Barry Rabe (1995), has researched the question of bringing about cooperation among groups and individuals in a community to deal with not-in-my-backyard phenomena, such as deciding on sites for waste disposal.

One situation characterized by cooperative pluralism occurs in health politics, when governmental regulations impact professional activities. In addition, federal health policy may, through Medicare and Medicaid funding, impact the financial aspects of some health services. For instance, Medicare sets requirements for the administration of anesthesia to its patients. A major issue is how closely doctors must supervise nurse anesthesiologists, which affects how the fee is apportioned to doctors or to nurses. Both groups are organized, and nurse anesthesiologists have a politically sophisticated lobby. But although nurses and doctors oppose each other on the issue of supervision, they cooperate with Medicare officials on other issues (Larson, forthcoming). Clinical psychologists oppose granting social workers the right to provide psychotherapy under government funding, but at the same time, both groups may cooperate with government health officials to promote funding for the treatment of mental illness in general. Thus, two professions may fight over the allocation of resources in some area, but at the same time cooperate with a governmental agency to get more overall resources for the area (Larson, forthcoming).

Environmental policy in river basins seems to be one area that encourages cooperative pluralism. A major issue in river basin policy is the coordination of hydroelectric power generation with the quantity of water flow conducive to wildlife protection and flood control. Another issue is the problem of dams blocking the migration of fish. In some cases, a coalition advocates the removal of one or more river dams. Business interests are embodied not just in the electric power company but also in recreational businesses.

In the mid-1990s, a committee including Central Maine Power, Trout Unlimited, and American Rivers (an environmental group) met with representatives of federal agencies and New Hampshire and Maine agencies regarding the construction of fish passage facilities on the Saco River in Maine. A satisfactory agreement was reached. The Saco River agreement may have influenced the Federal Energy Regulatory Commission (FERC) to launch a national program in 1997 to enable such cooperative pluralist groups to form to discuss dam regulation on other rivers. Several such committees formed in Michigan and Wisconsin, and a major effort has been launched in conjunction with dam licensing policy on the Osage River in Missouri. The Osage committee includes five federal agencies, nine state agencies, and six interest groups, including the Conservation Federation of Missouri and the Marine Dealers Association. Agreements reached by this group would become FERC policy, but as of 2003, it is not clear whether agreement will be extensive. Negotiations about licensing river dams may be seen as part of a policy implementation process (Lowry, 2003).

COOPERATIVE PLURALISM AND POLICY IMPLEMENTATION

Concern about the economic effectiveness of federal policy is likely in certain issue areas, such as environmental policy, energy policy, and health policy. In addition, many people will be concerned about the enhancement of environmental or egalitarian values in these areas. Great difficulty in policymaking is likely to ensue as values of efficiency, equality, and environmentalism clash.

Such difficulties are likely to be prominent in the implementation phase of such policy areas as environment, energy, and health. Let us assume that Congress is able, on occasion, to pass general legislation to address problems in these areas, and that the president is sometimes willing to sign such legislation. Even so, the implementation of new laws is likely to run into a thicket of well-organized, opposed group interests. Groups will seek to delay implementation of laws by continual, protracted litigation, supervised by numerous able lawyers. Groups will continually seek to delay or block the application of regulations by appealing to the congressional amending process, other competing executive agencies that might support their point of view, the Office of Management and Budget, or the White House staff.

Still another difficulty occurs when state and local governmental units are incorporated into the federal regulatory process, as in the state implementation programs under federal clean air legislation (Rosenbaum, 1985). It seems possible that state and local governments and newly created local health councils will be incorporated into the implementation of a future national health insurance program. In the environment, energy, and health areas, however, Congress will not be able to foresee all important policy issues and promulgate clear legislative standards. Accordingly, the implementation process is likely to be especially important in these issue areas, and much of this implementation will be delegated to local councils. But policy could be subject to great delay as interest groups, well organized at both the national and the local levels, strive to influence the implementation of policy at the local level.

Of course, more problems with environment, energy, and health policy will arise if Congress cannot pass significant legislation due to political deadlock among interest groups, even though a preponderant majority of the informed public wishes a policy change. For example, if this situation were to occur in relation to cost controls on federal expenditures for the treatment of kidney dialysis patients, one outcome might be that local health councils or state governments would negotiate a policy for themselves through mechanisms of cooperative pluralism. In other words, future environment, energy, and health policy might feature congressional inaction, leading to the delegation of decision-making authority to local administrative bodies, some of which might adopt the practices of cooperative pluralism.

CONCLUSION

The study of cooperation among groups, including cooperation among those that simultaneously have adversarial relations, is a potentially fertile field for the development of a theory of political process. At present, we can conclude with the general point, agreed on by almost everyone, that America is not a corporatist political system at the national level but is neopluralist (G. K. Wilson, 1981). But another question immediately follows. Is there corporatism, or elements of corporatism, at the state or city level of government? Are there elements of corporatism in some issue areas at the national level or, much more likely, at the local level? Such restricted corporatism might be called cooperative pluralism, and plumbing its depths should be an important future task for research.

Finding cooperative pluralism would increase the understanding of American political and social structure. That may not interest some scholars, but we have seen another reason why cooperative pluralist findings are important. If we understand this phenomenon, we may want to establish new institutions to increase the element of cooperation and planning in the policy process. This can be done, as with the Illinois Board of Higher Education, by establishing new institutions at the hub of a policy system network, institutions that regularly communicate with all significant actors in the system and are capable of researching, initiating, and gaining political support for general policies that have the widespread support of and engender coordinating actions by disparate actors in the system. Such policies are generally termed "plans," and they are sometimes useful in making public policy both representative and effective, at least in the sense of accomplishing goals in a timely fashion and reducing costs. This may be especially useful in getting public policy to work in the implementation stage, which often requires coordination among different governmental agencies at both the national and state levels.

There exists an academic field of research known as "planning" to complement the work of professional city planners and others working in this area. Unfortunately, there is little exchange of work between planning researchers and political science researchers. When political scientists, perhaps under the guidance of a theory of political process, become interested in cooperative pluralism, the two fields will be in a position to enrich each other.

For those who care about planning, we can say that pluralists can plan too, and as a matter of fact, some actors in pluralist policy systems seem to be doing planning with considerable success. We just have not studied this. But it is true that political process writers during the 1960s were very critical of theorists of planning. One impetus behind Lindblom's incrementalist theory was his critique of planning and operations research theories as being less democratic and effective than incremental policymaking in a political process having partisan mutual adjustment (Lindblom, 1959, 1965; Braybrooke and Lindblom, 1963).

Now theorists of policymaking seem to agree with Baumgartner and Jones's (1993) model of punctuated equilibrium of policy systems, rather than the incremental change model, although the former incorporates incrementalism as descriptive of routine behavior. The punctuated change model provides an important basis for the analysis of planning in the political process model. The role of the planners, as represented by the hub-and-spokes model, incorporates the introduction of punctuated changes in the system, such as the introduction of a new scheme of coordinated higher education institutions in California's master plan for higher education. Another concern for planning might be to mitigate the effects of punctuated change that are perceived as negative by many in the system. For instance, if there is a sudden burst of public criticism of nuclear power plants, leading to a de facto ban on the construction of new ones, the function of planning is to coordinate the effects of this punctuated change with the overall public policy concerning the production of electricity.

I want to make it clear that there are major limitations to linking planning with pluralist policy areas. Specifically, this link is possible only when there is neopluralism, as described in chapter 4. The link between pluralism and planning cannot exist unless rather strong countervailing interest groups are active in a policy area. In addition to this, to use network theory language, there must be a hub-and-spokes model for the argument about planning to apply. If there is a hollow core, this link between pluralism and planning does not apply. Similarly, if a policy area is characterized by niche politics, the argument does not apply.

As I maintain in this chapter, we cannot have a precise idea about the scope of the linkage between pluralism and planning because we do not have a clear idea about the extent of neopluralism versus niche politics and hollow cores. Thus, we need more research to assess the cooperative links among interest groups, including frequently opposed interest groups in the neopluralist systems, so that we have a clearer perception of the possibilities of establishing cooperative planning institutions amidst pluralism.

In addition, I have restricted my discussion to the contemporary American political system. Influenced by the work of Philippe Schmitter, American political scientists actually give considerable emphasis to cooperation among interest groups in their research about European politics. Accordingly, my argument for greater attention to cooperation among interest groups does not apply to studies of European policymaking, and a detailed discussion of European corporatism would divert from the central narrative of this book.

To return to political process theory, it is relatively well positioned to consider issues of cooperative pluralism and planning compared with other major theories. Structural social and political theory seldom considers specific matters such as how to plan for changes in public opinion about nuclear power plants or whether institutions should be implanted to create hubs for policy systems having a hollow core. Institutional theorists have shown an interest in cooperation within the context of legislatures (Kiewit and McCubbins, 1991) but do not seem to have much impetus to study the existence of cooperative pluralism or types of planning institutions. Rational choice theorists prefer to consider situations in which the preferences of actors are given, whereas planning, at least as considered herein, is concerned with the development of a new set of preferences for the actors. Sociological network theory, in contrast, fits in very well with the study of cooperative pluralism and the creation of planning institutions.

Cooperative pluralism and planning, then, provide a wide-open field for the development of a theory of the political process. We have been expanding neopluralism and political process theory to include the study of social movements, a historical dimension, and a common interest dimension. At this point, let us turn to assessing the inherent boundaries of an emergent political process theory.

8
Issues and Power

Political process theory may be seen as developing along two different lines. In chapters 2 to 7, I treated the development of political process theory along one line—the study of political power. There are a number of models of power for the study of a policy area, or perhaps for the study of a city or national system. These models are elitism, pluralism, multiple elitism, corporatism, statism, cooperative pluralism, and neopluralism. We are left with the question of how to differentiate types of neopluralist policy systems.

By 2003, there is little that is surprising about this observation. One might conclude that the major models of power have already been discussed by scholars. In the 1980s, there seemed to be a controversy, in that new writings on statist power criticized pluralism as an alternative model of power (Krasner, 1978, 1984). But there seemed to be no pluralists to contradict those who argued that the state has autonomous power over policy on many occasions (Almond, 1988). Further, the leading writer on statist theory, Theda Skocpol (1992), upon becoming interested in the American welfare policy process, treated the subject in many ways like a process theory, examining the power of interest groups within civil society and their relationship to the passage of legislation at the federal and state levels. In contrast, James Q. Wilson (1980) and his students, whom many might have assumed to be pluralists, emphasized the role of professionalism within partially autonomous state agencies in causing changes in public policy.

Since political scientists of different backgrounds now largely agree in their discussions of models of political power, we need only apply this knowledge to different policy areas in the United States and other countries. Since scholars would regard this as "applied" research, it does not have the disciplinary emphasis and prestige of advancing new theories. Still, there are many scholars concerned with specific policy areas, such as public health policies, who would appreciate and be interested in the application of political science models of power to specific areas, such as the analysis of professional regulation. It seems to be a sign of a disciplinary inferiority complex that political science does not pay much attention to such applications of its theories, in contrast to economics, for instance.

But there is a whole second line of theoretical development in political process theory. This is "where the action is." This line of thought deals with the question, "power over what?" Such theory is implied by the basic assumptions of political process theory as worked out by Bentley, Truman, Simon, March, and Dahl (see chapters 1 and 2). The assumptions of political process theory include the idea of process itself, the idea of power as causation, the idea of a subjective definition of interests, and the idea of specific domains or arenas of power (i.e., power over what?). Power as causation cannot be quickly generalized from one area of political action to other areas, according to this assumption. Power may be different in different issue areas. One must observe the process of policymaking in different areas before making conclusions about power in those areas. This was clearly a basic train of thought in pluralism as it became political process theory.

Dahl (1958, 1961b) used the "power over what?" argument against C. Wright Mills (1956), Floyd Hunter (1953), and other elitists. In *Who Governs?* Dahl persuasively showed that power might vary in different issue areas of politics. But in a startling manner, this same argument was turned against Dahl and the other pluralists. If power varied with issues, then who had the power to decide which issues were the subject of contention? If one must study power over what, who determined the "what"?

This, the "two faces of power" argument, became the anti-pluralist critique that most disturbed the pluralists of the 1960s. As presented by Bachrach and Baratz (1962), this argument first conceded the validity of the pluralist findings in *Who Governs?* but argued that the significance of the study was severely limited. Bachrach and Baratz agreed that Dahl had accurately described who had power on the three issues studied—but that was a description of only one face of power. The critics argued that there is a second face of power—power over which issues get on the agenda of the policy process—and that this agenda-setting power is often more significant than having power over the issues actually debated.

The pluralists lost no time in rejoindering that the two faces of power concept was not amenable to the conduct of empirical studies. Which events that did not happen, or *nonissues,* should one study? the pluralists asked. Isn't the choice of nonissues, presumably blocked by some agenda-setting power, a subjective choice of the scholar? If we resort to the two faces of power, wouldn't the empirical study of power dissolve into irresolvable controversies over the significance of various nonissues and hypothetical references to the supposed sources of agenda-setting power (Polsby, 1980; Scott, 1990, 72)?

The pluralists argued that empirical scholarship must accept the idea of self-defined interests, and that the important issues in politics are those that the participants themselves think are important. The pluralists bolstered this generalization by noting that the issues studied in *Who Governs?* were prima facie important: urban renewal policy in the urban renewal capital of the United States; public education; and party nominations for mayor, a key step in citizen control of the city government (Polsby, 1980, 200–201).

Still, there was no denying the extremely persuasive quality of the two faces of power argument—after all, agenda manipulation is part of almost everyone's intuitive idea of power. Moreover, the criticism was strengthened by the gradual realization, especially after Steven Lukes published his book *Power: A Radical View* (1974), that there are actually *three* faces of power. In other words, one can distinguish the power of intimidation from the power of hegemony. In the case of intimidation, the powerless conceive of something they want, but they never act to get it because they fear punishment by the powerful. In the case of hegemony, the powerless never even conceive of some possible goal, because they have been socialized to think in terms of support for the status quo, legitimated by a set of cultural values, norms, and beliefs, exercising cultural hegemony in support of the existing social system. Earlier, the Italian radical Antonio Gramsci (1971) developed the idea of hegemony to explain why so many workers rejected socialism. Following Lukes, in the book *Power and Powerlessness,* political scientist John Gaventa (1980) applied the concept of hegemony, or the third face of power, to explain the political quiescence of the inhabitants of an Appalachian valley.

Pluralists and quasi-pluralists set forth a few conceptual systems to deal with the two faces of power argument (I was one of these), but their ideas did not support additional empirical research (Frey, 1971; McFarland, 1969; Wolfinger, 1971). Sensitive to the point that the critique seemed to undermine empirical studies, critics Bachrach and Baratz (1970) and also Cobb and Elder (1972) put forth theoretical frameworks for the study of agenda setting, but these never actually caught on, especially in comparison to the work of John Kingdon, published years later in 1984.

Probably the most widespread and effective critique of pluralism was the flawed argument that pluralism is tied to the status quo (see chapter 9). But the most devastating argument against pluralism on strictly scholarly grounds was that the pluralist theory of power could not deal with the generation of the issues of politics and was therefore a superficial approach to the study of politics. However, research over the last forty years shows that this anti-pluralist argument is now obsolete.

DEALING WITH THE NONISSUES QUESTION

About forty years have passed since "Two Faces of Power," and we can now see that within the continuity of the development of political process theory, the nonissues question has been dealt with. It does not pose a major obstacle to the development of policymaking theory that some had supposed. Let us consider the several different ways, developed over forty years, of dealing with the nonissues problem.

First, the nonissues question is a bigger stumbling block for the consideration of power in a political system as a whole, rather than for the analysis of a single area of public policy. The two (or three) faces of power continue to be an obstacle to the discussion of power in an entire society or political system, but there are conventions for dealing with these questions. The power elite theorist C. Wright Mills (1956) used examples mainly from national security policy, especially those involving possible nuclear war or the risk of conventional war. Multiple-elite theorists generally stress the weakening of the American state, thereby implying the dominance of business decision-makers over all three faces of power (see chapter 3). Statists argue that the state has been more significant in the United States and in European societies than American political science has allowed (Krasner, 1978; Skowronek, 1982). Corporatists observe that corporate decision-making applies to basic decisions affecting a nation's economy but does not apply to all issues, such as national defense, immigration, and so forth (Katzenstein, 1985). Still, power elitists, old-style pluralists, multiple elitists, neopluralists, statists, and corporatists all have reason to be troubled by the nonissues critique in dealing with power in an entire society. But the neopluralist paradigm concentrates on the study of power within particular issue areas of politics. Here the three faces of power seem less troubling.

There is not a lot of commentary in the study of policymaking concerning the three faces of power. One reason for this is simple. If one studies policymaking on a certain issue, that issue is part of the "first face" of power. It is out there and can be studied; it is not repressed by intimidation or hegemony. Those studying air pollution policy or open employment policy are interested in just those things. It is not relevant to question whether some other political issues are not studied because of intimidation or hegemony. The scholar did not intend to study anything other than the policy topics being pursued.

But even if thousands of scholars have published research on individual areas of public policy without concern for the nonissues problem, this does not advance much from the work of Dahl and Polsby. However, there is a different way of looking at the data. Somehow, we often focus on the analysis of power in an entire society because of radical criticism, such as that emanating from Mills or from Marxist writers of various types. In answering the questions posed by a writer implicitly or explicitly advocating revolutionary change, it seems that we must try to discuss everything important and in general.

We do not do this when we analyze a single policy area, but research on specific policies leads to a second approach to the nonissues problem. When we have in-depth knowledge about a policy area and its issue network, we see that various unusual, perhaps radical issues have been voiced. In the suppression of such advocacy, we can then gather data about the control of the agenda, perhaps by intimidation or by cultural hegemony. For instance, in civil rights policy, the issue of the payment of reparations to African Americans for slavery is brought up at a number of points, such as by members of the Chicago City Council, and one can observe what then happens. Or within most environmental policy areas, a few spokespersons in the issue network advocate radical policies, such as the elimination of gasoline-burning automobiles, nuclear power plants, or genetically modified agricultural products or massive subsidies for solar-heated housing. Although such issues might not seem radical to traditional Marxists, to others, they imply massive shifts in economic resources and major changes in lifestyle for tens of millions. The point is that such radical proposals are not nonissues; they are routinely put forward within issue networks, and one can do empirical research on the limitation or repression of such ideas within the discursive politics of an issue network, from powerful opposing business forces, and from the indifference of elected politicians. And if certain issues that once seemed radical or extreme, such as blocking construction projects to preserve species of worms or garter snakes, actually get enacted into law and practice, we can ask why this happened in terms of power relations within a policy area.

Thus, Heclo's (1978) concept of "issue network" not only provides some idea about how interest groups are sustained in spite of the logic of collective action, it also provides an idea of how the three faces of power can actually be studied. Most policy issue areas do register statements and actions by radical intellectuals; eccentrics; advocates of those with little power, such as the homeless or disabled children; academics aspiring to be noticed by advocating unusual policy suggestions; foreigners publishing evaluations of American policies in domestic and foreign journals; and even writers, filmmakers, and other artists of imagination. This is not to say that American public policies are rife with imaginative, eccentric, radical, or economic-leveling enactments; however, such suggestions are frequently voiced, and ignoring, repressing, or defeating them is something that can be studied with standard research techniques, such as those used by Robert Dahl.

Further, as described in chapter 5, issue networks encompass spokespersons for social movements and social movement organizations, both conventional lobbyists and unconventional radical activists. Social movement lobbies may pick up, amplify, and redefine issues from the more radical movement groups. For example, the demand for reparations may be picked up by the Urban League as another justification for aid to predominantly African American schools. Homosexual politicians may restate demands from groups of disruptive AIDS patients as advocacy for accelerating the introduction of new drugs for mass treatment. In such cases, we can observe how a radical demand becomes transmuted in the policy process. In any case, it appears that much more can be observed and understood than at first seemed possible, in spite of the three faces of power critique.

John Kingdon's agenda-setting theory, as stated in his *Agendas, Alternatives, and Public Policies* (1984), has been very influential among scholars who study public policymaking and may be seen as a third way of dealing with the faces of power problem, in addition to the foci on particular policy process and issue networks affecting a process. Basing his theory on the "garbage can theory" of complex organizations developed by Michael Cohen, James G. March, and Johan Olsen (1972), Kingdon views the policymaking process as multiple sets of event streams, specific to different areas of policy. (This is one of the basic assumptions of pluralism.) Within each particular policy event stream, there circulate for years a set of policy problems, as constructed by participants, and a set of proffered policy solutions, as constructed by other participants. Normally, there is little linkage between problems and solutions, but during relatively small "windows of opportunity," political entrepreneurs link a problem with a solution and put this forth as a policy suggestion to gain reelection and power, and probably because of some belief in the public interest. The window of opportunity is defined by a surge of popular interest in an issue and a widespread demand for government action on that issue. With regard to most matters, this political opportunity lasts for a relatively short time.

Thus, in Kingdon's terms, one could study nonissues by scrutinizing a "policy community" (a term synonymous with the more generally used "issue network") and the policy streams acted on by that community. Within the policy streams, the scholar could observe agents proffering problems and solutions a long way from a window of opportunity, and one could refer to these as nonissues. Study of the second or third face of power would consist of observing the obstacles preventing the nonpreferred alternatives from gaining consideration in a window of opportunity. Certainly, such study could use standard empirical methods.

Kingdon's agenda theory needs to be combined with an appreciation of the complexity of issue networks to move the theory away from old-style pluralism. As noted, all kinds of unconventional, radical, and egalitarian proposals spring up somewhere in an issue network. Such unusual proposals may be phrased in terms of definitions of problems or proposed solutions to problems. A scholar following Kingdon's theory would be in a position to observe such unusual constructions of problems and solutions and to describe power relations in reaction to these unusual proposals. This would make good progress in dealing with the nonissues problem.

Still, Kingdon's theory is not greatly removed from the ideas of Dahl's pluralist method. One might find agenda control through intimidation using Kingdon's theory, but one might have difficulty describing instances of control through hegemony. Our understanding of the faces of power has moved ahead through Kingdon but meets a certain boundary, that of hegemony.

A fourth consideration in dealing with the faces of power is the logic of collective action. In terms of Kingdon's policy streams and policy community, due to the collective action problem, some interests may not organize and thus not put forth problems or solutions. In addition, such organization of interests may be necessary to establish a window of opportunity. In the language of chapter 4, countervailing power groups must organize to offset the power of producer groups in a policy area. Sufficient countervailing organization will enable such groups to advance their own problem and solution constructions and, furthermore, will allow governmental agencies the autonomy to propose still more problems and solutions. Thus, if interest group sustainers offset the logic of collective action, nonissues become issues within Kingdon's policy event streams. However, if countervailing power is not organized, the event streams become "frozen," or at least do not move very far, because events are controlled by the dominant coalition of multiple-elite theory. Such a coalition will act to repress change by keeping other actors from participating in the policy area and by repressing the expression of new problem or solution constructions through intimidation or hegemonic domination.

In attempting to be empiricists and positivists, political scientists at one time might have avoided referring to environmental or consumer interests, when such interests were not advocated within the political system and might be self-defined by a very small number of those supposed to have such interests. But since the problems of organizing collectively have become better known, political scientists go at least as far as economists in recognizing that externalities exist and can become part of scholarly study. *Externalities* refers to the external costs of an economic action, those costs not registered in a market. For instance, air pollution imposes external costs on those who must breathe it, but there is no market to get the factory owner to pay for the costs of pollution. One then speaks of a "market failure" (Coase, 1960).

Political scientists now speak of environmental, health, and consumer interests in "internalizing" such external costs, that is, making the beneficiary of the economic action pay all the costs of that action. If there is no feasible way of doing this, then from the standpoint of market theory, there is a legitimate case for government to regulate the imposition of external costs. That is, government can act to correct the market failure.

If there is no collective action to rectify a situation of external costs, the political scientist might refer to this as an example of a nonissue, and then examine the situation. A strict application of collective action theory would probably result in the observation of the usual organizational dilemma of everyone being "free-riders," hoping that someone else will organize to rectify the situation, hoping that someone else will take the time and money to do this, since the costs of organizational activity are greater than the benefits for any single individual. But since individuals are not always motivated solely in cost-benefit terms, there would probably be cases of attempted organization to remediate the market failure, and such failures would provide instances of the wielding of power. In contrast, if no one ever recognized the injustice of the imposition of external costs, this would be a case of hegemony, difficult to analyze using the empirical methods of the neopluralists and thereby providing a boundary for the use of neopluralist theory (Crenson, 1971).

To deal with the faces of power, a fifth consideration that could be assimilated into pluralist methods is the examination of historical cycles and trends, as illustrated in chapter 6. Thus, if past observation of a policy area reveals evidence of cycles or trends in policy, one might observe the present situation of policymaking and look for the submergence of behaviors, which is more evident when the policy area is in its "different" state. For instance, during traditionalist eras of politics, requiring loyalty oaths from teachers and other public employees may be a major issue, whereas requiring such oaths may be a nonissue during liberal, reform periods. Or in some city, assumption of public ownership of the local electric utility may be an issue during a period of reform politics but a nonissue during traditionalist, pro-business eras, such as the 1920s, 1950s, and 1980s. In the last 100 years, public action in the regulation of meatpacking has waxed and waned, with concern becoming more intense after incidents of food poisoning, such as the one that occurred from tainted hamburgers sold by the Jack-in-the-Box restaurant chain in the state of Washington. During those periods when there is little public concern about the regulation of meatpacking, a student of food safety policy is on firm ground in referring to this as a nonissue. Similarly, in many cities, the issue of police using guns when making arrests comes and goes, flaring up in reaction to the shooting of suspects. Again, during a year or two when no one makes police shootings an issue, the researcher has good grounds for referring to this as a nonissue and for commenting on the causes of the lack of activity. A researcher might learn a lot about the processes of change within a policy area by looking for such nonissues and examining the processes of power, intimidation, and hegemony that temporarily repress the advocacy of such hidden issues.

The sixth and final consideration outlined here is the study of "hidden narratives," a concept from postmodernist historical studies. Michael Foucault and other postmodernist historians and literary critics take the position that most of the seemingly important documentation of the past actually reflects the viewpoint of dominant elites, who (so to speak) chronicle the issues that are important to them, describing them from the point of view of elite power-holders. Postmodernists view such history as biased to the perspectives of elites, and they seek to compensate for this by compiling historical evidence about the character of everyday lives and the behavior of ordinary people. As such, they are less interested in grand political events and military campaigns and concentrate instead on behavior in the marketplace, modes of speech, manner of dress, sexual behavior, consumption of food, festivals and carnivals, folk art, and so forth. Using such methods, political scientist James C. Scott points toward the study of "hidden narratives," social and political interpretations by ordinary people expressed in behaviors such as marketplace conversation, festivals and carnivals, public rituals, song and dance, jokes, and reinterpretation of elite symbols (e.g., proclaiming loyalty to the tsar, but arguing that the tsar is being misled by foreign advisers). The idea of hidden narratives by dominated people is familiar to Americans in the example of slaves singing hymns in the fields, apparently exhibiting a devotion to the master's religion but actually expressing an identification with the Israelites' escape from slavery. The plantation master might cite a lack of resistance to indicate that his slaves are content with their lot (the elite narrative), but the postmodernist would observe that the songs and meetings of the slaves exhibit signs of a hidden narrative, expressing their resistance to their situation. In other words, the postmodernist studies seemingly routine events in everyday lives to search for evidence of nonissues. Such a scholar then comments on the sources of intimidation that are preventing the open expression of such issues, as does Scott (1990) in his study of hidden narratives among premodern European peasants and contemporary Malaysian farmers.

In terms of studying policy process and power today, the method of hidden texts would lead one to do anthropological study in such places as churches, taverns, school social events for students or parents, street-corner society, and so forth. One would be interested in hearing hidden narratives about the nature of schools, police use of force, and other issues of concern, even though these issues had been only weakly articulated within the political system, or perhaps not at all in terms of communication understood by political elites.

At first, it might seem odd to cite postmodernist history as contributing to the development of the political process paradigm. But on further consideration, we recognize that both the postmodernists and the old-style pluralists want to eliminate any interpretation of data that simply uses information communicated by the powerful among the people studied. The pluralists, however, would prefer to do survey research and to interview persons not in the elite stratum, but of course, this is impossible in studies of the past. In using historical materials, pluralists would be leery of the interpretive leeway in the deconstruction of a folk song, for instance, but their own methodological commitments must lead them to be sympathetic to such scholarly efforts. Or, to put it another way, both postmodernists and pluralists dislike Marxist and other theoretical attempts to impose an interpretation on popular behavior, and both insist that great attention be paid to the social constructions expressed by the people studied.

The difference between the postmodernist and the pluralist is that the postmodernist generally regards social science theory and methods as just another interpretive construction imposed by a scholar on the data and believes that such a construction is likely to be linked to the context of power relations within academic life. The pluralist, in contrast, would criticize the postmodernist for ignoring the need to build interpretive frameworks beyond the data of a particular historical context of action. In any case, both might agree on the usefulness of anthropological study of hidden narratives for uncovering nonissues and the three faces of power.

COMPARATIVE ANALYSIS

Certainly, introductory political science teaches that if one wishes to learn about nonissues, one must do a comparative study of political systems. If an issue occurs in the politics of several systems, but not in a system that otherwise seems similar, we can ask, why not X? What caused X not to happen? In such a case, we have empirical grounds for selecting the X, as it is something that readily occurs in similar circumstances. Thus, X is not something selected arbitrarily, perhaps reflecting personal ideology or wish fulfillment.

Surprisingly, comparative analysis was not tied to pluralist theory (the beginnings of political process theory) to any great extent in dealing with the nonissues question. One major reason for this was the exhaustion of community power studies in the early 1970s. As is well known, after the publication of hundreds of journal articles and dozens of books failed to result in a scholarly consensus across disciplines, researchers and scholars became bored with the field of community power studies and went on to other interests. Community power studies then collapsed as a research field. But if there had been continuing interest in the field, researchers likely would have used comparative analysis to find out why some communities experienced a political issue, while similar communities did not. For instance, protest against "police brutality" against African Americans is a major issue in some communities but is lacking in others that might seem to have a problem with police brutality. Or some communities might experience an active politics for the improvement of public parks, while this issue is absent in other similar cities. Interviewing processes might shed some light on issue development in cities, and although this increases the cost of an urban politics study, it is still surprising that such techniques were seldom used in dealing with the question of pluralism and nonissues (an exception is Crenson, 1971).

One way of dealing with nonissues is exemplified in Paul Peterson's study *City Limits* (1981), the dominant research study in the urban politics and policy field for about a ten-year period. Using a type of rational choice model, Peterson stated that urban elites seek to maximize economic development by striving to keep taxes low, in tax-rate competition with other cities vying for business development, and by minimizing tax-eating redistributional expenses, such as programs for the poor. This, then, provides a standard for the evaluation of nonissues, because one could ask why a city might depart from this model, such as when New York City spends public money to maintain a large public hospital system (Fuchs, 1992).

The "city limits" model thus places a "rational man" model at the center of the analysis, something that many scholars would not accept. Thus, after 1990, the alternative model for comparing urban policymaking and the derivation of issues has been Clarence Stone's (1989) regime theory model (based on a study of Atlanta), in which it is hypothesized that different cities have different sets of norms about politics and proper political policies related to the urban economy and business. Such regimes and their norms have a major impact on how actors interpret the need to address some issues but not others. For instance, in Atlanta, Stone found a regime based on collaboration among African American politicians in control of the city government and downtown business interests, incorporating well-to-do persons, almost all of whom were white. The regime's norms had the effect of suppressing politics about issues concerning poor blacks, on the one hand, and prosperous whites seeking to block the construction of economic development projects in their neighborhoods, on the other hand. In a system having different norms, such as the "progressive" regime cities of San Francisco or Santa Monica, different norms would lead to a politics considering issues that were suppressed in Atlanta (Clavel, 1986). Regime theory is considered in more detail later.

If political process theory seems to have fallen short in the comparative analysis of issue generation among cities, what of the more obvious task of comparing policy issue areas within the United States? John Kingdon's work, as noted earlier, is based on the comparison of issue agendas in Washington, D.C.; specifically, he considers eleven health issues and twelve transportation issues (Kingdon, 1984, 230). An important, similar study to Kingdon's is *Agendas and Instability in American Politics* by Frank R. Baumgartner and Bryan D. Jones (1993). Their research is based on data gathered in the comparison of events in national policy areas, particularly nuclear power, pesticide promotion and regulation, tobacco policy, and national policy toward cities. Their work is widely known for the observation of "punctuated equilibrium" in public policy; that is, policy proceeds by means of relatively sudden changes that punctuate longer periods of slow change. This finding is memorable to political scientists because it contradicts the conventional wisdom that American politics is incremental (small, gradual changes), as popularized in the earlier work of Charles E. Lindblom. For those who think in these terms, the Baumgartner and Jones model has replaced the Lindblom model of policy change, partly because the new model incorporates the incremental model as descriptive of routine politics but not descriptive of the "high politics" concentrated in short periods of time (see chapter 4).

In *Who Governs?* Dahl takes a few steps toward a theory of issue development. At the time of that study, New Haven, Connecticut, had an urban renewal program that, in relationship to the size of the city, was perhaps unparalleled in the country. This program became a major issue because the mayor believed that an active urban renewal program would enable him to form a base of support, uniting Democratic voters and Republican business leaders in a broad coalition for his reelection. Implicitly, in this older pluralist theory, politicians seeking reelection introduced or furthered political issues to gain votes or other types of political support. Certainly, this would be the perspective of rational choice theory, as it developed (Downs, 1957).

As a work based on the comparative analysis of national issues, *Agendas and Instability in American Politics* carried such observations to a point of greater inclusiveness. According to Baumgartner and Jones, issues are introduced and advanced not just by legislators, mayors, and presidents seeking their own reelection. Issues are introduced also by interest groups and by the judicial system. And, in a way not well described in the literature, issues are introduced by governmental agencies seeking to stabilize and expand their programs after an initial burst of enthusiasm for their establishment (e.g., new government support for nuclear-powered electricity, pesticide usage, new types of grants for cities). Because Baumgartner and Jones use institutional language, rather than Kingdon's entrepreneurs as initiators, their study reads somewhat broader than Kingdon's. In any case, Baumgartner and Jones's comparative study of national issues is certainly empirical and, like Kingdon's work, shows that political process theory can, in an empirical research fashion, discuss and theorize how issues get onto the political agenda, the agenda that stipulates the "what" in "power over what?"

Agendas and Instability in American Politics exhibits a true process orientation. Issues and the political agenda are not defined in one locus, such as the presidency or the Supreme Court. More significantly, a single issue is not likely to be defined in one locus, but through a process of political interaction among institutions and interest groups. Actors in different loci have different goals, and the various actors seek to define and redefine an issue in ways suitable to the policy goals of each.

Although issues frequently are defined in the course of political interaction, issues may also arise exogenously, that is, from outside a policy system. For example, scientific developments, such as the development of atomic energy or new pesticides, result in new policy issues as enthusiasts seek government support in spreading the new technology (Baumgartner and Jones, 1993, 57–102). But there is no such thing as an "objectively" defined exogenous issue. The meaning of such nonpolitical events is interpreted by actors in politics. Is the new technology a boon? Does it incur undue risk? To what extent should government act to spread the new technology? These are matters of interpretation.

Baumgartner and Jones are very aware of the importance of interpretation in the definition of interests. They use the term *image* and refer to contention among political actors to get others to see an issue and events in terms of an image favorable to the actor. They see that frequently a Downsian policy cycle, in which events are constructed optimistically, is followed by a Schattschneider policy cycle, in which previously established institutions are viewed critically, with increasing participation by reformers (nuclear power, pesticide, government aid to cities, and support for tobacco are their examples). Not only suddenly appearing exogenous events but almost all policy events are given different images by participants, as political issues are defined in the process of political struggle (Baumgartner and Jones, 1993, 103–25, 239).

Equally important to image construction in Baumgartner and Jones's discussion of the issue agenda is what might be called "the economy of attention." Political actors are in contention to define some issues as more important than others, as ones that should come to the attention of high-level decision-makers such as legislators and chief executives. Implicitly, then, other issues are defined as not pressing or not as issues at all, and thus may be left to decision-making at the routine level of policy subsystems (B. D. Jones, 1994).

The centrality of such matters of issue definition in policy processes is persuasively demonstrated by Baumgartner and Jones. But these authors are left out on a theoretical limb. Previous scholars were convinced that the nonissues criticism of political process theory was a theoretically devastating point; therefore, with the exception of Kingdon and a few others, not much work was done to develop the theory of issue development and its relationship to image construction. Such work in *Agendas and Instability in American Politics* needs to be linked to a theoretical context that is simply not there, but is manifested only in scattered islands of research conclusions. In addition, it seems that there must be links among the six types of arguments that political process scholars developed to deal with the nonissues question (policy networks, Kingdon's theory, social movements, and so on).

Social movement theory, a more advanced theory than political process theory, struggled with a similar question, in that social movements usually involve a redefinition of social issues, the construction of new social images, and the imputation of new types of meaning. In social movement theory, this is called *issue framing*, a term that would seem to be productive for political science. Framing theory, then, might be adapted to the study of political processes as a way of understanding "power over what?" as political actors contend to define, or to frame, the nature of political issues.

FRAMES, ISSUES, AND POWER

Frame analysis, taken just as a vocabulary, is a way to circumvent misunderstandings from the use of the term *ideology*, now used in many different ways by many different groups of academics (Benford and Snow, 2000; Snow, Zurcher, and Ekland-Olson, 1980; Snow, Rochford, Worden, and Benford, 1986). Although there was some influence from psychiatrist Gregory Bateson, frame analysis was initiated by social psychologist Erving Goffman (1974), famous for his dramaturgical analogies for "the presentation of self in everyday life." Frame analysis, accordingly, is based on theatrical metaphors and is a cousin to such expressions as *roles* and *narratives*.

Frame analysis has to do with *attention* and *context*. The "framer" (one who does the framing) communicates with an audience by calling attention to certain actions—a social situation, a political problem—that might be said to be placed on "center stage." Human attention is limited, and the framer wants to call his or her issues to the attention of the audience. While an issue or situation is framed, other issues or situations are relegated to the backdrop, to the dressing rooms, or, most likely, are eliminated from the theater. In addition to the call for attention, the framer sets forth a context for the situation or issue that is framed. If the action is a statement, a kiss, or a fight, so to speak, what is the context for this action? What is the nature of the "play"? What is the context of meaning for the action that is framed?

Politics then involves the manipulation of frames—with "stage directors" attempting to get audiences to listen to their messages and to interpret those messages within the context, or "script," preferred by each director. Politics may then manifest a conflict among differing frames of interpretation for events, with the directors attempting to outdo each other in getting larger audiences and more public support for particular interpretations or frames. A particularly significant example involves calling attention to some group suffering social discrimination in the context of the concept of justice as the protection of "individual rights," therefore requiring action by government to protect such rights, known in the literature as the "rights frame" (Benford and Snow, 2000, 618–19). At some point, a rights frame will be countered by the "limited government" frame, in which attention is called to the new regulations necessitated by a rights law and the difficulties such regulations could cause to business or public administration.

Each of the six modes of study of nonissues may be linked to frame analysis. Policy networks are normally the main locus for framing issues, often a specialized activity involving only a small fraction of the public. Should there be greater regulation of nitrogen oxides, and how harmful are such emissions to the public health? What about fine particulate emissions—just how fine is "fine," how damaging to the lungs, and what should the government do? Such issues are framed by participants in the air pollution network.

As discussed earlier, and as emphasized by leading political scientists such as Redford, Schattschneider, and Baumgartner and Jones, much of the substance of politics concerns whether issues move out of the policy networks and into major forums, such as Congress or the higher federal courts. Much of the substance of issue framing involves the presentation of issues as involving fewer or greater "audiences" and participants (Schattschneider, 1960; Redford, 1969; Baumgartner and Jones, 1993; B. D. Jones, 1994).

There may be attempts to frame policy networks in other ways in addition to high politics versus routine politics. One significant issue frame was Samuel Gompers's view of labor policymaking, in which issues were defined as involving particular crafts, rather than all workers in a factory or industry. And, according to Gompers, craft-oriented policy networks should exclude the national government as a participant in labor policy. Gompers's framing of the preferable composition of labor networks was central to labor politics in the early twentieth century.

As noted, if policy networks "shout down" the presentation of unpopular issue frames, this is an observable event in the process of policymaking.

Kingdon's theory of agenda setting can be viewed in terms of frame analysis. One might call attention to the occurrence of "Kingdon framing," in which an entrepreneur develops a new frame, linking a preexisting problem and solution within the context of the history of such problems and solutions and the context of the window of opportunity in which the public (the audience) is demanding a new frame (Kingdon, 1984).

Discussions of externalities are a type of discussion about injustice. Attention is called to a situation in which a producer is making others pay for some of the costs of production, thereby involuntarily subsidizing the profits. When it is framed this way, most persons in our culture view this situation as unjust. If externalities are generated but no one is challenging the situation, there is a strong reason to ask why this is so, and whether an alternative frame has been generated to justify the production of externalities. (Government regulations that produce inflation are one such alternative.) One may then analyze the situation in terms of political power.

If there is some truth to my presentation of cycles in political time (see chapter 6), then much American politics consists of attempts to frame policies as "extreme" and as contrary to the values of mainstream, middle-class persons. One efficient way to launch a powerful framing process is to allege that a "scandal" is occurring, calling attention to some action as corrupt or otherwise outrageous in terms of widely shared values, and therefore needing correction. This sometimes results in a contest between those who allege business corruption, needful of reform laws, versus those who allege that reform elites are seeking to impose an alternative value system on government and society.

The discussion of hidden narratives is a different mode of discourse about issue framing. The narratives are hidden because of perceptions that the open expression of certain views will lead to punishment by the powerful. Power imbalances mean that certain issue frames cannot be expressed in public, although the sensitive anthropologist is able to observe this and report it as indicative of who holds political power.

We see, then, that the six types of studying nonissues are all closely linked to frame analysis, and we might conclude that further application of frame analysis will be helpful in studying power and nonissues.

ISSUES AND THE USE OF FRAME ANALYSIS

As noted, Baumgartner and Jones stress the importance of issue definition occurring within the process of political interaction; persons do not always first define the issues and then engage in politics to deal with the issues previously defined. Similarly, social movement theorists stress that movement issues are often framed during the process of movement activity.

This brings us back to the study of political science. If Plato symbolizes the study of justice, Hobbes the study of the state, Locke the study of individuals associating by contract, and Marx the study of conflict and inequality, what about Machiavelli? Some may think that no one was more political than Machiavelli, but has not the study of political strategy in domestic politics been neglected? One reason for that neglect seems to be that after the nonissues criticism of pluralism, political scientists became convinced that the study of political strategy was a matter of no great importance, in comparison to power structure or institutions of rules. Since I have demonstrated that scholars should no longer be intimidated by the nonissues criticism, it may be time to give more attention to political strategy.

One mode of attention exists: that of rational choice theorists depicting the manipulation of conduct so that preexisting structures of rules and institutions will tend to bring about a desired goal. The major contribution of William Riker (1986) is his emphasis that the core of politics is the manipulation of issues, particularly in elections, and that the nature of issues for political contention is usually not a given. In a disciplinary division of function, the job of the political process theorists is to show how such new issues are framed, including the selection of goals to be pursued (in some models) by rational choice (Carsey, 2000).

Ideas of leadership can be tied with strategy and issue framing. To cite Riker's well-known example of issue manipulation, Senator Warren Magnusson of Washington reframed an issue from a proposal to transport nerve gas from Japan across his state for incineration in Oregon to the issue of the executive branch doing this in violation of the Senate's right to be consulted in implementing a treaty with Japan. Senator Magnusson succeeded in convincing many other senators to see the issue in the new frame, so we might call this an example of leadership (Riker, 1986, 110; Baumgartner and Jones, 1993, 30). One mode of leadership, then, is causing changes in the political process by effective framing of an issue. In this use of the term, an exercise of *leadership* is not necessarily desirable to those opposing the goals of the successful issue framer.

Creative reframing of an issue is an instance of leadership, hence an instance of political power. Frame analysis thus should be at the center of the study of political leadership; defining the issues is likely to be as important as the skillful use of resources (e.g., the mayor making key phone calls or offering political benefits for support) and is likely to be more important than the identification of leadership traits, unless these are tied to a politician's capacity to frame issues. Frame analysis gives the theory of political process a key to understand political leadership.

A similar perspective holds for the understanding of political lobbying in the contemporary American system. Marie Hojnacki and David C. Kimball (1998) provided strong evidence that lobbying is more often about activating a legislator who already agrees with the lobbyist than about persuading undecided legislators or bringing around legislators who were initially opposed. A legislator can expend attention and political resources on a limited number of issues, although there may be many other goals that are favored by a legislator but are not a top priority. Thus, the task of the lobbyist is often to persuade a legislator to move an issue up on the legislator's list of priorities. Kingdon inquired of policy leaders in his interviews: "What's on the front burner?" (Kingdon, 1984, 224). The legislator is like a busy chef; it is not that the chef does not like a particular dish, but that he or she is too busy with other dishes to work on those on the back burner.

This is the situation referred to in frame analysis. It is not that the lobbyist is trying to change the mind of the legislator, but that the lobbyist wants the legislator to work on a new issue, or "dish." The lobbyist must frame the situation to make the issue a center of attention, within a context of concern to the legislator. This usually means getting the legislator to think that the issue is somewhat more important in gaining reelection support than previously thought.

Lobbyists seek to successfully frame issues, and the most successful lobbying sometimes involves simultaneously lobbying those who were once thought to be on different sides of some issue. For example, Senators Ted Kennedy and Dan Quayle were thought to have opposing views on expanding government aid to the unemployed, but by framing the issue as government aid to private business to retrain displaced workers, Kennedy and Quayle could cosponsor a bill. And whereas Quayle could support free trade with Mexico but Kennedy might be skeptical about the loss of American jobs, both Kennedy and Quayle could support the job retraining act, especially as Quayle was under reelection pressure from unhappy, displaced workers losing their jobs in the automotive parts and steel industries (Fenno, 1989). Research attention can be diverted from such situations when researchers ask the question, derived from both rational choice theory and common sense: do lobbyists give more attention to those already in agreement rather than those opposed, or vice versa? (Austen-Smith and Wright, 1994; Baumgartner and Leech, 1996; Hojnacki and Kimball, 1998). Power is involved in the framing of an issue so that few are opposed to the framer's position on that issue.

One aspect of frame analysis is the occasional rapid spread of some particular frame; this might be categorized as different applications of the same "master frame" in the terminology of social movement theory (Benford and Snow, 2000, 618–19). This phenomenon occurs during times of "punctuation," or sudden jumps in policy (Baumgartner and Jones, 1993, 2002). A leading example is that the civil rights frame of African American social protest in the 1950s and 1960s was adopted by several other large groups, such as women, Latinos, gays and lesbians, Native Americans, the disabled, and so forth. This was issue definition; it was amenable to observation by empirical methods, and it could be studied by political process theory, including social movement theory. The use of the civil rights frame led to events indicating political power in various issue areas or at the local government level.

The rapid spread of an issue frame similarly occurred during the Progressive reform period of 1900 to 1914, in which reformers interpreted policies in various economic sectors to be under the control of corrupt, often monopolistic corporations, often in collaboration with local political machines. The Progressive reform frame included the action prescription of exposing the corruption and passing new legislation in the public interest, which would then be implemented by neutral, scientific administrators, often in independent commissions removed from political control. According to this frame, in order to get effective political action in the public interest, new political institutions would be needed, such as nonpartisan elections, the initiative, the referendum, city planning, "scientific government" through neutral commissions, an extended civil service, and citywide elections. The Progressive movement started at the level of state government and was emulated by the national government under President Theodore Roosevelt. One might say that there were hundreds, perhaps thousands, of separate Progressive movements at the city, county, and state levels, generally adopting the same or a very similar action frame. This frame was related to the widespread diffusion of policy and institutional innovation (not all of it progressive) within the American political system.

As noted in chapter 6, the manifestation of such reform frames depends on an increased level of political and social movement participation, which is difficult to sustain for more than a decade. After this, the size of the audience receptive to the reform frame and willing to act on its basis steadily decreases. Counterframes are likely to flourish; one counterframe is that those advocating change may be influenced by subversive foreign ideologies (as in 1920); another is that continued reform represents an expansion of repressive government control, which brings the additional problem of inflation (as in 1980).

Another source of issue definition is the judicial system. Of course, as Baumgartner and Jones observe, issues are framed in the process of interaction, so as policy scholars, we must view the formulation of judicial decisions and subsequent policies in the overall policy context. (Civil rights decisions are made in the context of the civil rights movement, the initiation of a legal campaign by the NAACP, black voting in the North, and so on.) Nevertheless, within American politics, we can accept the idea that the judiciary often has a major impact on the formulation of issues.

It is intriguing to view the similarities between legal processes and frame analysis. Law is supposed to be a process in which specific issues are correctly placed within the established legal framework. The legal system calls attention to certain issues; they are placed on stage before an audience. Prosecutors and defenders then speak to the issue of where some situation should be placed within the legal code. In trials or other discussions of legal issues, adversaries are contending as to the correct frame for some situation. The appropriate frame is determined by the audience—judge or jury. As in other situations involving issue framing, strategy can play an important role. The best lawyers develop the best strategies of framing an issue in a way persuasive to the audience. In some cases, strategy is exhibited in a legal campaign, as in the famous NAACP campaign to discredit "separate but equal," which started with a suit involving law schools, an example particularly persuasive to judges. The legal system diffuses the adoption of a new frame for some situation. A superior court accepts a frame and binds inferior courts to this interpretation of events. Or a successful legal framing of an issue in one court is sometimes followed by many lawsuits, using similar reasoning, in many other state or federal district courts. Then there is the master frame of all the master frames—constitutional law. The legal process strives to apply constitutional doctrines (frames) to numerous specific situations.

The Supreme Court establishes another master frame of frames—deciding which issues are suitable to be treated by the legal system, as opposed to the political system. This is obviously basic to issue definition and, as such, is important to the analysis of power. The legal system redistributed power among segregationist elites and African Americans by taking up civil rights cases. By stating that legislation cannot limit the right of a wealthy politician to spend money on his or her own political campaigns, a political advantage is given to wealthy campaigners (who, however, are often defeated).

Judicial bodies may have a role in the exercise of countervailing power against issue area elites. Widespread but diffused majorities are disadvantaged by the logic of collective action. To counteract this, environmentalists and other interest groups bring lawsuits against units of issue area subgovernments when their policies can be alleged to be contrary to legislation controlling the area or to violate one's rights as a citizen. Given limited resources, such lawsuits are often a relatively effective strategy to gain countervailing power. The goal is to get the judiciary to frame policy issues as legal issues, as a way to obtain countervailing power. In other words, the routine power of subgovernments is often challenged judicially to obtain a high politics situation, neopluralism, and countervailing power. This is done through reframing an issue in the courts (Galanter, 1974; Yarnold, 1990; McCann, 1998, 207–9).

The study of the legal process is part of the study of the policy process. Interacting with other institutions, courts help define issues. This activity certainly can be studied empirically. As with policy networks, we can observe lawsuits that fail and analyze why they failed in terms of social power. The links between frame analysis and legal process analysis are numerous and, although beyond the scope of this study, are likely to be formulated by other scholars as part of the new political process theory.

Power, issue formation, and frame analysis can be linked with planning, as it is treated in chapter 7. A plan is a frame; a plan calls attention to a problem and states a formulation for action, against a context to establish meaning. In our society, this meaning is a stipulation that institutions and individuals must act together and develop a near consensus to establish some program in the interests of almost everyone. A common referent is land-use planning. For example, when building a transportation facility, a few persons may be in a position to block action on behalf of the whole. A near consensus probably implies cooperative pluralism, in which ordinarily opposed interests find that they have something in common and cooperate among themselves and with government to achieve this common goal.

Of course, a plan is political. The planners develop an action frame (plan), seek to get others to adopt the perspective of the frame, and work in the policy arena to get political support for the plan. Often this means that they are at the hub of a policy network, communicating and coordinating the actions of others to gain support for the action frame (plan). In the process of such politics and communication, the plan is likely to be altered in important respects.

Planning described by frame analysis helps comprehend one type of issue development. Political power is involved. The plan reflects interpretations of social issues favored by some and, more important, leaves out interpretations favored, or potentially favored, by others—the nonissues. In my interpretation of American public policy, cooperative pluralism and planning phenomena are much more common than is suggested by the current literature. Certainly, such phenomena can be studied empirically by political process theorists no longer intimidated by the nonissues critique.

REGIME THEORY

Political process theory can be furthered by incorporating "regime theory." This term was simultaneously developed by scholars in international relations theory and in urban politics theory, apparently independently of one another (Krasner, 1983; Stone, 1989). In both schools of analysis, regime theory expresses the intention of studying systems of action by viewing the power aspects as closely linked to a culture or to values, norms, and beliefs, or what I prefer to call "frames." In international relations, this is expressed in John Ruggie's (1983) well-known term *embedded liberalism,* descriptive of a system of action in international trade, most indicative of the power of the United States and Western European countries, a system of action understood in terms of neoliberal trade theory. Embedded liberalism is opposed to another view of international trade generally held by developing countries, whose governments propose major modifications of neoliberalism to protect developing economies and allow them greater autonomy with respect to the economic power of the United States and its allies. The generalization of this perspective by Krasner (1983) and Keohane (1984) is called "regime theory" and is applied to other sectors of international relations, particularly economic ones, but also to noneconomic areas such as human rights or arms-control "regimes." The point is that simply describing a structure of power is not enough for explanation and prediction. Within a regime, one also needs to understand the dominant interpretive frames, which may change in the process of interaction, producing different outcomes. Within the human rights area, for instance, the U.S. government rejects the generally accepted action frame defining the need for an international court of justice, and this rejection has an effect on international relations. If the U.S. government should change its interpretation of the international court, events would be changed. To understand such events, it is not enough to say that the United States is the world's only superpower, because the international court exists without U.S. support. One needs to apply a frame analysis and question the possibility of the United States changing its position; this is called by some regime theory.

In the field of urban politics, Clarence Stone (1989) established a parallel form of analysis. Stone was dissatisfied with standard pluralist "who governs?" forms of analysis of city power structure (Dahl, 1961b); nor did he find "city limits" theory instructive of what he wanted to know (Peterson, 1981). Instead, Stone proposed urban "regime theory," in which the dominant system of political action is understood both as power and as a system of norms affecting coalition behavior and issue selection. Atlanta is governed by a coalition of African American elected officials in control of the city government who work with the leadership of the private-sector downtown business establishment. This is understood not just as a structure of power but as a set of norms (frames) instructing that the two groups must work together for the overall good of the city, which is highly dependent on the continuing economic growth of its downtown businesses. This growth regime would then posit downtown development projects, which would override environmental concerns, expressed by white neighborhood groups, or to expenditures directly on behalf of poor African Americans (Stone, 1989; but see Ferman, 1996).

Both the international relations theorists and Stone, the urban theorist, want a theory that incorporates both "power as causation" and "power–over what?" This happens to be the next step in the articulation of political process theory. Something like regime theory can be extended to cover the numerous separate policy areas of domestic politics, as well as politics in cities and towns. In fact, regime theory might be called the observation of institutionalized frames, incorporating relatively long-lasting frames that can, however, be both reinforced and undermined in the process of political action.

These ideas "plug into" the concerns about multiple elitism, reform cycles, high politics, Schattschneider's expanding zones of conflict, Baumgartner and Jones's punctuation, and so forth. As Baumgartner and Jones (1993, chaps. 4–6) point out, if policy areas are controlled by limited subgovernments, such elites are likely to have some normative scheme that legitimates their control. During periods of "punctuation," the normative scheme is challenged, and this challenge is not just epiphenomenal to other strategies of power. In our society, regime norms usually involve some statement of the relationship of a policy area to government, and subgovernmental regimes generally articulate frames stipulating the need for "experts" and "free markets" to control rather than ill-advised reformers and government officials. Regime norms need to be restated in relation to different areas of politics. It is difficult to discern what is technical and what is political. Why have stockbrokers been more closely regulated than accountants?

Stone's regime theory is widely considered to be successful. International relations regime theory, at least, has a certain prestige and is evolving into a general intellectual position known as "constructivism" (Wendt, 1999). Some application from this work should enrich political process theory. This is not to say that regime theory provides the answer to "power over what?" But it is likely to be helpful. The discussion of frames provides a certain specificity and has achieved some success in two other fields. The hope is to avoid philosophical quagmires concerning meaning, interpretation, the construction of reality, and so forth. As Goffman (1974, 1) said, one might sponsor a lecture on socially constructed reality, but one must be sure that there is a place for the audience to park their cars.

CONCLUSION

Within the pluralist and political process framework, the consideration of power and issues presents a highly interesting intellectual story. In the beginning, Dahl's critique of Mills's ruling elite model relied on the idea that elite power must be linked to the study of issues—power over what? The two faces of power critique apparently defeated the pluralists on their own grounds; the pluralists could not answer who controlled the "what" in "power over what?" In turn, the pluralists replied that one could not empirically study nonissues or nonevents, somehow indicating the existence of power. An intellectual stalemate ensued.

Yet the next generation of scholars studying the American political process (Heclo, Kingdon, and Baumgartner and Jones), social movement researchers, and others showed how some issues were developed and progressed within the policy process, while other issues did not get far. And in principle, one could study a policy network and observe instances of the failure of politically extreme, radical egalitarian, and other unusual proposals being criticized and ignored. The progress of pluralist research on issue formation seems to have been slowed by a kind of intimidation springing from the two faces of power criticism. Nevertheless, by 1990, political process researchers produced some compelling results in studying power over issue formation.

It is my view that this type of pluralist or political process research about issue formation will be greatly expanded in the next generation of scholarship.

A first step is to invest more resources in comparative approaches to the study of policy areas. A second step is to experiment with integrative theories to give researchers perspective on their own work and how it is linked to the work of others. Integrative theory also has the effect of enhancing the prestige of a research field, helping to gain respect and support from the scholarly community.

I have presented frame analysis as a type of integrative theory to provide perspective on the study of power and issue formation. Frame analysis seems to point the way to integrating research in the areas of social movements, lobbying, interaction within policy areas, leadership, political strategizing, policy punctuation, the legal process, and planning. Frame analysis may then integrate these studies with the general question of power and issue formation. I may be optimistic about the uses of frame analysis. But some other theory or theories are likely to have the capacity to integrate studies of issue formation in the political process. Developing such theories will be a matter of some pleasure and pride for the next generation of scholars.

One argument about pluralism and the study of issues is that pluralism cannot study issue formation because pluralism is an ideology of the status quo. According to such criticism, pluralist theory can therefore treat only those issues presented by the status quo, and not the formation of new and different issues. But, as explained in the next chapter, this charge of theoretical adherence to the status quo is now obsolete.

9
The Boundaries of Pluralism

We have reviewed several conceptual criticisms of the 1960s pluralist theory of Dahl, Polsby, and others, including criticisms of the neglect of the multiple-elite possibility, the logic of collective action, the three faces of power, and the supposed neglect of the role of government. Here, let us turn to the more general, philosophical criticism that old-style pluralism was a system of ideas legitimating the social and political status quo.

Part of this criticism was rooted in the belief that pluralist theory concerned itself solely with the first face of power, the current major issues of the political system, accepting the definition of *political* as that which is currently held within American society. We have seen that since 1962, at least six different ways have been developed to deal with the three faces of power, so that in this respect, neopluralism need not be dismissed as an ideology supporting the status quo.

Critics of the pluralists argued that they seldom if ever criticized the current American political system (i.e., the one found in 1955–1965). Theodore Lowi Jr. (1969) stressed that the pluralists neglected the role of law in the system, particularly the potential for enacting directive legislation that could be enforced equally without compromises with powerful special interests. Prominent political theorists such as Peter Bachrach (1967) and Carole Pateman (1970) charged that Dahl and other pluralists were uninterested in participation by ordinary citizens and had put forth a supposedly empirical theory that actually legitimated rule by elites.

The pluralists of 1955 to 1970 did have problems with these questions, but as with the conceptual problems, the last generation of neopluralism has surpassed them. It must be recognized that the work typified by *Preface to Democratic Theory, Who Governs?* and other pluralist writings attempted to reflect a personal discipline to positivist methods, in which one's own values should be taken out of the research and in which human behavior is viewed as objective data (Dahl, 1956, 1961b). This was the message of the "behavioral revolution" in political science, which stated that political behavior should be studied according to the canons of the scientific method. From this point of view, the physicist does basic science and the engineer applies that science, the biochemist does basic science and the medical doctor applies it, and so the political scientists should do the basic science of political behavior, leaving the application to political activists, politicians, and their advisers.

Regardless of the philosophical defensibility of a hard-line positivist position, part of our data of human behavior indicates that this position is not taken seriously by a majority of political scientists. Although most political scientists agree that there is a place for those who do statistical studies of elections (thereby assuming that elections are important), or that equations written by rational choice theorists sometimes instruct us in the comparison with observed behavior, it is not possible in today's world for a leading school of political science to claim a mission of simply gathering and analyzing data without concern for human values and ethics and be taken seriously by most people.

This was realized by Dahl and others during the turmoil of the 1960s. Dahl, in a number of works, indicated his preference for citizen participation in the politics of small cities, a preference for Athenian democracy with all adults voting, and realistically assumed that not all important decisions could be made in town meetings (Dahl, 1970). *Who Governs?* actually screamed out the importance of competing political parties for the development of democracy, and certainly Dahl made clear his preference for party competition in his later work (Dahl, 1961b, 1971). Dahl's associate, Nelson Polsby (1983), along with many other political scientists, subsequently made clear a preference for strong, competitive political parties in America and showed concern about the decline of American political parties in the 1970s. During the last generation, writers in all schools of interpretation of power and policymaking—pluralist, multiple elitist, neopluralist, statist, corporatist—have stated their preferences for improving politics and society, both in America and elsewhere.

Aside from adhering to a positivism that is now obsolescent, the original pluralists were in the position of adhering to a "behavioral revolution" that was to displace most of the political science preceding it (Dahl, 1961a). Their observation was that political science had not become a systematic discipline such as economics, psychology, or even sociology, and that scientific methodology should be applied to the data of politics. (The distinction between the formal theory of economics and the behavioral theory of psychology was not very clear at the time.) Seeing their role as conducting basic research, not suggesting reforms, these behavioral scientists were dismayed at the dominant role of political reformers in discussions of politics, for the political reformers seldom had hard data to back their position, and in this view, reformers were seeking to foist on others political schemes based on personal emotions and biases.

Thus, unwittingly, most of the publications of the early pluralists have an ambience of support for the status quo, for their usual argument was that some well-intentioned reform scheme was backed by no data, and that researchers should gather and analyze data before suggested reforms were put into place. For instance, if a reformer said, "this city is run by an elite and we need more democracy here," the pluralist would say, "let's do research to find out whether this is really true, because there may be more democracy than you think." A reformer might say, "federal budgetary processes are inefficient, so let's process the budget using analytic categories." The pluralist would say, "let's see how the politics of the budgetary process actually works, because it may make more sense than you think it does." The reformer might say (in 1965), "Congress is run according to the seniority system, which is undemocratic and should be abolished." The pluralist would say, "let's understand the full range of the workings of Congress before we advocate change. The seniority system reduces conflict, for instance." And so on.

Let us sympathize with the pluralists' desire to stand back and study how the system actually works, nonissues and all. But as we look back, we see that the pluralists dug themselves into a pit. First, they advocated a purist positivist doctrine that was rejected by most political scientists. Second, they continually opposed the well-intentioned schemes of reformers and argued that change should wait until we had done the basic research on the workings of the system—all this during the 1960s, when more academics were clamoring for fast change than at any other time since the depression. Thus the pluralists became identified as legitimating the status quo, while actually they were dedicated, in ways that were sometimes misguided, to doing basic research about American politics.

Still another factor contributed to the pluralist identification with the status quo. The first generation of survey research after World War II put forth disturbing findings. Although political scientists were probably not highly optimistic beforehand about the virtues of mass political attitudes and knowledge (Lippmann, 1922, 1925), the findings of the Michigan Survey Research Center, social psychologists at Columbia, and other national surveys were actually rather shocking (Campbell, Converse, Miller, and Stokes, 1960; Lazarsfeld, Berelson, and Gaudet, 1960; Stouffer, 1962). Then it was discovered that most Americans could not name their congressman, adhered to a political party but were not interested in the issues in presidential elections, and seemed to reject the Bill of Rights. These findings looked even worse in light of the recent experience with German fascism in appealing to the masses and to the apparent appeal of Senator Joseph McCarthy to the American public, many of whom seemed ready to suspend civil liberties in the fight against communism. Such findings put out a yellow caution light to data-oriented political scientists who might otherwise advocate increasing participation by ordinary citizens.

Accordingly, the pluralist priority seemed to be to protect political parties and the competition between them, and then to gather the ordinary citizenry into politics, believing that the process of participation would teach citizens about the issues and the values of political tolerance and compromise (Dahl, 1961b, 315–25). Since the 1960s, an impressive array of research findings has shown that the ordinary citizen is better informed than we thought, votes on issues more than it first appeared, and, though not well informed, is at least capable of taking cues about voting (Sniderman, Brody, and Tetlock, 1991). Such citizens are also more tolerant, making many distinctions about the behavior of other citizens as related to their own views on tolerance. (In general, although great problems remain, the United States seems less racist and more tolerant today than in the 1950s.) As the original pluralists advocated, we now have more and better data and have less cause for worry about an insurgence of mass participation than some might have thought in 1965. Nevertheless, a reluctance at that time to advocate increased mass participation was another factor contributing to the identification of pluralism with support for the political status quo.

It must be admitted that under the attack of the behavioral revolution, the prestige of the study of public law within the political science discipline hit a low during the 1960s—its lowest point during the entire twentieth century. During earlier generations, constitutional law was seen as the centerpiece of the discipline, but being an interpretive, textual form of scholarship, it had to give way before the new data gathering and scientific analysis promulgated by the behaviorists. Behaviorists insisted that too much attention had been paid to the laws on the books, and too little attention to what people actually did in the realm of law. Behaviorists and pluralists had no research interest in jurisprudence. Consequently, Lowi's criticism of pluralism in *The End of Liberalism* (1969) was influential and telling, as he decried the pluralists' disinterest in law, making an opening for an apologia for multiple elitism. In Lowi's view, pluralist ideology had legitimated the tendency for government to enact weak laws, subject to bargaining with special interests in their enforcement, thus leading to something like a lawless state, incapable of planning consistent programs. Explicitly in Lowi's view, and implicitly in the work of others setting forth a multiple-elite model, the status quo in American politics is the tendency for the political system to fragment into numerous subgovernments, each controlled by special-interest coalitions, and since pluralist theory lauded the fragmentation of power while not criticizing its downside, pluralism seemed to them to legitimate the political status quo.

NEOPLURALISM, THE STATUS QUO, AND PARTICIPATION

If the 1960s pluralists dug themselves into a pit and seemed to legitimate the status quo, the turn of policymaking theory to dealing with islands of oligarchy and the logic of collective action restored the scholar to level earth. We have seen that the two faces of power critique have been dealt with by six separate methods, starting with the recognition of the need to consider the generation of externalities as a nonissue in light of the logic of collective action. (If there is pollution, but no one is protesting, there are still grounds for studying this.) The pluralists were caught in the extremes of the behavioral revolution, taking a rather strained position about not injecting values into the data, attempting to demonstrate why democracy is possible in light of the first findings of survey research, and exhibiting disinterest in public law. Further, 1960s pluralist research often seemed to defend the status quo because of the theoretical strategy of attacking ill-informed proposals of political reformers.

However, during the 1970s, policymaking theory, though it had its roots in pluralism, was able to free itself from such restraints. David Truman (1965) had early signaled the approaching end of the behavioral revolution, indicating that political scientists were less concerned about separating facts and values, and making way to restore the prestige of nonquantitative legal studies. With an accumulation of empirical research, pluralists and other research political scientists were less concerned about using the tactic of criticizing the reformers. Now they could criticize previous researchers. Further, the accumulation of research indicated that voters might be more rational than the first survey research indicated, and that the majority might be capable of political tolerance. During the 1970s, then, researchers influenced by pluralism did not publish the type of material leading to the criticism that they legitimated the status quo.

Certainly, the multiple-elite writers wrote about nonissues, avoided the extremes of the behavioral revolution, and overtly criticized the American political status quo. Further, after Olson's logic of collective action percolated through the discipline, virtually all political scientists had to support at least *some* increase in participation. In his work, Olson concluded that the organized few usually could defeat the unorganized many, thereby attacking the logical foundations of democracy itself. Social scientists thus had to be concerned about means of organizing interests in the face of the logic of collective action, or else resort to a defense of some form of oligarchical government. Since Olson's alternative of distributing selective benefits to group members did not completely solve the problem of collective action, some additional incentives were needed for representing interests, including the incentive of valuing participation as an end in itself. Thus, if one believes in democracy, Olson's theory implies some advocacy of participation.

True, a neopluralist position might be that Olson's paradoxes could be dealt with by more active participation by a minority (say, 10 percent) of citizens. Such would be enough to mobilize and maintain the citizens groups, ideological groups, unions, and even economic interest groups necessary for civil society in democracy. Accordingly, although the neopluralist model necessarily assumes participation, it need not be of a sufficiently broad scope to provide for "strong democracy," the vision of participatory democracy relying on a majority of citizens practicing politics beyond voting and occasionally contacting government officials (Barber, 1984).

In other words, the neopluralist model observes the existence of mobilized countervailing power groups in many policy areas. These countervailing power groups offset the control of the producer groups in the policy area, leaving political room for autonomous agencies of the government. To get countervailing groups, the neopluralist must support the mobilization and maintenance of a variety of citizens groups, unions, and even business associations, which sometimes provide countervailing power to one another (e.g., sugar growers versus Coca-Cola). And, since social movements are a major source of countervailing groups, the neopluralist model seems to imply support for a range of social movements, although not those that would restrain others from participating. Although empirical researchers usually do not explicitly advocate modes of political participation, such writers normally observe that Olson's logic of collective action often does not apply, and that it is a good thing to observe more participation than Olson would lead us to expect (Walker, 1991).

Another strand links Dahl's pluralist model to advocacy of increased participation. As noted, the self-definition of interests is a basic assumption of the old-style pluralism, as well as of the political process theory that developed from it. If, after 1970, one gets away from the extremes of adherence to positivism, one might advocate not just taking individuals' expressions of interests for granted but also the existence of political institutions that might help citizens discuss and learn about their own interests, which could then be expressed. Then one might advocate participation in such institutions to increase one's knowledge of politics and of one's own interests. This was the position taken by John Stuart Mill in *Considerations on Representative Government* (1958) and also by William K. Muir (1982), a student of Dahl's who participated in the *Who Governs?* study. Muir found that before a subsequent institutional decline, much of the behavior within the California state legislature consisted of members and staff teaching one another about political issues and various positions that might be taken on such issues. Muir approved of the successes of the legislature as a school of politics, and clearly a reader of his book might advocate the enhancement of such processes in other legislatures. Still, within even the old-style pluralist assumptions, it is only a small step to argue that political parties, elections, and leaders running for office best serve the polity if there is an understanding of how such institutions might teach the citizen-students about politics. Really, the only obstacle for a pluralist to advocate such positions was the now obsolete, extreme injunctions about the separation of facts and values.

Following Mill, Dahl, and Muir, in my book *Cooperative Pluralism* (1993), I observe that even while producer groups, countervailing groups, and autonomous agencies are in contention, under some conditions they might teach one another about policy alternatives and the interests that various parties have in such alternatives. A theorist might consider how to construct new participatory institutions to further such political learning.

In conclusion, developing past the 1960s, the neopluralist is not inclined to reject advocacy of increased political participation. On the contrary, the whole idea of neopluralism is dependent on getting individuals to support the mobilization and maintenance of interest groups that should not exist, if Olson's logic of collective action were totally correct. Neopluralism is thus logically dependent on a relatively expansive theory of participation.

WHAT PLURALISM CANNOT EXPLAIN

As we have seen, the neopluralist model of policymaking has emerged out of the original pluralist theory of the 1960s. An original theoretical statement was made, a statement that was both limited and extreme. These problems were subsequently dealt with, leading to a more developed, synthetic theory with a broader scope. However, there are limits to the coverage of the neopluralist theory. Perhaps a few logical positivists once believed, and a few rational choice theorists still believe, that there can be a single theory encompassing the study of politics. But the development of such an overarching theory seems to me to be unlikely.

We can view pluralist theory in this respect as analogous to Marxist theory and to corporatist theory. (Although I regard pluralism and corporatism as research findings in the study of power, these ideas were generalized and advanced as political philosophies in the early twentieth century.) Marx's original theory was brilliant but extreme—positing working-class consciousness, the state as solely a dependent variable, and expecting the arrival of an egalitarian utopia. In the twentieth century, Marxism was revised to make it more persuasive: Lenin's imperialist theory of exploitation, Gramsci's (1971) concept of capitalist hegemony, the view that the state might have considerable autonomy, as held by Miliband (1969) and others. Still, most scholars would see the explanatory power of Marxism to be limited as one deals with nationalism, civil rights policy, and so forth. Similarly, the theory of corporatism traces its roots to pre-twentieth-century Italian and Romanian theorists seldom read in American or British political theory courses. Original corporatist writers used extreme organic analogies about the nature of the society and tended to lend themselves to authoritarian, even fascist interpretation. But the reinterpretation of corporatism by Schmitter (1974) and others indicated that it could be developed as an analytic tool to understand decision-making in modern societies, including both democracies and authoritarian regimes. Still, few would make the argument that corporatism is the first theory one should use for understanding the interest politics and bargaining in such countries as the United States, the United Kingdom, and the new Russia.

Similarly, pluralism had its original, rather extreme statement by Bentley, Truman, and Dahl, with a first wave of revision by Olson, Lowi, and others, and a second wave of revision by James Q. Wilson, Jack Walker, and many researchers. And similarly, neopluralism cannot cover everything we want to know.

In particular, the neopluralist theory is not so useful to scholars who want to understand the "political development" of "state structures" and "legal institutions." Nor does it deal entirely with the concept of hegemony over politics. Nor is it a satisfactory basis for a radical political theory, whether Marxist or religious fundamentalist, seeking quick, revolutionary change in society. The neopluralist paradigm is based on the notion of studying processes of policymaking events, rather than studying the evolution of political structures. The latter scholarly concern is exemplified in the title of the widely read *Building a New American State: The Expansion of National Administrative Capacities, 1877–1920* by Stephen Skowronek (1982). This type of scholarly activity can be pictured as attempting to construct a "freeze frame" of a political or administrative issue at several points in time and trying to explain the changes in the institution, often with a theory of direction of change, toward increased "administrative capacity" or some theory of the characteristics of state modernity. Such theorists are likely to argue that the first task is to understand the political structures, as they shape the political process, studied by the neopluralists.

Although neopluralism can progress to study the three faces of power with the methods outlined above, it can go only so far to explain questions of hegemony. (Although I am not sure that other theories do such a good job, either.) For instance, one observes that, persuaded by the argument that the prescription drug market is not one with freedom of choice, most industrial countries allow the state to regulate the price of prescription drugs, but this is done only partially and indirectly by the American state in its purchase of pharmaceuticals for Medicare. In political discussions of this issue, it seems illegitimate in the United States to call for the federal government to set the prices of the leading prescription drugs. Instead, reform proposals call for individuals to be granted increased Medicare allotments for the purchase of prescription drugs. Some might see the central element in this policy situation as the cultural hegemony of neoliberalism or capitalism, in persuading reformers, union leaders, and the average voter that "big government" should not regulate the pharmaceutical industry, even though prices, profits, and the free market in this economic sector do not reflect usual competitive practice. Proposals for government price setting for prescriptions for everyone (not just those on Medicare) are not actually defeated in lobbying battles in the policy process; such proposals are seen as illegitimate to begin with and are thus only weakly advocated. Neopluralist observers would surely note the appearance of this type of policy proposal in an issue network and its rejection by others. However, the theory would have difficulty explaining why government regulation of prices is considered off-limits.

The neopluralist policy paradigm is not likely to interest scholars proposing a rapid, wholesale change in social and political institutions. Marxist writers are likely to envision new institutional structures, such as unions and a political party, assuming control of the state and thereby instituting major change. Fundamentalist theorists are likely to assume the appearance of a religious structure, such as an alliance of mullahs, rabbis, or ministers, which also would assume control of the state, instituting policies to eliminate secular political hegemony and introduce the hegemony of a religion. Such writers focus on political structures and domination through hegemony and are not likely to find the neopluralist theory very useful.

However, before we relegate the neopluralist paradigm to some conservative niche, let us recall that among democrats, at least, it is tied to ideas of increased participation by mobilizing many interest organizations, implying a politically active civil society. Further, the neopluralist theory can be linked with support for social movements, including working-class movements and even fundamentalist movements, as social movements are a major source for the mobilization of active, political groups.

Neopluralism can take on a radical tinge if it is combined with ecological activism, a political tendency comfortable with the combination of radical civil disobedience and conventional tactics of lobbying and litigation. Believing that "small is beautiful," ecologists cannot take comfort from the idea of seizing control of the state and using bureaucratic coercion to enforce radical ecological change in society.

Pluralism expanded its original bounds in dealing with the ideas of islands of oligarchy, the logic of collective action, interest group sustainers, social movements, government autonomy, lack of fairness in the balance of interest group power, cooperation, and corporatism; studying the three faces of power; lessening the link to the status quo; encouraging more political participation; and adding a historical dimension. But neopluralism has its boundaries, too, in dealing with structural change, political hegemony, and revolutionary change.

SYNTHESIS OF MODELS OF POWER

The boundaries of pluralism, or political process theory, exclude structural, hegemonic, and individual attitudinal theories. However, the boundaries of pluralism, expanded to neopluralism, converge and overlap with other models of power. We have seen that the elitist, multiple-elitist, pluralist, and neopluralist models of power converge (chapters 2–4). In chapter 7, we also saw the convergence of corporatist models of power with the neopluralist model. The pluralist model of the 1960s was usually applied to community power studies in America; it seldom had comparative applications. Thus, when Schmitter revived the corporatist model in 1974 as part of his comparative studies, it made sense to contrast it to pluralism, which had not found corporatism in America. But as far as I know, no pluralist ever wrote that corporatism was a false model or that corporatism could not exist. Pluralists had no special problems with the finding of corporatism based on decision-making studies, using the same methods as pluralists.

I used the term *statism* in chapter 4 to indicate the convergence of neopluralist findings of agency autonomy with the statist theory of a school of research flourishing in the 1980s. Under the famous slogan "bringing the state back in," Theda Skocpol, the leader of this school, and other scholars such as Stephen Skowronek, Stephen Krasner, and Eric Nordlinger argued that political scientists were paying insufficient attention to the state as an independent variable in political analysis. Whereas the arguments of Skocpol and Nordlinger were directed mainly to the field of comparative politics, "bringing the state back in" was applied to the study of American politics by Skowronek and Krasner. Certainly in the policymaking field, after the work of the pluralists and multiple elitists, the role of the state (or the autonomous role of administrative agencies) needed clarification. The statists argued that institutions make a difference, should be analyzed as stable structures influencing the political process, and should be understood in the context of their historical development, a history illuminated by a comparative sociology of institutional development. The statists also observed that because institutions have autonomy, the ideas of institutional leaders or of the professionals embodied in a bureaucracy make a difference. As such, the statists paid more attention to the role of professional values in public policy, ranging from Germanic theories of military staffing and forest management to various economic doctrines, such as Keynesianism (Krasner, 1978; Nordlinger, 1981; Skocpol, 1985; Skowronek, 1982).

The statist writings achieved considerable prestige, and thus the impact of these writers in the 1980s reinforced the neopluralists' observations of autonomous agencies. Indeed, though clearly indicating the importance of the power triad (producer groups, countervailing groups, and autonomous agencies), James Q. Wilson (1980) resembled the statists in much of his work, except that he, like the other neopluralists, studied the contemporary political process and left the study of historical institutional development to others. In fact, neopluralist writers did not object to the idea of "bringing the state back in" and did not engage in published controversies with the statists. As mainstream comparative politics scholar Gabriel Almond (1988) observed, statism was not very different from mainstream political science, which had generally accepted the idea that state agencies are able to act autonomously.

Thus, neopluralism has also converged with statism. There is nothing in neopluralism that prevents the observation that state agencies have acted autonomously. In fact, through its opposition of producer groups and countervailing power groups, neopluralism provides an important theoretical basis for expecting autonomous action by state agencies. There are, however, differences in emphasis between neopluralists and those trained in statist theory. The statists tend to be more historical and comparative in their perspectives and to give greater emphasis to the effects of professionalism and other ideas of those in government. Neopluralists tend to be more interested in the role of interest groups and in the analysis of contemporary policymaking processes (see chapter 4). However, these are differences in degree of emphasis only. Accordingly, as Skocpol (1992, 1999) studies American welfare policy and the history of American civil society, there is no longer a major division between statism and neopluralism. In decision-making studies, a neopluralist could very well find that a policy area is statist, a likely conclusion in the study of the Federal Reserve Bank and its policies. Neopluralists might simply accept Krasner's decision-making studies showing that American policy toward foreign nationalization of oil and mining interests resulted from policies of the State Department, not of interest groups (Krasner, 1978).

Political process theory has thus achieved a convergence of models of power. A different question arises when one asks about "the power of power," as did James March (1966) and William Riker (1964) during the time when the four initial pluralist assumptions were laid out. When power is defined in terms of causation, a model of power is a model of causation. And we all know about the complexities of causation in politics and policymaking. In this sense, power as causation may not be very helpful (McFarland, 1969). But now that political science has achieved a certain sophistication in the study of power, we should be able to admit that frequently we can do case studies and get useful information more by persistence than by elaborate methodological devices. With a certain amount of work, researchers can provide evidence of the plausibility of elite control, or neopluralist control, of a policy area, as was done in studies cited in chapter 4. We can study a policy niche (see chapter 8) and provide communicable evidence about whether it is controlled by a limited elite coalition. As James Q. Wilson (1980) and his students indicated, we can study policymaking to ascertain the role of state agencies and make some judgment as to whether they are rather dominant (statist) or part of a power triad. Power indicates which individuals and which institutions made things happen, and we often get a good idea of this, even though the exact lines of causation may be very complex. In actual practice, most political scientists seem content with case studies that indicate with a high degree of plausibility who has power. The main problem with such plausibility is the question of power and issue formation, which now seems to be at the leading edge of research.

10
Conclusion

In our reconsideration of pluralist theory, we have seen that this theory was not limited to the group theory of David Truman and other such writers, nor was it limited to the scholarly studies of power and American politics by Robert Dahl and those influenced by him. Pluralist theory continued to evolve after 1970 into a neopluralist synthesis that might better be termed *political process theory*.

We have seen that the basic concepts of the evolving pluralist theory have much to do with a concern for political process rather than being limited to concepts of power. Pluralist theory is presented here as basic ideas in a developing theoretical sequence. The first idea was the fundamental importance of studying political process, the flow of agents and events and their interaction over time. A second idea was the definition of power as an agent's ability to cause changes in the sequence of events in the process in the direction of the agent's goals. To this was added the importance of studying power and political process in particular policy domains rather than postulating some arena as generalizable to all the others. A fourth idea was the self-definition of interests by the actors studied rather than having the researcher posit goals from some outside theory. Actors' goals were likely to be defined and modified through the interactions within the political process, according to Lindblom's theory of partisan mutual adjustment; this theory was also called "incrementalism," after the observation that political processes seldom take sudden leaps in time. The first four ideas, put forth by the pluralists of the 1960s, remained as basic assumptions of evolving political process idea, but incrementalism, the fifth pluralist concept, was overturned by the concept of punctuated equilibrium.

Although not a pluralist, in the somewhat misleading conventional sense of the term, Mancur Olson Jr. provided a sixth idea with his "logic of collective action," indicating why many groups that might be expected to organize and participate in a political process would not do so. This is a major factor in creating the effect of islands of oligarchy variously known as subgovernments, iron triangles, little governments, and so on. In this situation, particularistic coalitions gain control over policy in some specific area, leading to a political system not controlled by a power elite but dispersed into hundreds of separate policy processes, many of them controlled by narrowly based elites.

Still, within the evolving process theory, this picture was soon contradicted by responses to Olson's theory, responses arguing that interest groups can organize

CONCLUSION 159

and maintain themselves because of patrons, underlying issue networks, and other factors. Therefore, the separate policy areas may have a richer participation than that supposed by Olson, Lowi, and other multiple elitists. One effect of this more balanced participation is that groups might organize on two or more sides of a policy issue, leading to a power balancing process and preventing the control of governmental administrative agencies by a single interest coalition with stakes in that area. This phenomenon, observed by many researchers, might be termed *agency autonomy,* that is, governmental agencies are frequently autonomous actors in a policy process.

Social movements add an element to the policy process and to the evolving pluralist theory. Social movements in America normally spin off groups that become active in policymaking and that tend to be supported by contributors not following Olson's cost-benefit calculations. Movements thus create a greater pluralism in a policy process, tending to produce additional countervailing power to narrow coalitions that might otherwise dominate.

Finally, researchers who might be styled "neopluralist" accept the previous ideas but clearly do not argue that just because a plurality of groups is organized a policy process will be fair and adequately representative. The process may be complex, but business or another type of group may dominate, and the whole idea of fairness and representation is largely a matter of normative preferences.

This neopluralist outlook is apparently shared by a wide variety of political scientists conducting research into the operations of various policy processes in the American pubic sphere. I believe that I am reporting what many scholars actually think and what they do as they observe policy processes, even though they may not term their work neopluralist.

This research sequence has produced a number of models of power that can be applied to a particular policy process. Rejecting the idea of a power elite applied to a whole country or to the policies of a particular city, this developing theory came up with Truman's group theory (groups control, but with countervailing power), Dahl's pluralism (fragmentation into separate policy processes with dispersed power), multiple elitism (fragmented processes frequently controlled by narrow coalitions), neopluralism (fragmentation, many groups, but not necessarily balanced power), and even cooperative pluralism (opposed groups that also cooperate within some policy process). In addition, researchers using such pluralist theory do not necessarily assume that this is a "paradigm," implying that corporatist or statist models of power do not apply in America. Although these two models are more useful for explaining policymaking in certain European countries than they are for explaining American policy processes, neopluralist researchers seem capable of accepting the existence of such patterns of power in American policy, if there is convincing evidence.

This evolving research sequence has thus produced useful ideas for understanding power and policy processes: the original pluralist model, multiple elitism, neopluralism, cooperative pluralism, and the possibility of statism and a limited corporatism. These models can be linked to suggestive hypotheses, as stated in chapters 2 to 4. I view this as a definite accomplishment for political science, one that the discipline should be proud of.

CONCEPTUAL TOOLS AND RESEARCH SITES

What research applications for political process theory, as I define it, might be developed? I see this as a matter of combining conceptual "tools" with research "sites," that is, particular areas of research within the fields of politics and public policy. First, let us review the conceptual tools, before we discuss their applicability to the sites.

A first conceptual tool is the idea of *political process* itself—the flow of agents and events within some policy area over time. Then, let us stick with the idea that political process theory has evolved through a line of models of power and is now tackling a second line of questions regarding issue formation and power. The second conceptual tool, then, is *models of power.* These are elitism, pluralism, multiple elitism, neopluralism, corporatism, and statism as applied to a policy area or areas. The third conceptual tool may be defined as a major characteristic of the power structure of a policy area or areas, the *advocacy coalition.* This is a relatively long-lasting alliance of political actors cutting across the usual descriptive categories: interest groups with executive branch units, legislative branch units (e.g., committees), elected officials, aspiring politicians, supporters in the media, and various other experts. The advocacy coalition consists of a subset of the members of a policy network in coalition for several years to achieve one or more policy goals. A fourth conceptual tool is *cooperative pluralism*—the existence of common goals among normal adversaries and some joint action by these adversaries to achieve a common goal. Governmental units may be a part of cooperative pluralism.

Five more conceptual tools have to do with issue formation. Tool five is *frame analysis*—understanding the definition of issues by contending actors and coalitions. What is stated as the top priority for action, and what are the contextual reasons given for the action frame? What is the strategic interaction among actors in the process of frame definition? What are the effects of using different frames, and who gains and loses in the process of framing issues? A sixth conceptual tool is *policy niches.* Recent research has shown that very specific policy areas or niches are defined by the actors. Such niches usually have only a few interest groups and lack political contention. Research by Gray and Lowery (1996) and Browne (1990) shows that actors in the policy process strive to carve out policy niches, meaning that there is a constant tendency in policy-making to define issues very narrowly. Can we then observe the dynamics of this process in many policy areas?

A seventh conceptual tool is that of the *policy regime,* a stable normative pattern that is accepted as legitimate by participants, thereby affecting their behavior. As indicated by Clarence Stone's (1989) work, in American public policy, important norms may govern the relationship between leading governmental decision-makers and economic decision-makers. Is there a widely accepted norm that government should act minimally in some policy area? Is there a norm that a governmental organization should assist leading economic actors, and perhaps vice versa? This, too, is sometimes linked to frame analysis and policy niche creation (norms frame a niche as relevant to only a few).

An eighth tool is *social movement theory* and its concepts. How do movements impact power structure? What are the effects of movements on the policy process? In a policy area, do governmental units act as a patron (resource provider) for a political movement? Do politicians structure policy to encourage (provide political opportunities for) a movement? Do movements create interest groups? Do such groups provide countervailing power to policy elites?

Social movements frame issues; this is fundamental to their activities. Movement frames may be transformed into policy regime norms; for example, the issue frame of sexual harassment is now part of policy regulation and implementation practices. Movements are a major source of policy punctuation. Movements normally oppose policy niches as part of the activity of social mobilization for new social goals, as defined by movement issue frames. Movements are a source of groups in advocacy coalitions; noninstitutional movement tactics may be used in alliance with the institutional lobbying and litigation tactics of a coalition.

A ninth tool is the concept of *policy area punctuation*. Are there sudden changes in policy? What are the sources of such changes? Are the sources exogenous or endogenous to the politics of the policy area? Are they related to new policy frames and to the appearance of political movements? Was a normative regime broken down, perhaps by the actions of an advocacy coalition?

Now let us discuss the application of these conceptual tools to various "sites" of research. In other words, the neopluralist concepts are "carried" to different areas of study. The most general site is the policymaking process, usually as applied to a particular policy. The process plays an unusual role in this study; it is both a tool and a site. This is because it is one of the basic assumptions of political process theory: politics and policy are to be studied in terms of the interactions among various political agents in sequences of related events over time. In other words, the concept of process defines what is to be studied, or the tool defines the sites. This definition of what is to be studied is reinforced by another of the four basic assumptions of political process theory: one political process may differ significantly from other political processes. It follows that there are many significant political processes to study, that is, there are many different sites for the application of political process theory.

The application of models of power to the policy process has been a topic throughout this book. Elitism, pluralism, multiple elitism, neopluralism, statism, and corporatism are understood as models of policymaking, in which *power* refers to the process of realizing goals in the public policymaking arena. Models of power can be applied to specific areas, such as making policy for higher education in Illinois, or to more general ones, such as making policy for higher education within the federal government. They can apply to specific national policies, such as policymaking for each separate agricultural commodity—corn, wheat, soybeans, peanuts, tobacco, oranges, apples, beef, wool, and so forth. The models can apply to high-priority decisions, such as setting interest rates by the Federal Reserve and the banking system, or deciding whether to spend $100 billion for a new supersonic jet fighter.

In comparative politics, one may wish to state a generalization about an entire political system in terms of power structure: pluralist, corporatist, statist (e.g., Japan, France). Or sometimes, one may wish to make similarly general statements about city or community politics (elitist, pluralist, corporatist). In such cases, one is aggregating the most significant policy areas and making a general statement of such areas taken together. I consider this making generalizations at the macrolevel about policy processes. I would categorize it as a generalization from specific policy processes and link the two together for purposes of discussion.

Again, in stating a political process theory of policymaking, I do not intend to imply that this must be the only theory of policymaking. For instance, there are institutional theories of policymaking, such as those that study the development of state institutions (see below). In addition to process and power structure, seven other conceptual tools (advocacy coalition, cooperative pluralism, frame analysis, policy niches, policy regime, social movement theory, policy area punctuation) were discussed previously.

A second site for political process theory is the study of *interest groups*. In effect, a major argument of this book is that advances in the study of interest groups have been the major site for advances in the study of political process theory, at least since 1975. Thus, with Truman's *The Governmental Process* and the group theory of the 1950s, the study of interest groups was identified with the study of the political process (Garson, 1978). From *Who Governs?* in 1961 to the early 1970s, community power studies were the major focus of political process theory (Dahl, 1961b; Polsby, 1980). After this, the focus switched back to interest group theory and the examination of interest groups in the political process, existing and acting contrary to expectations based on the logic of collective action.

The conceptual tools have already been discussed in terms of the study of interest groups. Although this book may not contain revolutionary new ideas about the study of interest groups, I argue that certain types of interest group study are key in the developing, broad theory of the political process. In particular, study of the role of interest groups in issue formation seems to be the next step, going beyond the development of the models of power. I believe that frame analysis would be useful here (Baumgartner and Leech, 2001; Baumgartner, Berry, Hojnacki, Kimball, and Leech, 2000; B. D. Jones, 1994).

As we discover policy niches, more attention needs to be paid to how they are created and maintained and to their overall weight within the political system. At first glance, it seems that the mode of study described as multiple elitism should be applied, but at a more specific level than formerly. Olson's logic of collective action explains why few groups form; Schattschneider's concepts about manipulating the scope of conflict are helpful; the theory of punctuation applies at a more specific level; Gray and Lowery's vision of groups searching for niches in the environment seems to apply. Again, we are not discussing whether there is an iron triangle to build and develop scores of nuclear electric power plants; niches refer to issues such as the production and regulation of cesium (a radioactive element). Policy niches may seem to be of only secondary importance, but if there are a thousand of them, this is an important factor in the study of the political process.

Some attention needs to be paid to the relationship among interest groups and the tools of frame analysis, regime, and punctuation. Perhaps the major effect of interest group activity is their operation and maintenance of regimes applying to particular policy areas, in a fashion parallel to Stone's regimes applying to the politics of an entire city. Interest groups and their lobbyists can be seen as communicating to legitimate favorable issue frames and then institutionalize them, so that we may speak of a policy regime. For instance, electric utilities will try to persuade the public of the advantages of local enforcement of air pollution laws by state governments rather than by the federal government, using the frame of "grassroots control versus federal bureaucracy." As this frame becomes institutionalized, we have a particular relationship between utilities and national and state governments legitimated as a regime. Punctuation applies, because although the regime continues to change only incrementally, some social movement or exogenous event may cause a sudden policy punctuation, perhaps to the extent that the regime no longer exists (e.g., increased control by the federal Environmental Protection Agency). Political process theory would see the study of interest groups as moving in such a direction, generally following such work as *Agendas and Instability in American Politics* (Baumgartner and Jones, 1993).

Interest groups frequently work in coalitions, but these coalitions are usually not the ad hoc coalitions formed to lobby a legislature on a specific issue, nor are they permanent coalitions (with staffs) to lobby a legislature, such as the coalition on disability questions (Shapiro, forthcoming). More attention needs to be paid to the role of interest groups in organizing and maintaining advocacy coalitions that last ten years or more and incorporate government decisionmakers, politicians, friendly media, and academic experts.

A third site for the political process theory is *urban politics and policymaking*. Pluralist theory was intended by Robert Dahl (1961b), Nelson Polsby

(1980), and other researchers to apply to urban politics. Accordingly, models of power can be used to model urban politics, from Dahl's pluralism to later versions of pluralism and even corporatism, if that should be observed in a city. Those who advocate a "growth machine" model of urban policymaking, those who see that city policy is driven by a collaboration of government and developers to increase real estate values, are arguing a type of elitist theory (Logan and Molotch, 1987). However, if we use a neopluralist model and find many seemingly disparate cities to be pluralistic, not controlled by growth machines or power elites, then we need to differentiate types of pluralism. Stone (1989) did this in his regime theory, in which he described Atlanta politics as a relationship among the mayor and the executive branch, big business, and African American groups to use resources to develop the downtown, while distributing benefits within black neighborhoods. Actually, this regime might be characterized as cooperative pluralism or as a type of corporatism.

My impression is that a reading of tens of thousands of pages of studies in urban politics and policymaking would reveal not only extensive discussion of power structure but also considerable discussion of the eight other conceptual tools. However, I am arguing in this book that more focus should be given to the eight tools as they apply to the urban research site. For instance, is it possible that advocacy coalitions are often, or even usually, the basic factor driving policy, as opposed to elections, mayors, and city councils? To what extent is urban politics characterized by cooperation among normally opposed political actors (e.g., advocacy coalitions) because everyone in a city is in the same boat regarding overall economic development, the environment, and policies of the federal government? We might hypothesize that cooperative pluralism is more important at the urban level than at the level of Washington policymaking.

Stone has made the concept of "political regime" a widely used tool for the analysis of city politics. He uses this tool to characterize the overall politics of Atlanta, but specific policy areas (e.g., highway construction) in Atlanta would also embody the political regime. Similarly, we might ask whether normative regimes can be detected not only in other cities but also in specific policy areas within cities, even those without an overall political regime. For instance, a city might have a downtown development regime like Atlanta's but have a decades-old tradition of separate governance of and widespread support for park development in its neighborhoods.

Frame analysis applies to urban politics. Some cities might have long-standing competition among master frames, such as the development issue frame versus the environmental protection frame. For a time in Atlanta and Dallas in the 1950s, the dominant frames were preservation of racial segregation versus conciliation to enhance economic growth. The maintenance of an issue frame over time sometimes produces the long-lasting urban political regime, as the conciliation frame in Atlanta produced the cooperative regime among black politicians and white downtown businesspeople (my interpretation of Stone, 1989).

Niche theory implies a constant tendency to reframe issues at the narrowest level of generality, leading to control by one or a few actors. To what extent does this explain urban politics? To some extent, the traditional urban machine was a niche creator; aldermen or other local officials controlled a limited turf and provided resources to the machine in exchange for control over government benefits and public jobs. Has political reform put an end to the normal process of creating urban policy niches?

Different urban policies affect the local appearances and actions of social movements, as stated in the initial research about political opportunities and social movements (Eisinger, 1973; McAdam, 1982). In turn, social movements lead to the organization and maintenance of urban interest groups (sometimes acting in coalitions). This relationship affects pluralism, issue framing, and the possible construction of political regimes.

More attention can be paid to punctuation in urban policy processes. This can be related to exogenous factors outside of the city, such as national social movements or major economic changes. Or punctuation can be endogenous, as in Dahl's description of how an energetic mayor created a comprehensive urban renewal project (Dahl, 1961b). The dominant hypothesis here is that cities are like national policy areas—policy is usually incremental but can suddenly change in sharp shifts. A major goal is to understand why such shifts occur.

A fourth site for the tools of political process theory is the *study of regulation,* which is linked to models of power. For instance, both economist George Stigler (1975) and political scientists such as Theodore Lowi (1969, 1979) emphasize the tendency of regulated groups to capture the regulatory agency and, along with supportive legislators, to redefine existing regulations and promulgate new ones in the interests of existing businesses in the area being regulated. This is an example of the multiple-elite theory of power. James Q. Wilson (1980) and his associates argue that a balance of power among interest groups is often found, so that public interest groups or competing business groups exercise countervailing power to businesses striving to defeat regulation. In Wilson's view and in my own, this competition among groups provides leeway for governmental agencies to initiate policies on their own, outside of interest group control. Models of power and the study of the policy process are central to the study of regulation (see chapter 4).

The concept of the advocacy coalition was developed from Paul Sabatier's interest in the implementation of environmental regulations (Mazmanian and Sabatier, 1989). We know that government regulations are not always readily implemented according to the intentions of the legislature. In many policy areas, such as environmental policy, an advocacy coalition must act to back up the enforcement of regulations; otherwise, regulated producer groups will exercise power to block enforcement. This is much the same point as stating that countervailing power (see chapter 4) is necessary to have governmental agency autonomy, although the advocacy coalition concept emphasizes that the countervailing coalition is broad, probably including governmental agencies, and long-lasting.

I wrote about cooperative pluralism after studying interest group behavior in the areas of strip-mining and air pollution regulations (McFarland, 1993). One might investigate the prospect that interest groups, battling one another on some regulations, might find a way to cooperate in supporting other regulations, thereby making the policy process more effective.

The other tools applied to regulation call forth an interesting hypothesis. Bureaucracy may not expand, acting in a centralized fashion, as seems implicit in the Weberian tradition. Instead, niche-seeking behavior constantly fragments bureaucracy, implying a need to enhance centralizing tendencies for democratic control (see chapter 4; B. D. Jones, 1994). The hypothesis is that, at the federal level, perhaps 2,000 separate groups are constantly acting to isolate policy into "micro islands" in which a few or even just one group participates in policymaking. In most cases, niche behavior is accompanied by issue framing, such as the master frame that "the federal government cannot understand and regulate specific technical and local activities." Anti-regulation regimes develop as such issue frames remain accepted for a decade or more. The mechanisms of the reform cycle and punctuation come into play as the niche-controlling elite overplays its hand, leading to outrageous subsidies exposed by the media or to scandals, such as radiation leaking into the environment. Regulation is thus about framing, regulatory regimes, niche behavior, and punctuation (see chapters 4 and 8).

A fifth application of the conceptual tools is to the *study of policy implementation*. Will laws be implemented as Congress intended? In some instances, is it even possible to implement the legislative intention? Following the numerous problems in implementing President Johnson's Great Society program, including its urban policy aspects, policy implementation studies were current in public administration. But my impression is that by the late 1980s, scholars were largely finished developing the framework of implementation theory (Pressman and Wildavsky, 1973; Peterson, Rabe, and Wong, 1986; Mazmanian and Sabatier, 1989). Regulatory policy overlaps a great deal with policy implementation, so the previous section about regulation applies to implementation. Thus, again, a supportive advocacy coalition is usually necessary for policy to be implemented in the way intended by the legislature. Effective implementation can be destroyed by the niche behavior of interest groups reframing an issue. Again, intervention from a higher level of government may be necessary to advance effective implementation if a policy has been fragmented into a number of action niches.

Effective implementation is sometimes a matter of perception. The successful construction of a river dam is effective implementation to some, but to others it is not effective unless extensive environmental controls and compensatory policies are instituted. Implementation is thus tied to issue framing, being effective according to one frame and not effective according to another. Policy evaluation and implementation are thus linked to the framing strategies of the political participants. It is easier to implement simple policies that are technical in nature (build a dam) and harder to implement more complex policies (provide compensatory water flows, maintain fish migration patterns). One oppositional strategy is to work to complicate a policy and delay its implementation, making effective implementation difficult and costly, which leads to the collapse of the whole endeavor. This can be done through the strategic introduction of new frames, making issue definition very complex, and through normal niche politics, as different groups seek to carve out their own turf.

A strategy of complex framing and delay is a rational use of scarce resources for environmentalists, other public interest lobbyists, and sometimes for local governments seeking to block new public works or other public action. Accordingly, there may be a need for the public to compensate by encouraging cooperative pluralist practices, such as exchanges in which the blocking group is granted benefits (such as side payments) in return for limiting the complex framing and delay tactics (McFarland, 1993).

Political movements must have some impact on policy implementation to be effective, unless their goal is to revolutionize the political system. In light of the reform cycle and the theory of policy punctuation, political movements need to spin off interest groups to energize advocacy coalitions to provide policy backup for the implementation of movement policy goals.

A sixth site for the application of political process tools is the *study of federalism*. Various levels of governmental agencies simultaneously participate in federalist policy processes. Such processes might be described as pluralist, captured by a coalition, neopluralist, cooperative pluralist, corporatist, or statist. Federalism is not simply a system of rules coordinating the levels of government; it is also a policy process. And as such, political process theory applies to federalism.

Federalism enhances the need to use the idea of an advocacy coalition. Within a policy process, one frequently observes national, state, and local governmental agencies acting together in a coalition, probably with other actors too. For instance, to deal with a polluted river, the federal Environmental Protection Agency may work with one or more state environmental agencies and with one or more county or urban environmental units; at the same time, the National Park Service may be involved, together with state and local park units, and so forth. Environmental interest groups and various politicians may be part of such an advocacy coalition, whereas defenders of dams, such as electric utilities and the national Bureau of Reclamation, may be part of the countercoalition. Understanding advocacy coalitions is at the center of understanding processes of federalism.

The idea of advocacy coalitions is related to the idea that units at different levels of government have different patterns of cooperation, according to the self-definitions of interest by such units. As Peterson, Rabe, and Wong (1986, 12–15) pointed out, one should not always assume political conflict when studying federalism. Some Department of Education and federal economic development grants and programs for cities did not have opponents, at least when analyzed on an individual basis. Interest groups or advocacy coalitions supporting such consensual grants would be in a position to establish a policy niche within the federalist system.

Other conceptual tools point to the idea of strategic maneuvering within federalist processes, a type of maneuvering that overlaps with my earlier observations about other sites for the use of theory. Policy participants seek to frame issues to use federalist processes to their advantage, looking to emphasize decision-making at the level of federalism favorable to themselves. The most famous example, of course, was the history-making struggle to take civil rights policy out of state and local hands and put it into national hands. This is just the most prominent of numerous strategic processes within federalism: insurance companies have worked for a century to be regulated by state governments; coal companies wanted state administration of the federal strip-mining laws; automobile companies prefer that California's authority to regulate emissions be limited by the national government, because historically, California regulates more strictly; and so forth (Orren, 1974; McFarland, 1993).

Strategic manipulation in federalism brings in observations about regulation, implementation, urban policy, and niche politics. Policy actors will seek to create and control a policy niche to limit regulation and implementation contrary to their own goals. They may seek to fragment the regulation and implementation process so that it is controlled by scores of different state and local governments. For this, the master frame of "local government is better," "government at the grass roots," or "participatory democracy" is commonly applied (McConnell, 1966). Unfortunately, the political theorists of democracy have not dealt with the problem that niche-seeking behavior is a basic trend in modern, complex political processes and that participatory theories of democracy are used as frames to further the existence of unrepresentative policy niches.

Of course, the reform cycle and policy punctuation work within federalism, such as in countering the tendency toward niche-seeking behavior. Political movements in the United States often work to force an issue to be considered at the national level, as in the case of the civil rights movement or environmentalism. Countermovements work to keep issues at the local level, such as trying civil rights or environmental cases in local courts. But this is not to say that movements for political change do not seek to change policies at the state and local levels. The Prohibition movement started with the states and eventually became a constitutional amendment. The gay rights movement gets little support in Congress, so it works predominantly to change local and state policies.

A common tendency in the political process, then, is for interest groups to be engaged in niche-seeking behavior, framing issues accordingly to limit the effects of regulation and policy implementation. The niche seekers eventually may be challenged by a social movement and by an advocacy coalition (including movement supporters), and important instances of policy punctuation occur when the anti-niche coalition reframes the issue and obtains new national legislation and establishes a new institution for regulation and implementation (Baumgartner and Jones, 1993; B. D. Jones, 1994).

A seventh site for the application of political process tools is *planning by governmental agencies*. This topic was already considered in chapter 7, where I argued that opposed interests may seek out their joint interests, which provides a political basis for planning in the pluralist state. Other models of power can provide perspectives on the political basis of planning, such as an alliance among a nationally organized political party, business association, and single labor federation as a basis for planning under corporatism. Based on pluralist theory, Aaron Wildavsky (1979) contended that the effectiveness of planning is limited because policy processes are too complex and unpredictable, making it unlikely that planners can predict future events and the interactions of political agents with such events. Charles Lindblom (1965, 1977) apparently concluded that constructing economic plans for a nation could be good for the economy and could promote economic equality, but that the plan should operate as an incremental process, as a frame for defining issues, regulations, and implementation processes. But according to Lindblom, sudden changes in policy under a plan would yield consequences too complicated to predict.

Obviously, a plan states a frame for action. Planning is framing issues. Planning sets priorities for government action. A successful plan establishes norms of behavior; it sets up a policy regime. (Of course, as in Stone's Atlanta, regimes can exist without being planned.) For instance, as noted in chapter 7, Illinois' plan for higher education established norms: the coordinating board usually adopts measures unanimously, after lengthy staff work; governors and legislators are reluctant to institute higher education measures that have not been approved by the coordinating board. Some political scientists may take the view that plans are political and thus need not be studied, because politics is the important thing. Of course, plans are political, but we need to see them as frameworks for issue definition and for a political process; in addition, plans may be linked to advocacy coalitions, supporting or opposing a plan, and to the functioning of a policy regime.

A plan is a means to oppose niche behavior. In the higher education field, for instance, we can hypothesize that every college and every department seeks to make itself into a niche, defined as controlling its own budget without influence from any outside agency. At times, niche behavior may constructively manifest expertise, but at other times, it may tend toward behavior that is not widely supported outside of the niche. A plan is a means to set forth criteria and to legitimate policy norms to control niche behavior.

An eighth research site for the application of political process theory is *American political development studies*. Although historical studies of American politics have always been part of the discipline, a self-conscious group of political scientists, styling its research as American political development, formed around 1980. The first mark of such studies was the application of ideas about the state to American government, producing a research interest in the development of the American state. In particular, this meant research to understand the continuity of state institutions: sets of organizational practices and rules, associated professional beliefs, and continuous and consistent application of laws and rules by state organizations (see the journal *American Political Development;* see also, e.g., Berk, 1994; Orren and Skowronek, 1994; Sparrow, 1995). The pathbreaking work in the field by Stephen Skowronek (1982) was entitled *Building a New American State: The Expansion of National Administrative Capacities, 1877–1920,* and it treated such issues as the development of the national civil service, the profession of forestry in service to the state, the development of a central professional military staff, and the beginnings of the Interstate Commerce Commission.

At first, it seemed as if such studies were directly opposed to the political process interpretation of public policy. It seemed that the spirit of American political development research was based on the idea that too much attention had been paid to the effects of interest groups and politicians interacting in political processes to influence public policy. For instance, Stephen D. Krasner's *Defending the National Interest: Raw Materials Investment and U.S. Foreign Policy* (1978) cogently demonstrated that although many had blithely assumed that oil companies controlled U.S. policy regarding the foreign nationalization of energy properties, it was actually the professional bureaucracy of the U.S. State Department that had the controlling influence. In other words, a state institution had the most power in deciding whether to use force or the threat of force to stop the nationalization of American oil and gas properties. Such research indicates that the political process theory of politics must incorporate the activities of state institutions as part of the policy process to be analyzed, recognizing that state institutions often have considerable autonomy from group pressure. However, as demonstrated in chapter 4, the neopluralist version of political process theory accepts state institutions as important actors within the policy process.

American political development studies are particularly interesting with regard to policy process theory, in that the institutional studies are likely very complimentary of the process theory. An important hypothesis is that new state institutions cannot retain an important degree of autonomy unless they are supported within the political process. This is demonstrated in chapter 4, in the argument that countervailing power groups must balance the influence of producer groups to gain agency autonomy, that is, to prevent the development of a subgovernment. The national Interstate Commerce Commission (ICC) did not gain sufficient support within the political process to act as an autonomous state institution, effectively regulating the railroads; instead, the ICC became captured by the railroads. In contrast, the Forest Service acquired support from conservationists, some hunters, and recreational interests in the first fifty years of the twentieth century, so that it was seen as having considerable administrative capacity, marked by the enforcement of rules developed by professional foresters (Kaufman, 1960). The hypothesis is that countervailing power is necessary for the stability of a new institution in American political development.

The operations of punctuated equilibrium in the policy process, as described by Baumgartner and Jones (1993) and outlined in chapter 4, are linked to the development of new political institutions. Unlike the pessimistic image of the reform cycle (see chapters 4 and 6), in punctuated equilibrium, policy shifts to a different plane. Policy is not recaptured by formerly dominant interests because of the development of new state institutions and the support of professionals working within those institutions. Increased public attention and a new issue frame lead to a redefinition of policy, new laws, and new institutions.

Political process theory hypothesizes that the new institutions developed in punctuated equilibrium must receive the support of additional countervailing power if they are to survive as autonomous. Without the development of such countervailing force, it is hypothesized that producer interests will recapture the policy after public participation in that policy area wanes due to decreasing public attention. Whether this actually happens, and under what conditions, is a matter for empirical research. But in any case, political process theory links the theoretical tool of punctuated equilibrium to the understanding of American political development.

THE FUTURE EVOLUTION OF POLITICAL PROCESS THEORY

What will political process theory look like one or two decades hence? Obviously, I cannot be too specific about this. The preceding text reflects the base of political process theory in the study of American politics. But it seems possible that this somewhat parochial quality will lessen, especially as political process theory is applied to sectors of international relations. Both political process theory and international relations theory evolved the concept of political regime, apparently independently of each other (Krasner, 1983; Stone, 1989; Bole, 1995). International relations scholarship is not limited to national security issues but extends to what I call "international policy processes." These seem to be more numerous and significant with the increase of globalization, as international interest groups and multilateral corporations attempt to lobby national states and international organizations. For instance, there is a human rights policy process involving national governments, sectors of the United Nations, the new international criminal court, Amnesty International, and local within-country groups and social movements, with protest groups, state officials, and international officials banding together in advocacy coalitions (comparable to the international anti-apartheid coalition; Klotz, 1995).

Process theory is built on the four categories of process, power as causation, separability of issue areas, and subjective definition of interest. These assumptions are not limited to the study of American politics but can help gain an understanding of the policy process elsewhere (e.g., environmental policy in Japan). With observations based on the four assumptions, the scholar can gain some initial understanding of what happens in a policymaking process in some other country. Probably most of the tools will be useful elsewhere, but some of them may not be applicable, and political culture and different institutions may indicate that new tools will be useful. The scholar's initial knowledge will have implications for the use of sites; for example, federalism will not be useful in unitary states, and decision-making processes among military officers is a policymaking site in Turkey and other nations. But in general, I expect that political process theory will evolve so that it frequently refers to comparative politics studies and to international relations policies.

The applicability of political process theory to comparative politics shows us something about the role of theorizing in the social sciences. On the one hand, the role of theory is to interpret and simplify the complexities of observed phenomena. The process example is that the theory starts with four relatively simple assumptions: process, power as causation, separability of issue areas, and subjective definition of interest. On the other hand, there are seventy-two categories for the process theory if we combine each of the nine tools with each of the eight sites. This is a complex theoretical activity.

Useful theory may be both simple and complex. It evolves from the simple to the complex. As relatively simple assumptions are applied to interpret, explain, and predict various forms of activity, new generalizations and concepts are formed to understand different types of activity. The new generalizations and concepts replace, modify, and subsume those developed earlier. The process of theorizing is cumulative. It produces a relatively complex network of generalizations and concepts that can be traced back to relatively simple assumptions.

TOWARD A PROCESS THEORY OF POLITICS

Political theorists might now consider whether the array of models of power applied to many types of political processes can be further generalized. One need for generalization is indicated by the use of the term *pluralism* or *neopluralism* to describe the politics of a whole country. *Pluralism* is clear in indicating that a country is not corporatist, statist, an authoritarian dictatorship, totalitarian, and so forth. But this leaves the United States, Canada, Britain, Italy, India, and South Africa in the same category. As corporatist politics is distinguished, one might refer to a distinction between "market pluralism" and "social democratic pluralism" (Katzenstein, 1985). Another distinction might be based on institutions to deal with ethnic or religious conflict, such as Lijphart's (1969) category of consociationism, in which leaders of segmented ethnic or religious communities negotiate questions of representation and major government policy. In any event, Dahl's basic concept that pluralism is defined in the analysis of separate issue areas prevents useful generalization to an entire country, a problem for the developing theory of pluralism and process.

A basis for generalizing pluralist process theory can be seen in portions of this book. First, we see that four major criticisms of pluralism are not devastating but are limited in nature and actually contribute to the continuing development of pluralist theory. There is nothing in pluralist theory that prevents consideration of governmental units as an autonomous variable in politics. Pluralist theory does not have to suppose that all interests are mobilized into a fair balance of power within the political process, although it is incumbent on pluralist theory to explain why groups exist in spite of Olson's logic of collective action. Pluralist theorists must admit that their theory has its bounds in application, and that pluralist theory is limited in its treatment of hegemony and nonissues. Nevertheless, at least six approaches for dealing with these questions have been developed. Although pluralists avoid putting forth radical constructs about what actors should want, even if the actors are not conscious of such wants, pluralists are by no means bound to support the social status quo. For example, neopluralist theory points the way to a friendly attitude toward social movements and to constructing new interest groups to represent widely dispersed interests, which are difficult to organize due to the logic of collective action.

The historical chapter demonstrates that a pluralist process analysis can acquire historical depth, as in trying to generalize about a century of politics in issue areas. One need not agree with that particular analysis to see that pluralist theory asks questions about how politics in some issue area proceeds from one model of power to another, whether there are cycles in such dynamics, and whether the dynamics of one policy area might spill over into other areas. In addition to elitist control giving way to neopluralist control, which then cycles back to elitist control, one can postulate an array of other models, such as cooperative pluralism changing into neopluralism (competition, no cooperation) and then back again, and so forth.

We have seen that pluralist and process theories are bounded by theories relying on concepts of stratification or hegemony. Most social scientists concluded after the extensive community power debate of the 1960s and 1970s that pluralists and stratificationists were talking past each other. They were using different theories and considered different issues to be important. Pluralists convinced most political scientists that pluralism was a better theory to explain political processes in the local community. But pluralists did not try to answer the question of whether the social stratification of wealth and prestige enhanced the norms of capitalist hegemony, limiting the goals sought by non-elite groups. Other social scientists may consider such questions to be more important than the study of political process and models of power. In this sense, process theories and hegemony theories may be said to be different theoretical paradigms, here meaning two theoretical projects with very different concepts, research procedures, and definitions of significant questions. Unlike the picture of theory in Thomas Kuhn's *The Structure of Scientific Revolution* (1962), however, these two paradigms continue to exist side by side, and one is unlikely to replace the other.

One might assume one type of theory of society that purports to explain the distribution of resources of wealth and prestige and also tries to explain why certain interpretations of the nature of society have gained hegemony. Such a stratification-hegemony theory leaves room for another type of theory focusing on the development and operation of political-legal institutions. There are basically two types of institutional theories. One focuses on the development of legal and political institutions, such as the evolution of the state in European and other societies (Nordlinger, 1981; Skowronek, 1982; Evans, Rueschemeyer, and Skocpol, 1985; Orren and Skowronek, 1994). A second type of institutional theory is that proceeding from rational choice assumptions, focusing on how the nature of decision-making rules and other laws affect politics and political outcomes (Riker, 1982). The goal of the rational choice theoretical project is usually assumed to be the compilation of a general theory of political institutions, comparable to the work of economists in dealing with economic activity.

But given a system of resource stratification and cultural hegemony, and given both a historical and a rational choice theory of institutions, there remains leeway for asking questions about the political process acting within such frameworks. Individuals and political organizations are in continual interaction in a policy area, and such individuals and organizations are affecting one another's behavior after laws are passed, votes are taken, and executive orders are issued, and the process of interaction may completely alter the nature of the original institutional action. Similarly, through both everyday behavior and social movements, persons may be probing the limits of cultural hegemony over politics; they may be questioning existing political institutions and, in fact, may be acting outside such institutions with the aim of changing them. Such social movement activity and cultural challenges are readily linked to the flow of policy processes, and as is demonstrated in this book, theory about them is linked to political process theory.

If a more general process theory were developed, it would likely deal with certain theoretical questions. Such a theory would likely emphasize observations about political learning. Given pluralist theory's assumptions about process and about taking seriously the self-definition of actors' goals, and given the nature of the partisan mutual adjustment model, pluralist theory emphasizes that the behavior of the persons and organizations within an interactive process leads to changes in the goals of those concerned, and such changing definitions of goals and the interactive situation constitute a form of political learning. Other paradigms take goals as assumptions (rational choice theory) or look at sweeping changes in goals over long periods. The political process theory, in contrast, might answer the questions of those who are more interested in short-term political learning within political bargaining and negotiation processes.

A general process theory might be especially able to link institutional politics to social movement politics. Again, one may be interested in the short-term effects of social movements rather than century-long historical processes. Although resource mobilization scholars and the synthesizer Mark Lichbach (1995) have applied rational choice principles to social movements, many suspect that these movements, which are not well described by the logic of collective action, are best described as processes of action that definitely deny the value of containing themselves within existing institutions. However, the links among activities within institutional political processes and social movements might be described in a generalized neopluralist theory.

This theory could be linked to democratic theory. So far, pluralist theory has dealt with the issue of multiple elitism, that is, the tendency for democratic society to fragment into policy areas controlled by unrepresentative political coalitions. The neopluralist model of power provides an answer to this theoretical problem. A more generalized theory might take other such problems of democratic theory and contribute to the analysis of these problems.

The general process theory need not prove itself to be the best political theory, say, in contrast to institutional and hegemonic theories. But the new, general theory might be better at dealing with certain political and social situations than the institutional and hegemonic theories, thus proving its usefulness.

A RESEARCH SEQUENCE, NOT A REVOLUTION

Here, let us outline some lessons about the sociology and philosophy of developing theory and research in political science. Let us summarize the types of theories that exist in the area of the study of power, political process, and public policy.

In the reconsideration of pluralist theory, we have seen that the theory has proceeded in a sequence of four stages. Fist, there was a theory of political process, emphasizing interest groups, as exemplified by Bentley and Truman. Second was the development of the pluralist theory of power in issue areas and communities, as set forth by Dahl. Third came the multiple-elite theory, reinterpreting Dahl's work to assert that the fragmentation of power was a case of the few defeating the many in numerous important issue areas, as implied by Olson and Lowi. The fourth theory was the neopluralist synthesis, incorporating an expanded view of the formation and maintenance of interest groups, and recognizing the frequent autonomous action of state agencies.

Two other theories stand out as useful for the analysis of power, process, and public policy: statism and corporatism. Along with pluralism and multiple elitism, statism and corporatism might be termed "schools" in the study of political power. Schools of research may compete to explain the same phenomena, each with its favorite model. However, such schools can communicate with one another about theoretical issues and research procedures; one school may occasionally accept another's research as accurate and borrow from it, incorporating the results from another school into its own. In this sense, the neopluralists accept that multiple-elite interpretations are sometimes accurate, although the neopluralists see their own model as more frequently useful. Similarly, neopluralists agree that state agencies often have autonomy in the political process, although neopluralists pay more attention to a balance of power among groups causing state autonomy than do statist theorists. Neopluralists see nothing wrong with corporatism, if the evidence backs this model, although such evidence seems to pertain more to certain European countries than to the United States. Nevertheless, neopluralists might frequently observe an admixture of corporatism and pluralism in certain issue areas and at the local level of government.

In addition to the four stages of pluralist theory and to the idea of schools of research, I have referred to paradigms of theory, evoking Thomas Kuhn's landmark work *The Structure of Scientific Revolution*. My examples of paradigms for the study of power and public policy were stratification-hegemony theory, rational choice institutionalism, and historical institutionalism. This denotation of paradigms is based on the idea of a statement of a general social theory that posits certain questions as important to study, has certain basic concepts that its scholars seldom abandon, and implies a number of research procedures for scholarship. Unlike scholars within "schools," adherents to different paradigms are not likely to communicate well, do not use concepts from an opposing paradigm, and do not borrow research procedures from that paradigm. For instance, the process theorists are limited in their treatment of ideas of hegemony, which are central to neo-Marxists and others who argue that the stratification of resources is the basic variable in studying public policy outcomes. Conversely, hegemony theorists have little to say about the interactions of politicians, state agencies, interest groups, and social movements in a public policy process.

I argue that, in viewing pluralist theory, many political scientists have made a "Kuhnian mistake," while not implying that Kuhn himself would have done so. An oddity of the development of the pluralist research sequence is that its second stage, Dahl's theory of power, achieved sudden and widespread success in the study of American politics. During the 1960s, second-stage pluralism's success was so great as to tempt one to speak of a "new orthodoxy" or the "paradigm" for the study of American politics. Then, as rapidly as Dahl's views had been accepted, that acceptance collapsed, largely due to the four criticisms mentioned earlier. During the 1970s, students of American politics were likely to accept Lowi's critique of second-stage pluralism. This led to a Kuhnian mistake, in that second-stage pluralism was thought to be a paradigm in Kuhn's sense, a theory with concepts and research procedures to be completely overturned in a scientific revolution. But pluralism was not a general paradigm (which would be a general theory of political process); instead, it was a school of analysis working from certain models and research procedures, one that was still evolving with some rapidity.

For fifteen years, this misapprehension of pluralist theory did not have major ill effects. Researchers in the fields of public policy, regulation, and interest groups pushed forth the pluralist model to the third and fourth stages. The theory became less oriented to models of power and more oriented to studying the interactions of different types of actors (including government) within policy processes. But since 1985, theoretical development in this area has, in my view, slowed down because we have not understood how pluralism developed into political process theory.

This theory problem is not due to the unavailability of good research in the study of interest groups and of policymaking, such as the research about punctuation, advocacy coalitions, policy niches, and political regimes (see chapters 4 and 7). But except for aspects of punctuation theory, such research has been tied to rather particular fields. Advocacy coalitions are perceived as research findings about implementation; policy niches are a new conclusion in interest group theory; political regimes are the basis for the theory in urban politics that opposes the "city limits" theory (even though political regimes have also been a major theory in international relations). Policy punctuation, in contrast, has achieved widespread recognition because it is perceived as a theory encompassing Lindblom's instrumentalism and extending it.

This demonstrates the talent of the major pluralist writers Dahl and Lindblom. *Who Governs?* was not defined as a work about urban politics; it was defined as a contribution to the theory of power and also to the theory of democracy. Lindblom's work was defined as a general theory of policy processes in the context of democratic governance. The pluralists established a broad theoretical stage for their work, and their students and their critics, in their own ways, stepped onto this broad stage and were not confined to a sideshow unseen by most persons, regardless of the skill of the performers. After the emergence of neopluralism and the acceptance of corporatist and statist theories by 1985–1990, it seems that the curtain has been brought down on the broad stage of pluralism. There is no longer a "big tent" for the side players to go to. (The major exception to this confined definition of research is the Baumgartner and Jones theory of punctuation and issue development, which steps onto the pluralist stage constructed by Lindblom in his theory of incrementalism.)

One loss has been that researchers in many of the areas specified in this chapter (urban politics, federalism, planning, implementation, and so forth) lack a perspective on developing pluralist and process theories. Researchers in these other areas should have a bundle of theories and concepts immediately available for consideration in conducting research, the various theories of power and types of hypotheses examined in this book. But because of the widespread misapprehension of pluralist theory, such researchers do not have a clear sense of neopluralism and its concepts for the study of political process. No one in the discipline produced a major compendium of applications of neopluralism, analogous to David Truman's *The Governmental Process,* because no one recognized the usefulness of such a project. And even if someone had developed this idea, such a project would not have had great prestige within the discipline of political science.

Looking beyond neopluralism, extending it to historical analysis, and inspecting its boundaries, one can see the possibility of an important new paradigm developing, one concentrating on explaining the policy process and complementing theories based on institutions or on hegemony and stratification. But one is unlikely to share this perspective if one thinks that Dahl's theory of power and political process was overturned in a scientific mini-revolution, since the evolution of a theory of political process is the basis for the idea of its further generalization into a paradigm.

Political scientists and other academicians might think more highly of political science as a field if the discipline were not presented as a sort of Kuhnian carnival in which, every now and then, a new so-called paradigm is rolled out onto the shooting gallery, serving as a target for revolutionary sharpshooters until it is shot full of holes and a new theoretical target is put up in its place. When the paradigm is removed, there may be jeers and catcalls from some members of the audience, but in one respect, Kuhn is correct—most members of the audience have already strolled down the midway to participate in some other spectacle.

In reconsidering pluralism, we see that Dahl's theory was the second stage in a four-stage research sequence. It was not replaced, but evolved into something different. If properly understood, the fourth stage, neopluralism, is a considerable theoretical accomplishment. One need not accept the Victorian idea of the steady march of scientific progress; competing paradigms exist in the discipline, and such paradigms will coexist and compete for many decades in the future. Yet within such paradigms, there is likely to be steady progress in gaining knowledge through the development of particular research sequences (Laudan, 1984).

References

Ackerman, Bruce, and William T. Hassler. 1981. *Clean Coal/Dirty Air.* New Haven, Conn.: Yale University Press.
Adorno, Theodore W., Else Frenkel-Brunswik, Daniel J. Levinson, and Sanford R. Nevitt. 1950. *The Authoritarian Personality.* New York: Harper and Row.
Ainsworth, Scott. 1993. "Regulating Lobbyists and Interest Group Influence." *Journal of Politics* 55:41–56.
Almond, Gabriel A. 1988. "The Return to the State." *American Political Science Review* 82:853–74.
Austen-Smith, David, and John R. Wright. 1994. "Counteractive Lobbying." *American Journal of Political Science* 38:25–44.
Bachrach, Peter. 1967. *The Theory of Democratic Elitism: A Critique.* Boston: Little, Brown.
Bachrach, Peter, and Morton Baratz. 1962. "Two Faces of Power." *American Political Science Review* 56(December):947–52.
———. 1970. *Power and Poverty.* New York: Oxford University Press.
Balbus, Isaac D. 1971. "The Concept of Interest in Pluralist and Marxian Analysis." *Politics and Society* 1:151–78.
Banfield, Edward C. 1961. *Political Influence: A New Theory of Urban Politics.* New York: Free Press.
Barber, Benjamin. 1984. *Strong Democracy.* Berkeley: University of California Press.
Bauer, Raymond A., Ithiel de Sola Pool, and Lewis Anthony Dexter. 1963. *American Business and Public Policy.* New York: Atherton Press.
Baumgartner, Frank R., Jeffrey M. Berry, Marie Hojnacki, David C. Kimball, and Beth L. Leech. 2000. "Advocacy and Policy Argumentation." Paper presented at the annual meeting of the American Political Science Association, Washington, D.C., August 31–September 3.
Baumgartner, Frank R., and Bryan D. Jones. 1993. *Agendas and Instability in American Politics.* Chicago: University of Chicago Press.
———, eds. 2002. *Policy Dynamics.* Chicago: University of Chicago Press.
Baumgartner, Frank R., and Leech, Beth L. 1996. "The Multiple Ambiguities of 'Counteractive Lobbying.'" *American Journal of Political Science* 40:521–42.
———. 1998. *Basic Interests: The Importance of Groups in Politics and in Political Science.* Princeton, N.J.: Princeton University Press.
———. 2000. "Lobbying Alone or in a Crowd: The Distribution of Lobbying in a Sample of Issues." Paper presented at the annual meeting of the Midwest Political Science Association, Chicago, April 27–29.

———. 2001. "Interest Niches and Policy Bandwagons: Patterns of Interest Group Involvement in National Politics." *Journal of Politics* 63:1191–213.
Becker, Gary S. 1985. "Public Policies, Pressure Groups, and Dead Weight Costs." *Journal of Public Economics* 28:330–47.
Beer, Samuel H. 1976. "The Adoption of General Revenue Sharing: A Case Study in Public Sector Politics." *Public Policy* 24:127–95.
Benford, Robert D., and David A. Snow. 2000. "Framing Processes and Social Movements: An Overview and Assessment." *Annual Review of Sociology* 26:611–39.
Bentley, Arthur F. 1908/1967. *The Process of Government*. Chicago: University of Chicago Press. Reprint, Cambridge, Mass.: Belknap Press of Harvard University Press.
Berk, Gerald. 1994. *Alternative Tracks: The Constitution of American Industrial Order, 1865–1917*. Baltimore: Johns Hopkins University Press.
Bernstein, Marver. 1955. *Regulating Business by Independent Commission*. Princeton, N.J.: Princeton University Press.
Berry, Jeffrey M. 1977. *Lobbying for the People*. Princeton, N.J.: Princeton University Press.
———. 1978. "On the Origins of Public Interest Groups: A Test of Two Theories." *Polity* 10:379–97.
———. 1985. *Feeding Hungry People: Rulemaking in the Food Stamp Program*. New Brunswick, N.J.: Rutgers University Press.
———. 1989a. *The Interest Group Society*. 2d ed. Glenview, Ill.: Scott Foresman/Little, Brown.
———. 1989b. "Subgovernments, Issue Networks, and Political Conflict." In Richard A. Harris and Sidney M. Milkis, eds., *Remaking American Politics*. Boulder, Colo.: Westview Press.
———. 1999. *The New Liberalism: The Rising Power of Citizen Groups*. Washington, D.C.: Brookings Institution.
Bole, Shama. 1995. "Regime Theory in Political Science: Case Studies in Linkage." Ph.D. dissertation, University of Illinois at Chicago.
Boorstin, Daniel J. 1953. *The Genius of American Politics*. Chicago: University of Chicago Press.
Bosso, Christopher. 1987. *Pesticides and Politics*. Pittsburgh: University of Pittsburgh Press.
Braybrooke, David, and Charles E. Lindblom. 1963. *A Strategy of Decision*. New York: Free Press.
Browne, William P. 1988. *Private Interests, Public Policy, and American Agriculture*. Lawrence: University Press of Kansas.
———. 1990. "Organized Interests and Their Issue Niches: A Search for Pluralism in a Policy Domain." *Journal of Politics* 52:477–509.
———. 1995. *Cultivating Congress: Constituents, Issues, and Interests in Agricultural Policymaking*. Lawrence: University Press of Kansas.
Burnham, Walter Dean. 1967. "Party Systems and the Electoral Process." In William N. Chambers and Walter Dean Burnham, eds., *The American Party Systems: Stages of Political Development*. New York: Oxford University Press.
———. 1970. *Critical Elections and the Mainsprings of American Politics*. New York: Norton.
Burstein, Paul. 1998. "Interest Organizations, Political Parties, and the Study of Demo-

cratic Politics." In Anne N. Costain and Andrew S. McFarland, eds., *Social Movements and American Political Institutions*. Lanham, Md.: Rowman and Littlefield.
Campbell, Angus, Phillip E. Converse, Warren E. Miller, and Donald E. Stokes. 1960. *The American Voter.* New York: Wiley.
Carsey, Thomas M. 2000. *Campaign Dynamics: The Race for Governor.* Ann Arbor: University of Michigan Press.
Cater, Douglas. 1964. *Power in Washington.* New York: Random House.
Clarke, Jeanne Nienaber, and Daniel McCool. 1985. *Staking Out the Terrain.* Albany, N.Y.: SUNY Press.
Clavel, Pierre. 1986. *The Progressive City: Planning and Participation, 1969–1984.* New Brunswick, N.J.: Rutgers University Press.
Coase, R. H. 1960. "The Problem of Social Cost." *Journal of Law and Economics* 3(October):1–44.
Cobb, Roger W., and Charles D. Elder. 1972. *Participation in American Politics.* Baltimore: Johns Hopkins University Press.
Cohen, Michael, James G. March, and Johan Olsen. 1972. "A Garbage Can Model of Organizational Choice." *Administrative Science Quarterly* 17(March):1–25.
Cook, Constance E. 1998. *Lobbying for Higher Education: How Colleges and Universities Influence Federal Policy.* Nashville: Vanderbilt University Press.
Costain, Anne N. 1992. *Inviting Women's Rebellion: A Political Process Interpretation of the Women's Movement.* Baltimore: Johns Hopkins University Press.
Costain, Anne N., and W. Douglas Costain. 1983. "The Women's Lobby: Impact of a Movement on Congress." In Allan J. Cigler and Burdett A. Loomis, eds., *Interest Group Politics*, 1st ed. Washington, D.C.: Congressional Quarterly Press.
Costain, Anne N., and Andrew S. McFarland, eds. 1998. *Social Movements and American Political Institutions.* Lanham, Md.: Rowman and Littlefield.
Crenson, Matthew A. 1971. *The Un-Politics of Air Pollution: A Study of Non-Decisionmaking in the Cities.* Baltimore: Johns Hopkins University Press.
Culhane, Paul J. 1981. *Public Lands Politics.* Baltimore: Johns Hopkins University Press.
Dahl, Robert A. 1956. *Preface to Democratic Theory.* Chicago: University of Chicago Press.
———. 1957. "The Concept of Power." *Behavioral Science* 2(June):201–15.
———. 1958. "A Critique of the Ruling Elite Model." *American Political Science Review* 52(June):463–69.
———. 1961a. "The Behavioral Approach in Political Science: Epitaph for a Monument to a Successful Protest." *American Political Science Review* 55:763–72.
———. 1961b. *Who Governs?* New Haven, Conn.: Yale University Press.
———. 1968. "Power." In *International Encyclopedia of Social Sciences*, vol. 12. New York: Macmillan and Free Press.
———. 1970. *After the Revolution? Authority in a Good Society.* New Haven, Conn.: Yale University Press.
———. 1971. *Polyarchy: Participation and Opposition.* New Haven, Conn.: Yale University Press.
———. 1972. *Democracy in the United States: Promise and Performance,* 2nd ed. Chicago: Rand McNally.
Davis, Charles, and Sandra Davis. 1986. "Analyzing the Public Lands Subsystem."

Paper presented at the annual meeting of the American Political Science Association, Washington, D.C., August 28–31.
Davis, Otto A., M. A. H. Dempster, and Aaron Wildavsky. 1966. "A Theory of the Budgetary Process." *American Political Science Review* 60:529–47.
Derthick, Martha, and Paul J. Quirk. 1985. *The Politics of Deregulation.* Washington, D.C.: Brookings Institution.
Downs, Anthony. 1957. *An EconomicTheory of Democracy.* New York: Harper.
Dufour, Claude. 1998. "Mobilizing Gay Activists." In Anne N. Costain and Andrew S. McFarland, eds., *Social Movements and American Political Institutions.* Lanham, Md.: Rowman and Littlefield.
Edelman, Murray. 1964. *The Symbolic Uses of Politics.* Urbana: University of Illinois Press.
Eisenstein, James. 1973. *Politics and the Legal Process.* New York: Harper and Row.
Eisinger, Peter K. 1973. "The Conditions of Protest Behavior in American Cities." *American Political Science Review* 67:11–28.
Evans, Peter B., Dietrich Rueschemeyer, and Theda Skocpol, eds. 1985. *Bringing the State Back In.* Cambridge: Cambridge University Press.
Fenno, Richard F., Jr. 1989. *The Making of a Senator: Dan Quayle.* Washington, D.C.: Congressional Quarterly Press.
Ferman, Barbara. 1996. *Challenging the Growth Machine: Neighborhood Politics in Chicago and Pittsburgh.* Lawrence: University Press of Kansas.
Foss, Phillip O. 1960. *Politics and Grass.* Seattle: University of Washington Press.
Freeman, Jo. 1975. *The Politics of Women's Liberation.* New York: McKay.
Frey, Frederick W. 1971. "Comment: On Issues and Nonissues in the Study of Power." *American Political Science Review* 65(December):1081–101.
Fritschler, A. Lee. 1983. *Smoking and Politics,* 3d ed. Englewood Cliffs, N.J.: Prentice-Hall.
Fuchs, Ester R. 1992. *Mayors and Money: Fiscal Policy in New York and Chicago.* Chicago: University of Chicago Press.
Gais, Thomas L., Mark A. Peterson, and Jack L. Walker. 1984. "Interest Groups, Iron Triangles, and Representative Institutions in American National Government." *British Journal of Political Science* 14:161–85.
Galanter, Mark. 1974. "Why the Haves Come Out Ahead." *Law and Society* 9:95–160.
Galbraith, John Kenneth. 1952. *American Capitalism: The Concept of Countervailing Power.* Boston: Houghton Mifflin.
Gamson, William A. 1975. *The Strategy of Social Protest.* Homewood, Ill.: Dorsey Press.
Garson, G. David. 1978. *Group Theories of Politics.* Beverly Hills, Calif.: Sage Publications.
Gaventa, John. 1980. *Power and Powerlessness: Quiescence and Rebellion in an Appalachian Valley.* Urbana: University of Illinois Press.
Gelb, Joyce, and Marian Lief Palley. 1982. *Women and Public Policies.* Princeton, N.J.: Princeton University Press.
Gobeyn, Mark James. 1993. "Explaining the Decline of Macro-Corporatist Political Bargaining Structures in Advanced Capitalist Societies." *Governance* 6:3–22.
Goffman, Erving. 1974. *Frame Analysis: An Essay on the Organization of Experience.* Cambridge, Mass.: Harvard University Press.

Goldstein, Judith. 1993. *Ideas, Interests, and American Trade Policy.* Ithaca, N.Y.: Cornell University Press.
Goldwater, Barry M. 1961. *The Conscience of a Conservative.* New York: Hillman.
Gramsci, Antonio. 1971. *Selections from the Prison Notebooks.* Edited and translated by Quinten Hoare and Geoffrey Nowell Smith. London: Wishart.
Gray, Virginia, and David Lowery. 1990. "Corporatist Foundations of State Industrial Policy." *Social Science Quarterly* 71:3–24.
———. 1996. *The Population Ecology of Interest Representation: Lobbying Communities in the American States.* Ann Arbor: University of Michigan Press.
———. 2000. "A Neopluralist Perspective on Research on Organized Interests." Paper presented at the annual meeting of the Midwest Political Science Association, Chicago, April 27–29.
Griffith, Ernest S. 1939. *The Impasse of Democracy.* New York: Harrison-Wilton Books.
Grodzins, Morton. 1960. "The Federal System." In President's Commission on National Goals, *Goals for Americans.* Englewood Cliffs, N.J.: Prentice-Hall.
Haider, Donald. 1974. *When Governments Come to Washington.* New York: Free Press.
Hansen, John Mark. 1985. "The Political Economy of Group Membership." *American Political Science Review* 79:79–96.
Hansen, Susan B. 1989a. "Industrial Policy and Corporatism in the American States." *Governance* 2:172–97.
———. 1989b. "Targeting in Economic Development: Comparative State Perspectives." *Publius* 19:47–62.
Hardin, Russell. 1982. *Collective Action.* Baltimore: Johns Hopkins University Press.
Harsanyi, John C. 1962. "Measurement of Social Power, Opportunity Costs, and the Theory of Two-Person Bargaining Games." *Behavioral Science* 7:67–80.
Hartz, Louis. 1955. *The Liberal Tradition in America.* New York: Harcourt, Brace.
Hays, Samuel P. 1957. *The Response to Industrialism: 1885–1914.* Chicago: University of Chicago Press.
Heberle, Rudolph. 1951. *Social Movements: An Introduction to Political Sociology.* New York: Appleton-Century-Crofts.
Heclo, Hugh. 1978. "Issue Networks and the Executive Establishment." In Anthony King, ed., *The New American Political System.* Washington, D.C.: American Enterprise Institute.
Heinz, John P., Edward O. Laumann, Robert L. Nelson, and Robert H. Salisbury. 1993. *The Hollow Core: Private Interests in National Policy Making.* Cambridge, Mass.: Harvard University Press.
Herring, E. Pendleton. 1929. *Group Representation Before Congress.* Baltimore: Johns Hopkins University Press.
———. 1940. *The Politics of Democracy.* New York: Rinehart.
Hirschman, Albert O. 1982. *Shifting Involvements: Private Interest and Public Action.* Princeton, N.J.: Princeton University Press.
Hochschild, Jennifer L. 1984. *New American Dilemma: Liberal Democracy and School Desegregation.* New Haven, Conn.: Yale University Press.
Hoffer, Eric. 1951. *The True Believer: Thoughts on the Nature of Mass Movements.* New York: Harper and Row.
Hojnacki, Marie, and David C. Kimball. 1998. "Organized Interests and the Decision of Whom to Lobby in Congress." *American Political Science Review* 92:775–90.

Hula, Kevin. 1999. *Lobbying Together: Interest Group Coalitions in Legislative Politics.* Washington, D.C.: Georgetown University Press.

Hunter, Floyd. 1953. *Community Power Structure.* Chapel Hill: University of North Carolina Press.

Huntington, Samuel P. 1981. *American Politics: The Promise of Disharmony.* Cambridge, Mass.: Belknap/Harvard University Press.

Jervis, Robert. 2002. "Politics, Political Science, and Specialization." *PS: Political Science and Politics* 35(2):188.

Jones, Bryan D. 1994. *Reconceiving Decision-Making in Democratic Politics: Attention, Choice, and Public Policy.* Chicago: University of Chicago Press.

Jones, Charles O. 1970. *An Introduction to the Study of Public Policy.* Belmont, Calif.: Duxbury Press of Wadsworth Publishing Co.

———. 1975. *Clean Air: The Policies and Politics of Pollution Control.* Pittsburgh: University of Pittsburgh Press.

Jordan, Grant. 1981. "Iron Triangles, Wooly Corporatism, and Elastic Nets: Images of the Policy Process." *Journal of Public Policy* 1:95–123.

Jordan, Grant, and William A. Maloney. 1996. "How Bumble-bees Fly: Accounting for Public Interest Participation." *Political Studies* 44:668–85.

Kariel, Henry S. 1961. *The Decline of American Pluralism.* Stanford, Calif.: Stanford University Press.

Katzenstein, Peter J. 1985. *Small States in World Markets.* Ithaca, N.Y.: Cornell University Press.

Katznelson, Ira. 1981. *City Trenches: Urban Politics and the Patterning of Class in the United States.* New York: Pantheon.

Kaufman, Herbert. 1960. *The Forest Ranger: A Study in Administrative Behavior.* Baltimore: Johns Hopkins Press.

Keck, Margaret E., and Kathryn Sikkink. 1998. *Activists beyond Borders: Advocacy Networks in International Politics.* Ithaca, N.Y.: Cornell University Press.

Keohane, Robert O. 1984. *After Hegemony: Cooperation and Discord in the World Political Economy.* Princeton, N.J.: Princeton University Press.

Kersh, Rogan. 2002. "Corporate Lobbyists as Political Actors: A View from the Field." In Allan J. Cigler and Burdett A. Loomis, eds., *Interest Group Politics,* 6th ed. Washington, D.C.: Congressional Quarterly Press.

Key, V. O., Jr. 1955. "A Theory of Critical Elections." *Journal of Politics* 17:3–18.

Kiewit, D. Roderick, and Mathew D. McCubbins. 1991. *The Logic of Delegation: Congressional Parties and the Appropriations Process.* Chicago: University of Chicago Press.

Kingdon, John W. 1984. *Agendas, Alternatives, and Public Policies.* Boston: Little, Brown.

Klein, Ethel. 1984. *Gender Politics.* Cambridge, Mass.: Harvard University Press.

Klotz, Audie. 1995. *Norms in International Relations: The Struggle against Apartheid.* Ithaca, N.Y.: Cornell University Press.

Knorowski, Carla. 2000. "Lobbying at the State Level: Higher Education Interests in Illinois." Ph.D. dissertation, University of Illinois at Chicago.

Kollman, Kenneth. 1998. *Outside Lobbying: Public Opinion and Interest Group Strategies.* Princeton, N.J.: Princeton University Press.

Kornhauser, William. 1959. *The Politics of Mass Society.* Glencoe, Ill.: Free Press.

Krasner, Stephen D. 1978. *Defending the National Interest: Raw Materials Investment and U.S. Foreign Policy.* Princeton, N.J.: Princeton University Press.
———, ed. 1983. *International Regimes.* Ithaca, N.Y.: Cornell University Press.
———. 1984. "Approaches to the State: Alternative Conceptions and Historical Dynamics." *Comparative Politics* 16:223–46.
Kuhn, Thomas S. 1962. *The Structure of Scientific Revolution.* Chicago: University of Chicago Press.
Larson, Sandra L. Forthcoming. "The Influence of Interest Groups on the Development and Outcome of Federal Agency Regulations: A Case Study of the American Association of Nurse Anesthetists and the American Society of Anesthesiologists' Influence on Health Care Finance Administration Regulation #482.45." Ph.D. dissertation in progress, University of Illinois at Chicago.
Laski, Harold J. 1921. *The Foundations of Sovereignty and Other Essays.* New York: Harcourt, Brace.
Lasswell, Harold D., and Abraham Kaplan. 1950. *Power and Society.* New Haven, Conn.: Yale University Press.
Laudan, Larry. 1984. *Science and Values: The Aims of Science and Their Role in Scientific Debate.* Berkeley: University of California Press.
Laumann, Edward O., and David Knoke. 1987. *The Organizational State: Social Choice in National Policy Domains.* Madison: University of Wisconsin Press.
Layton, Azza Salama. 2000. *International Politics and Civil Rights Policies in the United States: 1941–1960.* Cambridge: Cambridge University Press.
Lazarsfeld, Paul, Bernard R. Berelson, and Helen Gaudet. 1960. *The People's Choice,* 2d ed. New York: Columbia University Press.
Lenth, C. S., ed. 1997. *1997 State Secondary Structures Sourcebook: State Coordinating and Governing Boards.* Denver: Education Commission of the States.
Lichbach, Mark Irving. 1995. *The Rebel's Dilemma.* Ann Arbor: University of Michigan Press.
Lijphart, Arend. 1969. "Consociational Democracy." *World Politics* 21:207–25.
———. 1999. *Patterns of Democracy: Government Forms and Performance in Thirty-six Countries.* New Haven, Conn.: Yale University Press.
Lindblom, Charles E. 1959. "The Science of 'Muddling Through.'" *Public Administration Review* 19:79–88.
———. 1965. *The Intelligence of Democracy.* New York: Macmillan.
———. 1977. *Politics and Markets.* New York: Basic Books.
Lindblom, Charles E., and David K. Cohen. 1979. *Usable Knowledge: Social Science and Social Problem Solving.* New Haven, Conn.: Yale University Press.
Linz, Juan J., and Alfred Stepan. 1996. *Problems of Democratic Transition and Consolidation.* Baltimore: Johns Hopkins University Press.
Lippmann, Walter. 1922. *Public Opinion.* New York: Harcourt, Brace.
———. 1925. *The Phantom Public.* New York: Harcourt, Brace.
Lipsky, Michael. 1968. "Protest as a Political Resource." *American Political Science Review* 62:144–58.
Logan, J. R., and H. M. Molotch. 1987. *Urban Fortunes: The Political Economy of Place.* Berkeley: University of California Press.
Lowery, David, and Holly Brasher. In press. *Organized Interests and American Government.* New York: McGraw-Hill.

Lowi, Theodore J., Jr. 1964a. "American Business, Public Policy, Case Studies and Political Theory." *World Politics* 16:677–715.
———. 1964b. *At the Pleasure of the Mayor.* New York: Free Press.
———. 1969. *The End of Liberalism.* New York: W.W. Norton.
———. 1971. *The Politics of Disorder.* New York: Basic Books.
———. 1979. *The End of Liberalism*, rev. ed. New York: W.W. Norton.
Lowry, William R. 1998. "Public Provision of Intergenerational Goods: The Case of Preserved Lands." *American Journal of Political Science* 42:1082–107.
———. 2003. *The Politics of Restoring American Rivers.* Washington, D.C.: Georgetown University Press.
Lukes, Steven. 1974. *Power: A Radical View.* London: Macmillan.
Lynd, Robert S., and Helen M. Lynd. 1929. *Middletown.* New York: Harcourt, Brace.
———. 1937. *Middletown in Transition.* New York: Harcourt, Brace.
Maass, Arthur A. 1951. *Muddy Waters.* Cambridge, Mass.: Harvard University Press.
March, James G. 1955. "An Introduction to the Theory and Measurement of Influence." *American Political Science Review* 49(June):431–51.
———. 1966. "The Power of Power." In David Easton, ed., *Varieties of Political Theory.* Englewood Cliffs, N.J.: Prentice-Hall.
March, James G., and Johann P. Olsen. 1989. *Rediscovering Institutions.* New York: Free Press.
Margolis, Howard. 1984. *Selfishness, Altruism, and Rationality: A Theory of Social Choice.* Chicago: University of Chicago Press.
Matsler, F. G., and E. R. Hines. 1987. *State Policy Formation in Illinois Higher Education.* Normal, Ill.: Center for Higher Education.
Mazmanian, Daniel, and Paul A. Sabatier. 1989. *Implementation and Public Policy.* Lanham, Md.: University Press of America.
McAdam, Doug. 1982. *Political Process and the Development of Black Insurgency, 1930–1970.* Chicago: University of Chicago Press.
———. 1999. Introduction to *Political Process and the Development of Black Insurgency, 1930–1970,* 2d ed. Chicago: University of Chicago Press.
McAdam, Doug, John D. McCarthy, and Mayer N. Zald, eds. 1996. *Comparative Perspectives on Social Movements.* Cambridge: Cambridge University Press.
McCann, Michael W. 1986. *Taking Reform Seriously.* Ithaca, N.Y.: Cornell University Press.
———. 1998. "Social Movements and the Mobilization of Law." In Anne N. Costain and Andrew S. McFarland, eds., *Social Movements and American Political Institutions.* Lanham, Md.: Rowman and Littlefield.
McCarry, Charles. 1972. *Citizen Nader.* New York: Signet.
McCarthy, John D., and Mayer N. Zald. 1977. "Resource Mobilization and Social Movements." *American Journal of Sociology* 82(May):1212–41.
McClosky, Herbert, and John Zaller. 1984. *The American Ethos: Public Attitudes toward Capitalism and Democracy.* Cambridge, Mass.: Harvard University Press.
McConnell, Grant. 1953. *The Decline of Agrarian Democracy.* Berkeley: University of California Press.
———. 1966. *Private Power and American Democracy.* New York: Knopf.
McFarland, Andrew S. 1969. *Power and Leadership in Pluralist Systems.* Stanford, Calif.: Stanford University Press.

———. 1976. *Public Interest Lobbies: Decision Making on Energy.* Washington, D.C.: American Enterprise Institute.
———. 1983. "Public Interest Lobbies versus Minority Faction." In Allan J. Cigler and Burdett A. Loomis, eds., *Interest Group Politics,* 1st ed. Washington, D.C.: Congressional Quarterly Press.
———. 1984. *Common Cause: Lobbying in the Public Interest.* Chatham, N.J.: Chatham House.
———. 1987. "Interest Groups and Theories of Power in America." *British Journal of Political Science* 17(April):129–47.
———. 1991. "Interest Groups and Political Time: Cycles in America." *British Journal of Political Science* 21:257–84.
———. 1992. "Interest Groups and the Policymaking Process: Sources of Countervailing Power in America." In Mark P. Petracca, ed., *The Politics of Interests: Interest Groups Transformed.* Boulder, Colo.: Westview Press.
———. 1993. *Cooperative Pluralism: The National Coal Policy Experiment.* Lawrence: University Press of Kansas.
———. 2001. "Political Power." In Neil J. Smelser and Paul B. Baltes, eds., *The International Encyclopedia of the Social and Behavioral Sciences.* Oxford: Pergamon/Elsevier Science.
Melucci, Alberto. 1996. *Challenging Codes: Collective Action in the Information Age.* Cambridge: Cambridge University Press.
Micheletti, Michele. 1993. "Sweden: Interest Groups in Transition and Crisis." In Clive S. Thomas, ed., *First World Interest Groups: A Comparative Perspective.* New York: Greenwood Press.
Michels, Robert. 1959. *Political Parties.* New York: Dover.
Miliband, Ralph. 1969. *The State in Capitalist Society.* New York: Basic Books.
Mill, John Stuart. 1958. *Considerations on Representative Government.* New York: Liberal Arts Press.
Miller, Tim R. 1985. "Changes in the Utility of the Subsystem Model for Public Policy Analysis: The Status of Water Policy Making in the U.S." Paper presented at the annual meeting of the American Political Science Association, New Orleans August 29–September 1.
Mills, C. Wright. 1956. *The Power Elite.* New York: Oxford University Press.
Mitchell, Robert Cameron. 1979. "National Environmental Lobbies and the Apparent Illogic of Collective Action." In Clifford S. Russell, ed., *Collective Decision Making: Applications from Public Choice Theory.* Baltimore: Johns Hopkins University Press.
———. 1984. "Public Opinion and Environmental Politics in the 1970s and 1980s." In Norman J. Vig and Michael E. Kraft, eds., *Environmental Politics in the 1980s: Reagan's New Agenda.* Washington, D.C.: Congressional Quarterly Press.
Morgenthau, Hans J. *Politics among Nations. 1964.* 3d ed. New York: Knopf.
Morris, Aldon D. 1984. *The Origins of the Civil Rights Movement: Black Communities Organizing for Change.* New York: Free Press.
Morris, Aldon D., and Carol McClurg Mueller, eds. 1992. *Frontiers in Social Movement Theory.* New Haven, Conn.: Yale University Press.
Mowry, George E. 1962. *The Era of Theodore Roosevelt and the Birth of Modern America.* New York: Harper and Row.

Mucciaroni, Gary. 1995. *Reversals of Fortune: Public Policy and Private Interests.* Washington, D.C.: Brookings Institution.
Muir, William K., Jr. 1982. *Legislature: California's School for Politics.* Chicago: University of Chicago Press.
Murray, Francis X. 1978. *Where We Agree: Report of the National Coal Policy Project,* 2 vols. Boulder, Colo.: Westview Press.
Nadel, Mark V. 1971. *The Politics of Consumer Protection.* Indianapolis: Bobbs-Merrill.
Nadel, Mark V., and David Vogel. 1977. "Who Is a Consumer? An Analysis of the Politics of Consumer Conflict." *American Politics Quarterly* 5(January):27–56.
Nagel, Jack H. 1975. *The Descriptive Analysis of Power.* New Haven, Conn.: Yale University Press.
Neustadt, Richard E. 1960. *Presidential Power.* New York: Wiley.
Nie, Norman, Sidney Verba, and John R. Petrocik. 1976. *The Changing American Voter.* Cambridge, Mass.: Harvard University Press.
Niskanen, William A. 1971. *Bureaucracy and Representative Government.* Chicago: Aldine-Atherton.
Noble, Charles. 1986. *Liberalism at Work: The Rise and Fall of OSHA.* Philadelphia: Temple University Press.
Nordlinger, Eric A. 1981. *On the Autonomy of the Democratic State.* Cambridge, Mass.: Harvard University Press.
Oberschall, Anthony. 1973. *Social Conflict and Social Movements.* Englewood Cliffs, N.J.: Prentice-Hall.
Offe, Claus. 1984. *Contradictions of the Welfare State.* Edited by John Keane. Cambridge, Mass.: MIT Press.
Olson, Mancur, Jr. 1965. *The Logic of Collective Action.* Cambridge, Mass.: Harvard University Press.
———. 1982. *The Rise and Decline of Nations.* New Haven, Conn.: Yale University Press.
Orfield, Gary. 1975. *Congressional Power: Congress and Social Change.* New York: Harcourt Brace Jovanovich.
Ornstein, Norman J., and Shirley Elder. 1978. *Interest Groups, Lobbying, and Policymaking.* Washington, D.C.: Congressional Quarterly Press.
Orren, Karen. 1974. *Corporate Power and Social Change: The Politics of the Life Insurance Industry.* Baltimore: Johns Hopkins University Press.
Orren, Karen, and Stephen Skowronek. 1994. "Beyond the Iconography of Order: Notes for a New Institutionalism." In Lawrence Dodd and Calvin Jillson, eds., *The Dynamics of American Politics.* Boulder, Colo.: Westview Press.
Orum, Anthony M. 1972. *Black Students in Protest: A Study of the Origins of the Black Student Movement.* Washington, D.C.: American Sociological Association.
———. 2001. *Political Sociology,* 4th ed. Upper Saddle River, N.J.: Prentice-Hall.
Pateman, Carole. 1970. *Participation and Democratic Theory.* Cambridge: Cambridge University Press.
Peabody, Robert J., and Nelson W. Polsby, eds. 1963. *New Perspectives on the House of Representatives.* Chicago: Rand-McNally.
Peterson, Paul E. 1981. *City Limits.* Chicago: University of Chicago Press.
Peterson, Paul E., Barry Rabe, and Kenneth Wong. 1986. *When Federalism Works.* Washington, D.C.: Brookings Institution.

Pinard, Maurice. 1975. *The Rise of a Third Party,* rev. ed. Montreal: McGill-Queens University Press.
Pious, Richard M. 1979. *The American Presidency.* New York: Basic Books.
Piven, Frances Fox, and Richard A. Cloward. 1977. *Poor People's Movements.* New York: Pantheon Books.
Polsby, Nelson W. 1960. "Toward an Explanation of McCarthyism." *Political Studies* 8: 250–71.
———. 1963. "Two Strategies of Influence: Choosing a Majority Leader, 1962." In Robert J. Peabody and Nelson W. Polsby, eds., *New Perspectives on the House of Representatives.* Chicago: Rand-McNally.
———. 1971. *Congress and the Presidency,* 2d ed. Englewood Cliffs, N.J.: Prentice-Hall.
———. 1980. *Community Power and Political Theory,* 2d enlarged ed. New Haven, Conn.: Yale University Press.
———. 1983. *Consequences of Party Reform.* New York: Oxford University Press.
———. 1984. *Political Innovation in America: The Politics of Policy Initiation.* New Haven, Conn.: Yale University Press.
Pressman, Jeffrey L., and Aaron Wildavsky. 1973. *Implementation.* Berkeley: University of California Press.
Quirk, Paul J. 1989. "The Cooperative Resolution of Policy Conflict." *American Political Science Review* 83:905–22.
Rabe, Barry G. 1994. *Beyond NIMBY: Hazardous Waste Siting in Canada and the United States.* Washington, D.C.: Brookings Institution.
Redford, Emmette S. 1969. *Democracy in the Administrative State.* New York: Oxford University Press.
Riesman, David. 1953. *The Lonely Crowd.* New York: Doubleday Anchor.
Riker, William H. 1964. "Some Ambiguities in the Notion of Power." *American Political Science Review* 58(June):341–49.
———. 1982. *Liberalism against Populism.* Prospect Heights, Ill.: Waveland Press.
———. 1986. *The Art of Political Manipulation.* New Haven, Conn.: Yale University Press.
Riordan, William L. 1963. *Plunkitt of Tammany Hall.* New York: Dutton.
Ripley, Randall B., and Grace A. Franklin. 1984. *Congress, the Bureaucracy, and Public Policy,* 3d ed. Homewood, Ill.: Dorsey Press.
Rogin, Michael Paul. 1967. *The Intellectuals and McCarthy.* Cambridge, Mass.: MIT Press.
Rosenbaum, Walter A. 1985. *Environmental Politics and Policy.* Washington, D.C.: Congressional Quarterly Press.
Rothenberg, Lawrence S. 1992. *Linking Citizens to Government: Interest Group Politics at Common Cause.* Cambridge: Cambridge University Press.
Rourke, Francis E. 1968. *Bureaucracy, Politics and Public Policy.* Boston: Little, Brown.
Ruggie, John Gerard. 1983. "International Regimes, Transactions, and Change: Embedded Liberalism in the Postwar Economic Order." In Stephen Krasner, ed., *International Regimes.* Ithaca, N.Y.: Cornell University Press.
Sabatier, Paul A., and Hank C. Jenkins-Smith, eds. 1993. *Policy Change and Learning: An Advocacy Coalition Approach.* Boulder, Colo.: Westview Press.
———. 1999. "The Advocacy Coalition Framework: An Assessment." In Paul A. Sabatier, ed., *Theories of the Policy Process.* Boulder, Colo.: Westview Press.

Salisbury, Robert H. 1969. "An Exchange Theory of Interest Groups." *Midwest Journal of Political Science* 13:1–32.

———. 1984. "Interest Representation: The Dominance of Institutions." *American Political Science Review* 78:64–76.

Sayre, Wallace S., and Herbert Kaufman. 1960. *Governing New York City.* New York: Russell Sage Foundation.

Schattschneider, E. E. 1960. *The Semisovereign People.* New York: Holt, Rinehart and Winston.

Schelling, Thomas C. 1960. *The Strategy of Conflict.* Cambridge, Mass.: Harvard University Press.

Schlesinger, Arthur M., Jr. 1986. *The Cycles of American History.* Boston: Houghton Mifflin.

Schlozman, Kay Lehman, and John T. Tierney. 1983. "More of the Same: Washington Pressure Group Activity in a Decade of Change." *Journal of Politics* 45:351–77.

———. 1986. *Organized Interests and American Democracy.* New York: Harper and Row.

Schmitter, Philippe. 1974. "Still the Century of Corporatism?" *Review of Politics* 36: 85–131.

Schneider, Mark, John Scholz, Mark Lubell, Denise Mindruta, and Matthew Edwardsen. 2003. "Building Consensual Institutions: Networks and the National Estuary Program." *American Journal of Political Science* 47:143–58.

Schubert, Glendon. 1960. *The Public Interest: A Critique of the Theory of a Political Concept.* Glencoe, Ill.: Free Press.

Schumpeter, Joseph A. 1950. *Capitalism, Socialism, and Democracy,* 3d ed. New York: Harper.

Scott, James C. 1990. *Domination and the Arts of Resistance.* New Haven, Conn.: Yale University Press.

Selznick, Philip. 1953. *TVA and the Grass Roots.* Berkeley: University of California Press.

———. 1957. *Leadership and Administration.* New York: Harper and Row.

Shaiko, Ronald G. 1999. *Voices and Echoes for the Environment.* New York: Columbia University Press.

Shapiro, David B. Forthcoming. "A Network Analysis of the Consortium for Citizens with Disabilities (CCD) and a Theory of Policy Networks." Ph.D. dissertation, University of Illinois at Chicago.

Simon, Herbert A. 1953. "Notes on the Observation and Measurement of Power." *Journal of Politics* 15:500–516.

———. 1957. *Administrative Behavior,* 2d ed. New York: Macmillan.

Simon, Herbert A., Donald W. Smithburg, and Victor A. Thompson. 1950. *Public Administration.* New York: Knopf.

Skocpol, Theda. 1979. *States and Social Revolutions: A Comparative Analysis of France, Russia and China.* Cambridge: Cambridge University Press.

———. 1985. "Bringing the State Back In: Strategies of Analysis in Current Research." In Peter B. Evans, Dietrich Rueschemeyer, and Theda Skocpol, eds., *Bringing the State Back In.* Cambridge: Cambridge University Press.

———. 1992. *Protecting Soldiers and Mothers: The Political Origins of Social Policy in the United States.* Cambridge, Mass.: Belknap Press/Harvard University Press.

———, with the assistance of Marshall Ganz, Ziad Munson, Bayliss Camp, Michele Swers, and Jennifer Oser. 1999. "How Americans Became Civic." In Theda Skocpol and Morris P. Fiorina, eds., *Civic Engagement in American Democracy*. Washington, D.C., and New York: Brookings Institution Press and Russell Sage Foundation.

Skowronek, Stephen. 1982. *Building a New American State: The Expansion of National Administrative Capacities, 1877–1920*. Cambridge: Cambridge University Press.

———. 1993. *The Politics Presidents Make*. Cambridge, Mass.: Belknap Press/Harvard University Press.

Sniderman, Paul M., Richard A. Brody, and Philip E. Tetlock. 1991. *Reasoning and Choice: Explorations in Political Psychology*. Cambridge: Cambridge University Press.

Snow, David A., E. Burke Rochford Jr., Steven K. Wordon, and Robert D. Benford. 1986. "Frame Alignment and Mobilization." *American Sociological Review* 51(August):464–81.

Snow, David A., Louis A. Zurcher, and Sheldon Ekland-Olson. 1980. "Social Networks and Social Movements: A Microstructural Approach to Differential Recruitment." *American Sociological Review* 45:787–801.

Sparrow, Bartholomew. 1995. *From the Outside In: World War II and the American State*. Princeton, N.J.: Princeton University Press.

Stigler, George J. 1975. *The Citizen and the State: Essays on Regulation*. Chicago: University of Chicago Press.

Stone, Clarence N. 1989. *Regime Politics: Governing Atlanta, 1946–1988*. Lawrence: University Press of Kansas.

Stouffer, Samuel A. 1962. *Communism, Conformity, and Civil Liberties*. Gloucester, Mass.: Peter Smith.

Sundquist, James L. 1983. *Dynamics of the Party System*. Washington, D.C.: Brookings Institution.

Tarrow, Sidney. 1989. *Democracy and Disorder: Protest and Politics in Italy, 1965–1975*. New York: Oxford University Press.

———. 1995. *Power in Movement: Social Movements, Collective Action and Politics*. Cambridge: Cambridge University Press.

———. 1998. "The Very Excess of Democracy: State Building and Contentious Politics in America." In Anne N. Costain and Andrew S. McFarland, eds., *Social Movements and American Political Institutions*. Lanham, Md.: Rowman and Littlefield.

Thomas, Daniel C. 2000. *The Helsinki Effect: International Norms, Human Rights, and the Demise of Communism*. Princeton, N.J.: Princeton University Press.

Tilly, Charles. 1978. *From Mobilization to Revolution*. Reading, Mass.: Addison-Wesley.

True, James L., Bryan D. Jones, and Frank R. Baumgartner. 1999. "Punctuated Equilibrium Theory: Explaining Stability and Change in American Policymaking." In Paul A. Sabatier, ed., *Theories of the Policy Process*. Boulder, Colo.: Westview Press.

Truman, David B. 1951. *The Governmental Process*. New York: Knopf.

———. 1965. "Disillusion and Regeneration: The Quest for a Discipline." *American Political Science Review* 59(December):865–73.

Vogel, David. 1980–1981. "The Public Interest Movement and the American Reform Tradition." *Political Science Quarterly* 95:607–27.

———. 1989. *Fluctuating Fortunes: The Political Power of Business in America*. New York: Basic Books.

Waldo, Dwight. 1948. *The Administrative State*. New York: Ronald Press.

———. 1955. *The Study of Public Administration.* New York: Random House.
Walker, Jack L., Jr. 1966. "A Critique of the Elitist Theory of Democracy." *American Political Science Review* 60:285–95.
———. 1977. "Setting the Agenda in the U.S. Senate." *British Journal of Political Science* 7:423–45.
———. 1983. "The Origins and Maintenance of Interest Groups in America." *American Political Science Review* 77:390–406.
———. 1991. *Mobilizing Interest Groups in America.* Ann Arbor: University of Michigan Press.
Warner, W. Lloyd, and Paul S. Lunt. 1941. *The Social Life of a Modern Community.* New Haven, Conn.: Yale University Press.
Weber, Edward P. 1998. *Pluralism by the Rules: Conflict and Cooperation in Environmental Regulation.* Washington, D.C.: Georgetown University Press.
Weber, Max. 1946. "Class, Status, Party." In H. H. Gerthe and C. Wright Mills, eds. and trans., *From Max Weber: Essays in Sociology.* New York: Oxford University Press.
———. 1947. *The Theory of Social and Economic Organization.* Translated by A. M. Henderson and Talcott Parsons. New York: Oxford University Press.
Wendt, Alexander. 1999. *Social Theory of International Politics.* Cambridge: Cambridge University Press.
Wenner, Lettie M. 1982. *The Environmental Decade in Court.* Bloomington: University of Indiana Press.
Wessel, Milton R. 1976. *The Rule of Reason: A New Approach to Corporate Litigation.* Reading, Mass.: Addison-Wesley.
Wiebe, Robert H. 1967. *The Search for Order, 1877–1920.* New York: Hill and Wang.
Wildavsky, Aaron B. 1964a. *Leadership in a Small Town.* Totowa, N.J.: Bedminster Press.
———. 1964b. *The Politics of the Budgetary Process.* Boston: Little, Brown.
———. 1979. *Speaking Truth to Power: The Art and Craft of Policy Analysis.* Boston: Little, Brown.
———. 1980. *How to Limit Government Spending.* Berkeley: University of California Press.
Wilson, Graham K. 1981. *Interest Groups in the United States.* Oxford: Oxford University Press.
———. 1985. *Business and Politics.* Chatham, N.J.: Chatham House.
Wilson, James Q. 1973. *Political Organizations.* New York: Basic Books.
———, ed. 1980. *The Politics of Regulation.* New York: Basic Books.
Wirt, Fred. 1974. *Power in the City: Decision-Making in San Francisco.* Berkeley: University of California Press.
Wolfinger, Raymond E. 1971. "Nondecisions and the Study of Local Politics." *American Political Science Review* 65 (December):1063–80.
Woliver, Laura R. 1993. *From Outrage to Action: The Politics of Grass-Roots Dissent.* Urbana: University of Illinois Press.
Yarnold, Barbara M. 1990. *Refugees without Refuge: Formation and Failed Implementation of U.S. Political Asylum Policy in the 1980's.* Lanham, Md.: University Press of America.
Zald, Mayer N., and John D. McCarthy. 1987. *Social Movements in an Organizational Society: Collected Essays.* New Brunswick, N.J.: Transaction.

Index

AARP, 43, 68, 100
AFL, 90, 95
AFL-CIO, 118
AFSCME, 45
Ackerman, Bruce, 41
Actors, preferences of, 123
Administrative agencies, 10
Adversary coalitions, 52–56, 160–171
Agency autonomy, 48, 109, 159
Agenda, political, 74, 76, 94–96, 125
   Kingdon's theory, 128–130, 138
   manipulation, 126
Agendas, Alternatives, and Public Policies, 128–129
Agendas and Instability in American Politics, 55, 134–136, 163
   Downsian cycle, 135
   economy of attention, 136
   image construction, 135–136
   interest, definition of, 135
   process orientation, 135
   Schattschneider cycle, 135
Agriculture policy, 33–34, 36, 57–58, 98, 105
Ainsworth, Scott, 55
Air pollution policy, 40, 41–42, 45–46, 69, 70, 85, 114, 162
Air Products and Chemicals, Co., 114
Almond, Gabriel, 156
American Association of University Women, 64, 72
American Business and Public Policy, 47
American Capitalism (Galbraith), 98
American Council of Education, 54, 116
American Federation of Teachers, 45
American Lung Association, 42, 45

American political development studies, 170–171
American politics, general theories of, 81, 83
American Politics: The Promise of Disharmony, 81
American Public Health Association, 42
American Rivers (environmentalists), 119
Amnesty International, 171
Andrus, Ethel, 44
Anesthesiologists, nurse, 4
Anti-apartheid movement, international, 172
Anti-poverty program, 105
   community action councils, 68
Attitudes, political, 82

Bachrach, Peter, 125–126, 147
Banking policy, 70
Baratz, Morton, 125–126
Bargaining, political, 5
Basic Interests (Baumgartner and Leech), 12
Bateson, Gregory, 136
Bauer, Raymond, 16, 28
Baumgartner, Frank, 12, 13, 55–60, 86, 102, 121, 134, 137, 138–139, 144–145, 171, 177
Beard, Charles, 81
Beer, Samuel, 41
Behavioral revolution, 28, 110, 147–150
Bentley, Arthur F., 3, 4, 5, 9, 15, 20, 46, 47, 125, 175
Bernstein, Marver, 32
Berry, Jeffrey, 41, 54, 98
Bob Jones University, 68
Boorstin, Daniel, 81

Bosso, Christopher, 98
Browne, William, 57–60, 160
Brownlow, Louis, 98
Budgetary process, 9, 21, 24, 25, 26–27, 30, 56, 105
   excessive spending, 37
Bureaucracy, 38
Bureau of Land Management, 52
Burford, Anne, 99
Building a New American State (Skowronek), 154, 170
Burnham, Walter Dean, 79
Burstein, Paul, 71
Bush, George H. W., 99
Business groups, 48, 49, 165
Business mobilization, 90
Business power, 42, 48, 59–60, 86, 92, 93, 94, 96
Business Roundtable, 44

Campaigns and elections, 100
Center for Strategic and International Studies, Georgetown University, 113
Central Maine Power, 119
Christian fundamentalism, 70
CIO, 90
Cities, progressive norms, 134
Citizens groups, 42, 48, 55, 59, 66, 109
City Limits (Peterson), 133
City limits, theory of, 144, 177
Civil liberties, in U.S., 149
Civil rights movement, 63–65, 75, 88, 140–141
Class, concept of, 6, 20, 21 62
Clientelism, 32, 33
Clinton, William J., 100
Coalition building, 8
Cobb, Roger W., 126
Cohen, Michael, 94, 129
Columbia University, 149
Common Cause, 44
Communism, 93
Community power studies, 16, 19, 25, 40, 41, 108, 133, 155, 162, 173
Complex systems, 5, 8, 10, 22, 24, 41, 43, 54, 61, 79, 157, 159, 168
Conflict, scope of, 36, 38

Conservation Federation of Missouri, 119
Consociationism, 173
Consolidation Coal Co., 114
Constructivism, 145
Consumer lobbies, 69
Cooperation, 109
Cooperative pluralism, 3, 76, 108–123, 160–171
   definition, 108, 118
Cooptation of policy, 36, 38, 75
Corporatism, 2, 84, 106–109, 118, 121 127, 148, 153, 176, 177
Costain, Anne N., 41, 65
Costain, W. Douglas, 41
Counterframing, 141
Countervailing power, 10, 15, 33, 38, 41, 43, 46–50, 52, 55, 61, 66, 68, 74, 85–87, 90–93, 97–103, 109, 122, 130, 142, 151, 154, 165, 166, 171
Culhane, Paul J., 52, 98
Culture, 67, 143
Cycles. *See* policy cycles, reform cycles.
Cycles of American History, The (Schlesinger), 82

Dahl, Robert A., 2–11, 15–20, 22, 25–31, 33, 46, 47, 83, 105, 106, 110, 125, 127, 128, 129, 134, 147–148, 152, 153, 158, 159, 163, 175, 177, 178
Democracy, 14, 97, 107, 148, 150–151, 153
   in America, 2
   strong, 151
Department of Education, 168
Department of Energy, 42, 114
Department of Justice, 48
Derthick, Martha, 53
Detroit Edison Co., 114
Dexter, Lewis A. 16, 28
Distributory policy, 37, 74
   and subsidies, 37
Dow Chemical Co., 114
Downs, Anthony, 26
Durkheim, Emile, 3, 79

Ecological activism, 155
Economics, 34, 124, 130, 148
Edelman, 32, 34, 36–37, 66, 89

INDEX   195

Edgar, Jim, 117
Efficiency (policies), 37
Elder, Shirley, 41, 126
Elitism, 2, 16, 19, 21, 24, 25–26, 32, 109, 127, 145, 162
    Italian theorists, 3
Empiricism, 110, 125
End of Liberalism, The (Lowi), 4, 150
Enron scandal, 86
Entrepreneurs, political, 10
Environmental Defense Fund, 114
Environmental groups, 166
Environmental Law Institute, 114
Environmental movement, 72–73
Environmental policymaking, 52–56, 68, 99, 120
Environmental Protection Agency, 42, 43, 45, 48, 51, 52, 99, 118
Equal Employment Opportunities Commission, 51
Equal Rights Amendment (ERA), Illinois, 68
Excess in policy, 94–95, 101, 103, 138
Externalities (external costs), 7, 34, 89, 130, 138

Farm Bureau, 33, 44
Federal Communication Commission, 48
Federal Energy Regulatory Commission, 119
Federalism, 25, 40, 70, 166–168
Federal Reserve Bank, 69
Federal Trade Commission, 33, 51
Federation of Business and Professional Women's Clubs, 92
Forest Service, 171
Foucault, Michel, 66, 131
Foundations, 45
    Ford Foundation 45
Frame analysis, 3, 14, 67, 74, 76, 136–143, 160–171
    attention, 136
    context, 136
    ideology, 136
    institutionalized, 144–157
    judicial system, 141–142
    narratives, 136

regime theory, 143–145
    roles, 136
Frames, master, 72–73, 76, 137, 140
    environmental protection, 72
    rights frame, 72, 82
    Supreme Court, 142
Freeman, Jo, 41, 64
Friedman, Milton, 34
Fritschler, A. Lee, 52
Fundamentalism, religious, 65, 154

Gais, Thomas, 98
Galbraith, John Kenneth, 42, 98
Game theory, 3, 111
Garbage can model (organizations), 94, 129
Gardner, John W., 44, 71
Gaventa, John, 6, 126
Gay rights movement, 168
Gelb, Joyce, 41
Globalization, 171
Goffman, Erving, 136
Gompers, Samuel, 44, 137
Governmental Process, The (Truman), 2, 4, 27, 41, 80, 95, 104, 162, 178
Gramsci, Antonio, 126, 153
Grassroots ideology, 66
Gray, Virginia, 57–60, 75, 160, 162
Great Society program, 166
Group theory, 31, 42, 158, 175
Growth machine (urban), 163

Haider, Donald, 41
Hansen, Susan, 118
Harsanyi, John, 18
Hartz, Louis, 81
Hassler, William T., 41
Heclo, Hugh, 45, 49, 53, 54, 83, 94, 98, 128, 145
Hegemony, 16, 20, 34, 62, 126, 129, 130–131, 153, 154, 174, 176
Herring, Pendleton, 110
High politics, 51, 55, 85, 94, 134, 137, 142, 144
Hirschman, Albert, 89–80, 95, 96
Historical methods, 3, 32
Higher educational policy (states), 115–117
Hojnacki, Marie, 139

Hollow Core, The (Heinz, et al), 54
Hollow core, theory of, 111–113, 117–118
Hula, Kevin, 53, 118
Human rights policy, 144, 171
Humphrey, Hubert, 90
Hunter, Floyd, 125
Huntington, Samuel P., 81, 102

Illinois Board of Higher Education, 54–55, 115–118, 121, 169
Implementation (policy), 56, 61, 104, 164–166
  and interest groups, 120
Incrementalism, 5, 8, 11, 21, 22–23, 26–27, 29, 55, 63, 101, 104–106, 121–122, 134, 158
Industrialization, 92
Industrial policy, 118
Institutions and institutionalism, 1, 20, 36, 45, 46–47, 57, 61, 62, 74, 84, 87, 122–123, 135, 142, 152, 156, 162, 170
  American, 63
  historical, 176
  judicial, 5
  pluralist view, 28–31
  rational choice and, 176
Interest aggregation, 15, 21
Interest group coalitions, 162
Interest group formation, 95–96
Interest-group liberalism, 33, 74
Interest group stasis, 38
Interest group sustainers, 10, 40–46, 48, 50, 60, 76
  patrons as, 10, 44–46, 50, 64, 66, 159
  and representation, 9
Interest group theory, 16, 79, 80, 83
  ecological model, 58–60
Interest, subjective definition of, 6–7, 35
Interest groups, 1, 47
  balance of power among, 11, 14
  Penn State research, 3
  and representation, 36
Interest groups, study of, 2, 10, 27, 28, 31, 41, 43, 44, 162–163, 177
Interests, common, 109–111
Interests, concertation of, 107
Interests, consumer, 130

Interests, environmental, 130
International influences (policy), 102
International relations theory, 110, 143, 145, 171
Interstate Commerce Commission, 33, 170
Iron triangles, 33
Islands of oligarchy, 66, 67
Issue areas, 28, 32–33, 78, 83, 94, 134
Issue formation and political power, 11, 12, 13, 67, 83, 162
Issue networks, 45–46, 50, 51, 53, 66, 94, 98, 127–128, 154, 159
Issues, frame analysis, 138–143
Issues, public attention to, 56–57

Jenkins-Smith, Hank, 52–57
Job retraining policy, 140
John Birch Society, 93
Jones, Bryan, 55–57, 60, 86, 102, 121, 134, 137, 138–139, 144–145, 171, 177
Jones, Charles O., 40–41
Juridical democracy (Lowi), 47

Kaplan, Abraham, 17
Kariel, Henry, 32
Kaufman, Herbert, 33
Katznelson, Ira, 70
Kennedy, Edward, 140
Keohane, Robert O., 143
Kerner, Otto, 115
Kersh, Rogan, 14
Kimball, David, 139
King, Martin Luther, Jr., 65
Kingdon, John, 74, 94–95, 126, 128–129, 134, 135, 138, 140, 145
Klanism, 93
Klein, Ethel, 41
Knoke, David, 83
Kollman, Kenneth, 55
Kornhauser, William, 77
Krasner, Stephen, 47, 143, 155–157, 170
Kuhn, Thomas, 2, 12, 176–178

Labor unions, 75, 88, 92, 98, 137
Lasswell, Harold, 17
Laumann, Edward O., 54, 83
Laws, 56

Leadership, 139
League of Cities, 44
League of Women Voters, 64, 72, 92
Lee, Richard, 28
Leech, Beth, 12, 13, 57–60
Legal codes, 106
Legal studies, 20, 28, 30, 31, 110, 146, 150, 151
  law and society, 31
  legal process, 31
Lenin, V. I., 153
Liberalism, embedded, 143
Lichbach, Mark, 175
Lindblom, Charles E., 3, 5, 8, 9, 15, 21, 22, 25, 26, 27, 28, 30, 46, 56, 104, 105, 121, 158, 169, 177
Lobbies and lobbying, 10, 14, 35, 37, 38, 45, 54, 55, 58–60, 61, 67, 68, 115, 117–118, 139–140, 146
  signaling, 55
Lobbying Disclosure Act (1995), 58
Logic of collective action, 4, 9, 11, 12, 31, 38, 43, 47, 49, 60, 61, 74, 75, 76, 84–85, 89, 96, 105, 129, 142, 147, 151, 158
  free riders, 130
  selective benefits, 6, 10, 35, 43
Logic of Collective Action, The (Olson), 9, 49, 89
Logrolling, 38
Logue, Edward, 28
Lowery, David, 57–60, 75, 160, 163
Lowi, Theodore J., Jr., 2, 4, 33, 37, 47, 49, 66, 68, 70, 74, 83, 85, 98, 105, 106, 147, 150, 153, 159, 165, 175, 177
Lukes, Steven, 126

Machiavelli, 139
Macroeconomic policies, 107
Magnussson, Warren, 139
March, James G., 5, 17, 26, 94, 125, 129, 157
Marine Dealers Association, 119
Mayors' Roundtable, 44
Mazmanian, Dan, 56
McAdam, Doug, 64–65
McCarthy, John D., 41, 44, 64–65

McCarthyism, 70
McClosky, Herbert, 82–83, 94, 96–97, 102
McConnell, Grant, 32, 36, 47, 66, 68, 70, 98
McFarland, Andrew, 41
McGovern, George, 90
Marxism, 3, 6, 20, 81, 127, 153, 154
Market failure, 7, 34, 130
Medicare, 154
Michels, Robert, 3, 66, 68
Miliband, Ralph, 20, 153
Mill, John Stuart, 152
Mills, C. Wright, 125, 127, 145
Mitchell, William C., 41
Modernization, 78
Morgenthau, Hans, 110–111
Morris, Aldon, 64
Mucciaroni, Gary, 53
Muckrakers, 85
Muir, William K., Jr., 152
Multiple elitism, 13, 19, 23, 31, 32–39, 43, 45, 51, 52, 54, 60, 66, 68, 84, 107, 109, 110, 112, 127, 144, 147, 148, 151, 165, 175

NAACP, 56, 90, 142
Nadel, Mark V., 41
Nader, Ralph, 44, 70, 71
Narratives, hidden (postmodern), 131–132, 138
National Association of Counties, 44
National Association of Manufacturers, 44
National Coal Policy Project, 109, 111, 113–115, 117
National Education Association, 45
National Governors Association, 42, 44
National interests, 111
National Organization of Women, 68
Natural Resources Defense Council, 42
National Rifle Association, 69
National Wildlife Federation, 72
Nelson, Robert L., 54
Neopluralism, 2, 3, 5, 9, 10, 13, 39, 40–61, 66, 67, 71, 78, 84, 104, 108, 113, 121, 122, 124, 127, 131, 142, 148, 151, 153, 155, 156, 158, 159, 172, 175, 177, 178

Neopluralism *(continued)*
   state autonomy and, 40, 43, 48, 51, 52, 61, 68, 69, 70
   status quo, 150–153
Network theory, 26, 53–55, 61, 72, 111–113, 123
   hollow core, 54–55, 111–113, 122
   hub-and-spokes, 54–55, 113, 115–117, 121, 143
   policy networks, 10
Neustadt, Richard, 98
New Deal, 47, 88, 90, 92, 97
New Deal intellectuals, 85
New Freedom, 90
New Nationalism, 90
New York Times, 75
Niche theory, 57–60, 75. *See also* policy niche.
Niche politics, 122. *See also* policy niche.
Nonissues (study of power), 6–7, 124–146
Nonprofit groups, 44
Nordlinger, Eric, 155–156
Norms, 49, 134, 143–145, 161
   Max Weber, 78

Oberschall, Anthony, 64
Occam's razor, 26
Oligarchy, 66
Oligarchy, islands of, 32–39, 66
Olsen, Johan, 94, 129
Olson, Mancur, Jr., 4, 9, 11, 34–37, 43, 60, 64, 66, 74, 76, 89, 96, 105, 107, 151, 152, 153, 158, 159, 163, 175
OMB (Office of Management and Budget), 42, 120
Orfield, Gary, 92
Ornstein, Norman, 41
OSHA (Occupational Safety and Health Administration), 51, 52

Pacific Gas & Electric Co., 114
Palley, Marian Lief, 41
Paradigms (theory), 174–176
Participation, political, 80, 84–95, 103, 141, 147, 148, 149–152, 155, 168
Partisan mutual adjustment (Lindblom), 5, 8, 16, 22–23, 56, 63, 105, 121, 158, 174

Party alignment theory, 83
Pateman, Carole, 4, 147
Patrons, 159. *See also* interest group sustainers.
Peabody Coal Co., 114
Peak association, 116
Personality theory, 14
Peterson, Mark A., 98
Peterson, Paul E., 168
Pharmaceutical industry, 100
Pinard, Maurice, 64
Planning, 3, 21, 25, 54–55, 61, 68, 76, 104–123, 142, 160–171
   land-use, 143, 146
Pluralism, 1–31, 33, 38–39, 46–47, 76–77, 84, 104, 109, 110, 112, 121, 133, 144, 145, 148, 172, 175, 177
   behavioral revolution, 150
   boundaries of, 26, 147
   case studies and, 25, 31
   criticisms of, 4, 140, 173
   defining political, 147
   limitations, 26–27
   hyperpluralism, 104
   market, 173
   research procedure, 24–26, 32, 129
   reformers, 151
   social democratic, 173
   sovereignty, 104
   status quo, 27, 31, 126, 147–152
Policy areas, 6, 71
Policy communities, 83, 94, 129
Policy cycles, theory of, 51–52, 81, 83–103, 131, 138
   endogenous, 84–86
   macrocycles, 91
   microcycles, 91
   spiral cycles, 96–99, 102
   synchronicity, 87–92
   transition period, 92
   wave theory, 95–96
Policy implementation. *See* implementation.
Policy innovation, 37
Policymaking, 5, 6, 15, 53, 78–103, 151, 161
   European, 122

Policy market, 105
Policy networks, 53, 61, 137. *See also* network theory.
Policy niche, 3, 57–61, 157–171. *See also* niche theory, niche politics.
Policy regime, 160–171
Policy subsystems, 32–33
Political actors (definition), 20, 25, 28
Political agenda, formation, 7, 27. *See also* nonissues.
Political arena, 83
Political development, 78, 153
Political entrepreneurs, 25, 46, 53, 61, 74, 94–95, 105, 129, 135
Political learning, 100, 152, 174
Political machines, urban, 70–71
Political parties and elections, 25, 26, 47, 56, 79, 88, 152
Political parties, competing, 16, 19, 148, 149
Political process, concept, 4, 9, 160–171
Political process, general theory, 1, 4, 7, 8, 12, 14, 31, 62, 122, 124, 125, 132, 144, 145, 152, 155, 157, 158–175
Political process theory, four assumptions, 4, 16, 22, 25, 31, 40, 63, 76, 78, 112–113, 125, 158, 173
Political science, theory in, 1, 4, 78–79, 172
  applied, 13–14, 124
  arrow theories, 78
  circle theories, 78
  consolidation, 12, 13
  paradigms, 12, 13
  political development, 78
  research sequence, 13, 14, 178
Political strategy, 139
Political time, 78–80
Politics of Deregulation, The (Derthick and Quirk), 53
Politics Presidents Make, The (Skowronek), 79
Polsby, Nelson W., 15, 23, 28, 30, 46, 47, 127, 147, 163
Pool, Ithiel de Sola, 16, 28
Populism, American, 68
Positivism, 147–148, 153

Postmodernism, 131–132
Power and Powerlessness (Gaventa), 126
Power: A Radical View (Lukes), 126
Power, causal definition, 5–6, 11–19, 144
  amount, 18
  anticipated reactions, 18, 20
  base, 18
  coercion, 17, 18
  domain, 6, 18
  empiricism, 6, 18
  influence, 5, 17
  intention, 3, 5
  resources, 6, 19, 20
  scope, 18
  suggestion, as, 17
Power, case studies, 157
Power, in America, 24
Power, and issue formation, 124–146
Power, schools in the study of, 176
Power, theories of, 2, 3, 11, 14, 124, 155–171
Power, three faces of, 127
Power triad, 48, 49, 52, 61, 157
Power, two faces of, 4, 125, 145, 150, 154
Preface to Democratic Theory, A (Dahl), 29, 147
Presidency, theories of, 79–80
Process of Government, The (Bentley), 4
Producer groups, 48, 49, 61, 69, 84
Professional associations, 43
Professionalism (and public policy), 10, 49, 119, 124, 156
Progressive Movement, 72, 74, 81, 82, 88, 92, 95, 97, 110, 141
Prohibition Movement, 168
Public Administration, 97
Public interest groups, 41, 44, 49, 75, 98, 165
Public Interest Movement, 71
Public interest, the, 110
Public policy, 2
  study of, 10, 14, 48, 177
Punctuated change (policy), 3, 23, 55–57, 60, 61, 62–63, 69, 73, 76, 86, 96, 102, 104, 105, 122, 134, 140, 144, 146, 161–171
Purposive groups, 80

Quayle, Dan, 140
Quirk, Paul J., 53

Rabe, Barry, 119, 168
Rational choice theory, 1, 14, 43, 123, 133, 134, 140, 153, 168, 174
Rationality, bounded, 104
Reagan, Ronald, 51, 52, 86, 93, 99
Realism, 111
Redford, Emmette S., 32, 137
Reed, Ralph, 68
Reform cycles, 36, 38, 52, 55, 61, 78, 84–103, 144
  flattening of, 97–103
Reformers, political, 21, 75, 87
Regime Politics (Stone), 118
Regime theory, 133–134, 143–145, 160–171
Regulatory commissions, 110
Regulatory negotiation, 115
Regulatory policy, 34, 35, 37, 53, 73, 90, 119, 165–166
Regulation, study of, 177
Republican party, 100
Retired Teachers Association, 44
Revolution, studies of, 62
Riker, William, 26, 157
River basin policy, 119
Roe v. Wade, 101
Roosevelt, Theodore, 141
Routine politics, 51, 55, 85, 134, 137
Ruckleshaus, William, 99
Ruggie, John, 143
Rule of reason, 114

Sabatier, Paul, 52–57, 165
Salisbury, Robert, 58, 80
Santa Barbara oil spill, 86
Sayre, Wallace, 33
Schattschneider, E. E., 32, 36, 47, 137, 144, 163
Schlesinger, Arthur F., Jr., 80–103
Schlozman, Kay Lehman, 41
Schmitter, Philippe, 106, 122, 153, 155
Schumpeter, Joseph, 16, 26
Scott, James C., 131
Selznick, Philip, 32, 36
Shapiro, David B., 118

Shifting Involvements (Hirschman), 89
Sierra Club, 42, 72, 114
Sierra Club Legal Defense Fund, 42
Simon Herbert A., 5, 17, 25, 26, 104, 110, 125
Skocpol, Theda, 124, 155–156
Skowronek, Stephen, 79–83, 154, 155–157, 171
Smith, Adam, 3
Social construction, 132
Social movement theory, 3, 10, 40, 41, 45, 46, 50–51, 62–77, 161–171
  action repertoires, 64–65
  cooperation, 68
  cooptation, 68
  countermovements, 72–73, 74, 168
  cycles of, 69, 75
  definition of, 62, 71, 74
  density, 69
  development of, 63
  egalitarian, 90, 92
  entrepreneurs, 64
  identity formation, 65, 66, 67
  issue definition, 74, 95
  issue framing, 136, 139, 140, 146
  neopluralism, 92–94
  organizations (SMOs), 64, 68, 69, 128, 152, 159
  participation (political), 89
  planning, 68
  political opportunities, 65, 76, 95, 161, 165
  political process, 71–77
  punctuated change, 69
  rational choice theory, 175
  resource mobilization theory, 41, 43, 63–64, 66
  structure among, 68
  traditionalist, 93
Social structure, 54, 118
Sociology, 19, 44, 54, 63, 65, 77, 113, 118, 148
Social psychology, 1, 65, 136, 149
Spiral theories (policy), 96–99, 102
State, concept of, 46
State governments (U.S.), 58, 67
  gay and lesbian movement, 70

Statism, 2, 28, 79, 84, 87, 96, 110, 124, 127, 148, 155–157, 176, 177
  local state, 29
Stigler, George, 34, 37, 165
"Still A Century of Corporatism?" (Schmitter article), 106
Stone, Clarence, 118, 133, 144, 145, 161, 163, 169
Stratification theory, 20, 21
Strip-mining regulation, 115
Structure of Scientific Revolution, The (Kuhn), 2, 174, 176–178
Structural theory, 6, 14, 122
Subgovernments, 9, 10, 31, 32, 35, 39. 47, 48, 52, 60, 84, 96, 107, 144, 158
Subsidies (government), 37–38
Sundquist, James L., 79
Survey research, 149
Symbolic Uses of Politics, The (Edelman), 36
Symbolic interaction theory, 14
Symbols, political, 34, 66, 67, 89

Taft-Hartley Act, 92
Tarrow, Sidney, 65, 75, 77
Telecommunications policy, 70
Tennessee Valley Authority, 34, 36
Tierney, John T., 41
Tilly, Charles, 64
Tort reform, 70
Tocqueville, Alexis de, 77, 81
Truman, David B., 2, 3, 5, 9, 15, 20, 27, 28, 31, 40, 41, 42, 46, 47, 80, 95–96, 104, 110, 125, 151, 158, 159, 162, 175, 178
Trout Unlimited, 119
Turner, Frederick Jackson, 81

United Nations, 171
University of Michigan Survey Research Center, 149
Urban politics, study of, 108, 143, 144, 162–164
Urban renewal program, New Haven, 134

U.S. Chambers of Commerce, 44, 118
U.S. Civil Rights Commission, 52
U.S. Congress, 25, 36, 51, 58–60, 74, 100, 112, 120
U.S. federal courts, 51
U.S. President, 51
U.S. President's Council on Environmental Quality, 42
U.S. Senate, 24, 29

Veto groups, 104
Vietnam War, 88, 90
Violence, 75
Vogel, David, 41, 88, 90, 92

Wagner Act, 98
Walker, Jack L., Jr., 41, 44, 50, 64, 98, 153
War, 90, 101
Wave theory of interest mobilization, 80, 95–96
Weber, Edward P., 118
Weber, Max, 1, 3, 5, 17, 78
Wenner, Lettie McSpadden, 41
Wessel, Milton, 114
Where We Agree (National Coal Policy Project), 114
White Citizens' Councils, 93
Who Governs? (Dahl), 5, 8, 23, 27, 28, 29, 33, 83, 105, 125, 134, 147, 148, 152, 162, 177
Wildavsky, Aaron B., 15, 21, 28, 30, 46, 56, 104, 169
Wilson, James Q., 10, 48, 49, 51, 85, 124, 153, 156, 157, 165
Women's movement, 70, 73
Wong, Kenneth, 168
Woodrow Wilson Prize, 16
Workingmen's associations, 95

Yale University, Political Science Dept., 33

Zald, Mayer N., 41, 44, 64–65
Zaller, John, 82–83, 94, 96–97, 102

www.ingramcontent.com/pod-product-compliance
Ingram Content Group UK Ltd.
Pitfield, Milton Keynes, MK11 3LW, UK
UKHW021327180426
11947UKWH00017B/1478